PURITAN PAPERS

A Symposium of Papers Read at Three Annual
Puritan and Reformed Studies Conferences,
Westminster Chapel, London

PURITAN PAPERS

Volume 2
1960–1962

EDITED BY
J. I. Packer

FOREWORD BY
W. Robert Godfrey

P&R PUBLISHING
P.O. BOX 817 • PHILLIPSBURG • NEW JERSEY 08865-0817

CONTENTS

CONTRIBUTORS

I. Breward was professor at Uniting Church Theological Hall, Ormond College (Australia).

J. A. Caiger was minister of Gunnersbury Baptist Church, London.

G. N. M. Collins was professor of church history at Free Church College, Edinburgh.

W. H. Davies was minister of Blackpool Baptist Church.

B. R. Easter was vicar of Barston, Warwickshire.

F. R. Entwistle is chief executive of Inter-Varsity Press (UK).

Eifion E. Evans was a minister in the Presbyterian Church of Wales.

Alan Gibson was general secretary of the British Evangelical Council.

W. Robert Godfrey is president of and professor of church history at Westminster Theological Seminary in California.

J. Gwyn-Thomas was vicar of St. Paul's Anglican Church, Cambridge.

D. J. Innes was a Church of Scotland minister.

D. Martyn Lloyd-Jones (1899–1981) was first co-pastor and then pastor of Wesminster Chapel in London from 1939 to his retirement in 1968.

J. I. Packer is Board of Governors Professor of Theology at Regent College in Vancouver and executive editor of *Christianity Today*.

FOREWORD

W. Robert Godfrey

Puritanism has been controversial from its beginning. The principles and passions of the Puritans, along with the powerful attraction of their movement in the seventeenth century, made them profoundly influential in church and society. Their convictions and impact also made them very unpopular with many in their own day and ever since. The Puritans have had severe critics from the beginning. William Shakespeare, for example, disparaged them in *Twelfth Night*:

> MARIA: Marry, sir, sometimes he is a kind of puritan.
> SIR ANDREW: O, if I thought that, I'd beat him like a dog.

A popular song of the early seventeenth century accused them of hypocrisy:

> Pure in show, an upright holy man,
> Corrupt within—and called a Puritan.

Lord Macaulay, in a famous statement, caricatured them as killjoys: "The Puritan hated bear-baiting, not because it gave pain to the bear, but because it gave pleasure to the spectators."

Yet even Macaulay had grudgingly to recognize the fortitude and commitment of the Puritan: "The Puritan was made up of two different men, the one all self-abasement, penitence, gratitude, passion, the other proud, calm, inflexible, sagacious. He prostrated himself in the dust before his Maker; but he set his foot on the neck of the king."

Scholarship in recent decades has recognized the vitality and power of the Puritan movement for its lasting impact not only in religion, but also in politics, education, economics, and science. The great increase in knowledge about the Puritans and the recognition of their influence has done little, however, to change the widespread perception of the Puritans as busybodies who sought to eliminate pleasure from life, by force if necessary, in the service of their arbitrary and unattractive God.

In the light of these attitudes it is truly remarkable that about fifty years ago two young scholars conceived the idea of holding a conference on Puritanism as a practical help for pastors and Christians generally. Surely a modern conference largely devoted to the study of Puritan thought as a vital resource for the contemporary church would not commend itself to many. But O. Raymond Johnston and James I. Packer had an advantage over many: they had actually read the Puritans. They had so profited spiritually from their own study of the Puritans that they wanted others to share in the rich spiritual blessing that had been theirs. In the late 1940s they consulted with D. Martyn Lloyd-Jones, minister at Westminster Chapel, London, who enthusiastically embraced the idea and offered the chapel as a meeting place for what became known as "The Puritan Conference."

The first conference took place in December 1950. Six papers, each about an hour in length, were read over the course of two days, one in the morning and two in the afternoon. After each paper a discussion followed of about one hour, often a very vigorous exchange of ideas. The basic form of the conference has remained the same over the years. For nearly thirty years Dr. Lloyd-Jones chaired the sessions of the conference and from 1959 contributed an annual paper and led the discussions. His commitment to the conference reflected his conviction: "As I see things, it is of supreme importance for the future of the Christian faith in this country that we should experience a revival of interest in the literature of the great Puritans of the seventeenth century."[1]

James I. Packer organized the conference for many years and contributed regularly for the first twenty years. His keen study and analysis helped set a very high standard for the papers. His presentations, along with those of Dr. Lloyd-Jones, ensure that the volumes of the conference papers from those years are of great value.

No conference was held in 1970. Dr. Lloyd-Jones objected strongly to some of the ecumenical positions taken by Dr. Packer. Dr. Lloyd-Jones was approached by several men who asked him to chair a reconvened conference of the same character as the earlier ones. He agreed to do this, and so the Westminster Conference was held in 1971 and has continued to operate under that name.

The basic purpose of the conference has remained the same for the fifty years of its existence. As Dr. Packer wrote in a foreword to the 1958 conference papers,

> [the conference] exists because its organisers believe that historic Reformed theology in general, and the teaching of the great Puritans in particular, does justice to certain neglected Biblical truths and emphases which the church today urgently needs to re-learn. This is not, of course, to imply that Puritan expositions of Scripture are infallible and final, or that the Puritans always succeeded in balancing truth in exactly the right proportions; nor is it suggested (forsooth!) that the way to solve problems which face Christians of the twentieth century is to teach them to walk and talk as if they were living in the seventeenth. What is meant is simply that the Puritans were strongest just where Protestants today are weakest, and their writings can give us more real help than those of any other body of Christian teachers, past or present, since the days of the apostles.

The pursuit of that "real help" from the Puritans was very much the purpose of the conference. Again, Dr. Packer: "The interests of the Conference, therefore, are practical and constructive, not merely academic. . . . the aim of the Conference is to make a constructive application of what is learned to our own situation."

The conference played a vital role in reinvigorating evangelicalism with a strong Reformed influence in Great Britain and beyond. The decision to publish the conference papers annually in 1956 further extended its influence. God used this conference—along with the work of great preachers and scholars, the Evangelical Library, the Banner of Truth Trust, and other agencies—to renew British evangelicalism.

The historical importance of the Puritan Conference and its papers is clear. For that reason alone the decision of the den Dulk Christian Foundation to reprint these papers is sound and proper. But these papers are much more than historical documents, and the foundation—dedicated primarily to the publication and dissemination of Reformed literature—has seen that. The republication of these studies will continue their original purpose: to furnish Christians today with insight into the rich heritage of Puritan thought. In the shallowness, pragmatism, and confusion of much current evangelicalism, the depth, conviction, and steadiness of the Puritans can again help renew the churches.

Part 1

Increasing in the Knowledge of God

1960

1

PHILIP DODDRIDGE'S THE RISE AND PROGRESS OF RELIGION IN THE SOUL

Alan Gibson

"If to have conducted thousands to the feet of Christ and a crown of righteousness be high praise, then few uninspired books have greater honour than the *Rise and Progress*. We continue to regard it as the safest, completest and most effectual manual for anxious enquirers." So wrote an anonymous reviewer of Philip Doddridge's *The Rise and Progress of Religion in the Soul* in the *British and Foreign Evangelical Review* 1857, over a hundred years after the book's first publication in 1745. And even the modest author could say of it in his own lifetime:

This is the book which so far as I can judge, God has honoured for the conversion and edification of souls more than any of my writings. I cannot mention it without humbly owning that great hand of God, which has been with it and to which I desire, with unaffected abasement of mind, to ascribe all the glory of its acceptance and success.

It was a recommendation from a friend, as "one of the best books ever written," which persuaded William Wilberforce to read *The Rise and Progress,* and its reading led to his serious study of the Bible and conversion to Christ.

Some knowledge of the days in which Doddridge wrote may help our assessment of the book. The early eighteenth century was undoubtedly a time of religious and moral decline. Bishop Ryle in *The Christian Leaders of the Eighteenth Century,* writes of it as follows: "This was the period at which Archbishop Secker said in one of his charges, 'In this we cannot be mistaken, that an open and professed disregard of religion is become, through a variety of unhappy causes the distinguishing character of the age. Such are the dissoluteness and contempt of principle in the higher part of the world, and the profligacy, intemperance and fearlessness of committing crimes in the lower part, as must, if the torrent of impiety stop not, become absolutely fatal.' "

An analysis of the situation within the churches is found in these words from Mr. Poole-Connor's book, *Evangelicalism in England:*

There are times when the Body of Christ is called to enter into fellowship with her Head; to know what it is to have the sentence of death in herself, that she may trust, not in herself but in God that raiseth the dead. Such, during the eighteenth century was the experience of evangelicalism. . . . The decline was gradual. It manifested itself in the realm of theology first by a growing disinclination to build belief upon ecclesiastical or dogmatic authority. The teachings of the Fathers, the Schoolmen and the Reformers fell into the background; the Scriptures began to be employed more often as a buttress than a foundation;

reason rather than revelation became the court of appeal. . . . Speaking generally, the main object appears to have been to demonstrate the eminent reasonableness of Christianity rather than to show its Divine origin; to present it as a philosophy rather than as a revelation; all warmth of feeling being studiously eliminated in the process.

Let us be on our guard, however, from dismissing this period as *entirely* irreligious. There were exceptions to the prevailing apostasy, among whom were such unquestionable evangelicals as Isaac Watts and Philip Doddridge.

The dedication of *The Rise and Progress* to "The reverend Dr. Isaac Watts" is not just an act of kindness to a friend. Doddridge makes it clear in his preface that the book owes its existence to Watts's request. Watts had devised its scheme, especially the former part, and had hoped to write it himself, but being older and unwell, he urged Doddridge to undertake it instead; which Doddridge duly did.

However, although Doddridge was a disciple of Watts he is no mere amanuensis. The work is an expression of his own life and ministry. While he was anxious to acknowledge a debt to his mentor, it is clear that he wrote nothing which has not become his own by conviction and experience.

Philip Doddridge was born in the year 1702, the twentieth child of a London shopkeeper. John Doddridge, his grandfather, had chosen to resign his comfortable living at Shepperton-on-Thames shortly after the Act of Uniformity, while his maternal grandfather had been expelled from Bohemia for faithfulness to the Protestant cause. We are not surprised then, to see in Philip a love for the truth of Scripture. He was trained for the Nonconformist ministry at the academy of the Reverend John Jennings and spent the last twenty-one years of his life, from 1730 to 1751, as minister of the Independent Church at Castle Hill in Northampton.

We turn now to the book itself, in which the rise and progress of personal religion is "illustrated in a course of thirty serious and practical addresses suited to persons of every character and circumstance."

Introduction and Outline (Chap. 1)

As the title of the book implies, Doddridge begins by directing his attention to what he calls a "careless sinner." His aim, he says, is to awaken his subject until the latter feels himself under the just condemnation of the law. The gospel will then be brought to him and its way of acceptance described. After some assurance of genuine regeneration has been given, the reader is to be introduced to the high standard required of the Christian's life and assisted in preparing for its difficulties. He will be warned of the perils of spiritual decline, and encouraged to grow in grace. Eventually the established Christian will be exhorted to honor God by his life and in his death. Let the author explain his manner of handling this material:

> I shall not discuss these themes as a preacher might properly do in sermons, in which the truths of religion are professedly to be explained and taught, defended and improved, in a wide variety and long detail of propositions, arguments, objections, replies and inferences. . . . I shall here speak in a looser and freer manner, as a friend to a friend, just as I would do if I were to be a person admitted to a private audience by one whom I tenderly loved, and whose circumstances and character I knew to be like that which the title of one chapter or another of this treatise describes. And when I have discoursed with him a little while, which will seldom be so long as half an hour, I shall, as it were, step aside and leave him to meditate on what he has heard, or endeavour to assist him in such fervent addresses to God, as it may be proper to mingle with these meditations.

These prayers or meditations comprise from two to four pages at the close of each chapter. Doddridge intends the book not only to be read seriously but to be *thought over* in retirement.

Concern and Condemnation (Chaps. 2–7)

Here is Doddridge's own outline of these chapters:

> I will first suppose myself addressing one of the vast number of thoughtless creatures, who have hitherto been utterly unconcerned about religion, and will try what can be done, by all plainness and earnestness of address, to awaken him from this fatal lethargy, to a care (chap. 2), an affectionate and an immediate care about it (chap. 3). I will labour to fix a deep and awful conviction of guilt upon his conscience (chap. 4), and to strip him of vain excuses and his flattering hopes (chap. 5). I will read to him . . . that dreadful sentence, which a righteous and an Almighty God hath denounced against him as a sinner (chap. 6); and endeavour to show him in how helpless a state he lies under this condemnation, as to any capacity he has of delivering himself (chap. 7).

The first point of significance to notice is Doddridge's conception of *the man to whom he speaks*. Although he has called him a careless sinner he is more properly designated a "nominal Christian."

> I will suppose that you believe the existence and providence of God, and the truth of Christianity as a revelation from him: of which, if you have any doubt, I must desire that you would immediately seek your satisfaction elsewhere. But supposing you to be a nominal Christian and not a deist or a sceptic; I will also suppose your conduct among men to be not only blameless but amiable; . . . yet

with all this, you may "lack that one thing" (Mk. 10:21) on which your eternal happiness depends.

The primary application of this first section, then, is not so much to the man-in-the-street who is careless of any spiritual values but rather to the member of the congregation who is complacent but yet unregenerate. Doddridge proceeds to upbraid this man for his ingratitude in face of God's goodness:

> Is it a decent and reasonable thing that this great and glorious benefactor should be neglected by his rational creatures? by those that are capable of attaining to some knowledge of him and presenting to him some homage? . . . Nay, brutes far less sagacious and apprehensive have some sense of our kindness and express it after their own way. . . . What lamentable degeneracy therefore is it, that you do not know that you, who have been numbered among God's professing people, do not, and will not consider your numberless obligations to him.

Doddridge addresses the intellect, to shame his readers for their unreasonable neglect of God. By direct charge and natural analogy he appeals to their conscience to produce conviction of sin. His use of such argument, however, does not mean that, like the rationalists of his day, he has forgotten the *limitations* of fallen reason:

> Let it not be imagined that it is in any neglect of that blessed Spirit, whose office it is to be the great comforter, that I now attempt to reason you out of this disconsolate frame: for it is as the great source of reason, that he deals with rational creatures; and it is in the use of rational means and considerations that he may most justly be expected to operate.

It is his contention that conscience is the voice of God to the sinner, and we continually meet such phrases as, "I put it to your conscience," and "It is so contrary to the plainest principles of common reason." He treats the sinner throughout as a rational, and therefore a responsible, being:

> Your conscience tells you that you were born the natural subject of God, born under the indispensable obligations of His law. For it is most apparent, that the constitution of your rational nature, which makes you capable of receiving law from God binds you to obey it.

Some attention has been given to this point because we may be in danger of overlooking its importance. In our insistence upon the doctrine of total depravity and the necessity of regeneration for a saving appreciation of the truth of Scripture, we must not become Barthians and deny that there is any point of contact between God and the sinner. Doddridge reminds us what that point of contact is. The sinner's rational nature requires that we should approach him with arguments from Scripture directed to his reason, applying truth to his mind and appealing to the law of God written in his heart. Even by these standards there are sins for which his conscience will condemn him. By these standards, therefore, he is rendered inexcusable.

The Good News: Its Acceptance and Rejection (Chaps. 8–13)

Having discharged his responsibility in the "law-work," Doddridge now turns to the more congenial task of urging the gospel on his readers. He writes:

> I will joyfully proclaim the glad tidings of pardon and salvation by Christ Jesus our Lord, which is all the support and confidence of my own soul (chap. 8): And then I will give some general view of the way by which this salvation is to be obtained (chap. 9); urging the sinner to accept of it as affectionately as I can (chap. 10); though

nothing can be sufficiently pathetic, where, as in this
matter, the life of an immortal soul is in question. Too
probable it is that some will after all this remain insen-
sible; and therefore, that their sad case may not encum-
ber the following articles, I shall here take a solemn
leave of them (chap. 11); and then shall turn and address myself, as compassionately as I can to a most contrary character; I mean to a soul overwhelmed with a
sense of the greatness of its sins, and trembling under
the burden as if there were no more hope for him in
God (chap. 12). And that nothing may be omitted which
may give solid peace to the troubled spirit, I shall endeavour to guide its inquiries as to the evidences of sincere repentance and faith (chap. 13).

There are two main points we would make from this section.
First, we shall draw attention to Doddridge's conception of *God*
and second, to his *careful counsel* in evangelism.

The majesty of God dominates the author's thinking. Few in
our day possess such an exalted view of their Creator and Redeemer as Doddridge carries with him through this book. When
stressing the awful responsibility of the sinner he urges him to
"consider the majesty of the God you have affronted by inatten-
tion and wilful disobedience." We now find that the scheme of
gospel reconciliation is the expressed will of this same righteous
God.

Doddridge has that full-orbed view of the character of God
which comes from much reading of Scripture and meditation on
the Savior it reveals. He encourages his reader to consider the
wrath of God, His patience, His tenderness, His justice, His sovereignty, His eternity—each adduced at the appropriate moment
for the particular exhortation in hand. Would God that we all
knew Him as Doddridge did!

Let us now consider the approach Doddridge has to the declaration of the gospel. His realization of the importance of this
work has an effect on what he writes. One feels, in reading the
book, his intense *longing* for the salvation of the sinner. He con-

veys this desire in the painstaking care with which he pursues the sinner into every corner of his carnal confidence. His "Solemn address to those who will not fall in with the design of the gospel" is a cleverly construed appeal to the sinner's conscience to shake him into a concern of heart. Stanford, in a biography of the author, has complained that, "we know that his object is to lead a poor trembler to Christ, but he seems to us to be a long time about it." Doddridge is concerned, however, for genuine rather than speedy results, and desires thoroughness above all, in both himself as pastor and those whom he counsels. "I find it exceedingly difficult," he says, "to satisfy myself in anything I say to men where their eternal interests are concerned." He is in no hurry to congratulate the convert, but urges him to re-examine his own heart to see whether he yet possesses scriptural grounds for confidence before God.

In describing "the great vital act of faith" by which the sinner solemnly commits his soul into the hands of Christ, he ensures that submission is made to Christ in *all* his offices, as "unerring prophet," as "ever acceptable high-priest" and as "exalted sovereign." Furthermore, he stresses that this must be the language of the penitent's life as well as his heart.

The Christian Character (Chaps. 14–15)

This short section stands between the first half, on the rise of religion in the soul, and the later chapters, on its progress.

His description of the Christian character is the longest chapter in the work and is an abridgement of a book by a Dr. Evans entitled, *The Christian Temper*. Notice again the emphasis on self-examination:

> Happy will you be . . . in no inconsiderable degree, if you can say, "This is what I desire, what I pray for, and what I pursue in preference to every opposite view, though it be not what I have yet attained." Search then, and try "what manner of spirit you are of."

The way Doddridge approaches the Christian's sanctification seems to be this. He first states fully what is the *scriptural ideal* for the Christian character so as to make it clear that we are all far short of it. Then he shows that the genuine convert will want to attain this, and thereby he segregates the truly regenerate from the spurious. Finally he shows that this task is beyond the convert's own strength and that the enabling of God is an imperative need in the Christian's daily life. Once the convert has realized this, he will readily employ all the means at his disposal, to obtain God's help.

It would seem that some present-day counselling of converts tends to over-emphasize the importance of the means, with inadequate attention being given to the *effectual cause of sanctification*. The convert is told that now he is a Christian his great need is to grow. He *must* grow, and to grow he *must* read the Bible and *must* pray every morning. We would suggest that the failure of many to persist in complying with these *musts* is due to their not having a sufficient motive to do so. If the convert were told what God's intention for his character is, the truly regenerate would desire to attain it.

At this stage, then, Doddridge is more concerned to show the convert his continued need of God than to stress the means to his finding Him. "The production of religion in the soul," he writes, "is a matter of divine promise and when it has been effected, Scripture ascribes it to a divine agency."

Difficulties and Directions (Chaps. 16–21)

As some particular difficulties and discouragements attend the first entrance on a religious course, it will here be our first care to animate the young convert against them (chap. 16). And that it may be done more effectually, I shall urge a solemn dedication of himself to God (chap. 17); to be confirmed by entering into the full communion of the Church by an approach to the sacred table (chap. 18). That these engagements may be more happily fulfilled, we shall endeavour to draw a more particular plan of that devout, regular, and accurate course, which ought daily to be attended to (chap. 19); and because the idea will probably rise so much higher than what is the general practice, even of good men, we shall endeavour to persuade the reader to make the attempt, hard as it may seem (chap. 20), and shall caution him against various temptations, which might otherwise draw him aside to negligence and sin (chap. 21).

Like many of former generations but fewer of our own, Doddridge recommends that the young convert should follow his own example and enter into a formal, written covenant as an express act of dedication to the service of God. He explains its usefulness for binding the treacherous heart to God, for strengthening the will in temptation, and for prompting regular review of one's life in the light of its obligations. This act of surrender should be deliberate, cheerful, entire, perpetual, and solemn.

On the whole the rest of this section must be considered one of the most useful parts of the book. It is so full of scriptural, practical advice on preparing for the spiritual conflict of daily life. Apparently the ordinance of the Lord's Supper was too lightly esteemed in Doddridge's day. In commending it, he gives encouragement to "bear about with you a lively sense of the love of Christ which must animate you to break through all opposition." The nineteenth chapter, "on being in the fear of God all the day long," shows how we should regard God in the beginning, the progress, and the closing of the day. Its emphasis on lifting up one's heart to God while rising in the first moments of the day, and in his conscientious self-examination at its close, is especially impressive. Here are one or two sentences illustrating other aspects of Doddridge's advice:

> *On conscience:* "By acting contrary to the secret dictates of your mind, as to what it is just at the present moment best to do, though it be but in the manner of spending half an hour, some degree of guilt is contracted, and a habit is

cherished, which may draw after it much worse consequences."

On friendships: "I beseech you to consider, that those companions may be very dangerous, who might at first give you but very little alarm: I mean those who, though not the declared enemies of religion and professed followers of vice and disorder, yet nevertheless have no practical sense of divine things on their hearts.

The charge has sometimes been made against Doddridge that he gives us too many *rules,* and that this to the inexperienced reader may become a form of legalism. In these directions for daily life, this tendency is certainly present. In fairness to Doddridge, however, he has himself included a clear warning against this snare in the preface to the later editions. He also says at this point in the book:

I wish my reader may act on these directions, so far as they may properly suit his capacities and circumstances in life; for I would be far from laying down the following particulars as universal rules for all, or for any one person in the world at all times. With this precaution I proceed to the letter, which I would hope, . . . will not discourage any, the weakest Christian.

Decline and Discipline (Chaps. 22–25)

In this section more than any other we see Doddridge as a *pastor.* A. T. S. James has written of him, "he was a preacher and a tutor more than an author, and when he writes he has a congregation in front of him." James goes on to contrast him with William Law, and we must agree that *The Rise and Progress* is the work of a shepherd rather than a recluse. The beat of the pastor's heart makes Doddridge insist on God's employment of *means* to the working out of His decreed purposes. His conception of sovereignty never has a neutralizing effect on his view of responsibility. For example, the Christian whose spiritual life is in decline is exhorted to return to God immediately and told how to do so:

> While the darkness continues, go on in the way of your duty. Continue the use of means and ordinances; read and meditate; pray, yes, and sing the praises of God too, though it may be with a heavy heart. Follow the "footsteps of his flock" (Cant. 1:8); you may perhaps meet the Shepherd of souls in doing it. Place yourself at least in his way. It is possible you may by this means get a kind look from him; and one look, one turn of thought . . . may create a heaven in your soul at once.

If we were asked what is the one outstanding lesson of the book, we would point to the way in which the progress of religion in a man's soul is organically related to its rise. One cannot read this book and merely note a good point in an odd chapter. The early parts are foundational and the rest is built up from them. This is not one book on conversion and another on sanctification bound between the same covers, but it is a unity. The advice Doddridge gives his readers at the outset should be heeded: "Into whatever hands this work may come, I must desire, that before any pass their judgment upon it, they would please to read it through, that they may discern the connection between one part of it and another."

It is this connection, this continuity, which is so helpful. The way in which Doddridge has led the sinner to Christ has ensured that *this* convert has certain convictions. Because of his lofty conception of God, and the holy standard expected by God, he is conscious that he is still full of all manner of sins. As a result, Doddridge can now tellingly impress upon him that all his Christian experience is God's way of delivering him from his remaining depravity. This he does in his chapter on the "Christian struggling under great and heavy afflictions." The Christian is expected to pray, "I am much more concerned that my afflictions may be sanctified than that they may be removed." How many of us react in this way?

It is no wonder that many professing converts today do not seem to make progress in the Christian life, if the rise of religion in their soul has not been a thorough work of grace. This thorough work, with all its implications and humbling lessons, Doddridge here presupposes; as he is entitled to, for he has thoroughly instructed his reader in this early on, so that now in the later stages he is able to build on a sure foundation.

Growth and Glory (Chaps. 26–30)

Doddridge summarizes his final chapters in this way:

> We shall endeavour, in the best manner we can, to assist the Christian in passing a true judgment on the growth of grace in his heart (chap. 26), as we had done before in judging of its sincerity. And as nothing conduces more to the advance of grace, than the lively exercise of love to God, and a holy joy in him, we shall here remind the real Christian of those mercies which tend to excite that love and joy (chap. 27); and in the views of them to animate him to those vigorous efforts of usefulness in life, which so well become his character, and will have so happy an efficacy in brightening his crown (chap. 28). Supposing him to act accordingly we shall than labour to illustrate and assist the delight with which he may look forward to the awful solemnities of death and judgment (chap. 29). And shall close the scene by accompanying him, as it were, to the nearest confines of that dark valley, through which he is to pass to glory; giving him such directions as may seem most subservient to his honouring God and adorning religion, by his dying behaviour (chap. 30).

We have previously mentioned Doddridge's extensive and judicious employment of Scripture quotations. As James puts it,

"Many of the longest sentences are composed of texts pieced together from every corner of Scripture, and in the result the Bible speaks for itself." In two pages of the last chapter of the book there are nineteen portions of Scripture quoted, and in the meditation following chapter fourteen, there are fifty-four. In this respect Doddridge resembles many of the Puritan writers.

There are one or two occasions, however, when even Doddridge seems to lose sight of a scriptural emphasis. His single eye is fixed on the honor of God, but is it not a New Testament principle that God is to be honored by our seeking primarily the glory of Christ? This distinction may be seen in his exhortation to the exercises of habitual love to God and joy in Him. The tendency of his meditation is certainly warm and joyful, but we could have wished that a Rutherford or a M'Cheyne had been at his side to remind the convert to "run with patience . . . *looking unto Jesus,* whom having not seen we love, in whom, though now we see him not, yet believing we rejoice with joy unspeakable and full of glory." Does the title chosen for this book, *"The Rise and Progress of Religion in the Soul,"* overlook the second part of Paul's description of the true circumcision which is, "worship God in the spirit and rejoice in Christ Jesus"? We are not suggesting that there is any sense in which his doctrine of the Person or work of Christ is defective. It is not. But the Christ-centered vision is not always prominent, although it is present. He delights thus in the expectation of the Second Advent:

> Is it so delightful to receive the visits of Jesus for an hour? and will it not be infinitely more so to dwell with him for ever? "Lord," may you well say, "when I dwell with thee, I shall dwell in holiness, for thou thyself art holiness; I shall dwell in love, for thou thyself art love; I shall dwell in joy, for thou art the fountain of joy, as thou art in the Father, and the Father in thee."

This is more than religion, this is Christianity! But he has a tendency to lose sight of this emphasis.

The closing section of the book underlines some remarks we

made in the introduction to this paper regarding the author's personal life. It is apparent throughout that Doddridge is writing from experience and all that he writes he has himself put into practice. "I can truly and cheerfully say, that I have marked out to you the path which I myself have trod, and in which it is my desire still to go on. I have ventured my own everlasting interests on that foundation, on which I have directed you to adventure yours."

When we read him urging the established Christian to "exert himself for purposes of usefulness," we must remember that this was exemplified to the letter by his own zeal for good works. He was instrumental in opening a school for the poor, founding a county infirmary and, most interesting of all, was an earnest advocate of foreign missions. He projected a scheme for a missionary society and was keen to learn about Brainerd and to meet Zinzendorf and Whitefield. In 1741 he preached to ministers in Norfolk on "the evil and danger of neglecting souls," and we can imagine him including such questions as these which he later wrote in this book:

> Do you find your imagination teeming, as it were, with conceptions of schemes for the advancement of the cause and interest of Christ in the world, for the propagation of the gospel, and the happiness of your fellow creatures? And do you not only pray, but act for it; act in such a manner as to show that you pray in earnest? . . . Have compassion on those who dwell in a desert land; and rejoice to do something towards sending among the distant nations of the heathen world, that glorious gospel which hath so long continued unknown to multitudes.

And all this was written *before Carey was born!*

Orton's memoir is full of references to the consistency of Doddridge's life with his writings. His charity to other ministers, even to Arians and High Churchmen, has, we fear, unjustly put his own reputation for orthodoxy under suspicion. We quote again: "But to hate persons because we think they are mistaken, and to aggravate every difference in judgment or practice into a fatal and damnable error, that destroys all Christian communion and love, is a symptom generally much worse than the evil it condemns."

In these days of increasing interest in Reformed theology, this seems to us a very important lesson. Doddridge may not have been so acute a theological teacher as some would wish, but if theology means a knowledge of God, then he was certainly a practical theologian of the first rank.

The New Testament does stress the importance of the apostles' doctrine, but knows nothing of a merely intellectual apprehension of the Truth without any application of that Truth in the Christian life. What steps should we take, then, to ensure that our studies in Reformed theology lead to a different way of life, as well as a different scheme of doctrine? To produce the different way of life was Doddridge's grand aim for his book.

The measure of his success, only eternity will reveal!

2

JONATHAN EDWARDS
AND THE THEOLOGY OF REVIVAL

J. I. Packer

Jonathan Edwards, saint, scholar, preacher, pastor, meta-physician, theologian, Calvinist, and revival leader, lived from 1703 to 1758. He was a tall, reserved, soft-spoken man, strong-minded and humble-hearted. In 1727, after five years in the ministry, he became co-pastor of the large and fashionable church at Northampton, New Hampshire, where his grandfather, Solomon Stoddard, the grand old man of ecclesiastical life in the Connecticut Valley, now a patriarchal eighty-three, had ministered since 1669.

Northampton was a town of perhaps two thousand inhabitants, and its church was the best-known and most influential in New England outside Boston. Stoddard himself was almost idolized by the congregation, most of whom had grown up under his ministry. Two years later, in 1729, Stoddard's death brought his sixty-year pastorate to a close, and from then on Edwards was sole

21

minister. In 1734–35 and 1740–42 he saw remarkable movement of the Spirit of God in his congregation and, in the latter case, throughout all New England.

From 1743, however, Edwards was for various reasons in trouble with his church, and in 1750 he was dismissed from the pastorate because he insisted on restoring the demand, which Stoddard had dropped, for a personal confession of faith as the *sine qua non* of communicant church membership. Edwards then moved to a mission station in the frontier hamlet of Stockbridge, and it was here that he wrote his great treatises on the *Freedom of the Will* and *Original Sin*. In 1757 he was made President of Princeton College. He travelled to Princeton to take up his appointment in February, 1758. His first move was to be inoculated against smallpox; but the inoculation itself brought on fever, and in the following month he died.

Edwards was a Puritan born out of due time. It is hardly too much to say, with a recent writer, that Puritanism is what Edwards was. All his roots were in the theology and outlook of the founding fathers of New England, men like Hooker and Shepard, Cotton and Davenport. He was a true Puritan, first, in his *devotion to the Bible*. All his life he laboured, fearlessly and tirelessly, to understand and apply the Bible, and his written works (apart, perhaps from those on prophecy) reveal an exegetical acumen comparable with that of Calvin, or Owen, or Hodge, or Warfield. All his life he fed his soul on the Bible; and all his life he fed his flock on the Bible.

Again, he was a true Puritan in his *doctrinal convictions*. In a day when, as in England, a rationalistic Latitudinarianism—the "free and catholic" outlook of Charles Chauncy and his friends—was eating away the Puritan heritage, Edwards stood forth as an uncompromising and unashamed Calvinistic supernaturalist, diagnosing the fashionable view as Arminianism and opposing it, as the Puritans had opposed the Arminianism of their day, on the grounds of its religious implications. Edwards argued that Arminianism in any form—any form, that is, of the synergism which makes conviction of spiritual truth God's work, but conversion itself man's—undercuts true piety. It makes God less than

God; it is three-quarters of the way to deism, and halfway to real atheism. It destroys due reverence for God, because it denies our complete dependence on Him. It ministers to pride, by representing the decisive act in our salvation as all our own work. Thus it introduces a principle of self-reliance into religion; which is in effect to render religion irreligious, and to base the form of godliness upon a denial of the matter of it. These were Puritan points, and in making them Edwards showed himself a true heir of the Puritan tradition in theology.

In the third place, Edwards was a true Puritan in his view of *the nature of Christian piety*. In essence, Edwards maintained, godliness is a matter of glorifying the Creator by humble dependence and a thankful obedience. In Christian terms, this means acknowledging our complete dependence upon God, as for life and health, so for grace and glory, and loving and praising and serving Him for all that He has so freely given us through His Son. Edwards struck this note in 1731 in his first published sermon, a discourse on 1 Corinthians 1:29–31 entitled "God glorified in man's dependence." The theme of the sermon is that "God is glorified in the work of redemption in this, that there appears in it so absolute and universal a dependence of the redeemed on him." And it concludes thus:

> Let us be exhorted to exalt God alone, and ascribe to him all the glory of redemption Let us endeavour to obtain, and increase in, a sensibleness of our great dependence on God, . . . to mortify a self-dependent and self-righteous disposition. Man is naturally exceeding prone to exalt himself, and depend on his own power or goodness. . . . But this doctrine should teach us to exalt God *alone;* as by trust and reliance, so by praise. *Let him that glorieth, glory in the Lord.* Hath any man hope that he is converted and sanctified . . . that his sins are forgiven, and he received into God's favour, and exalted to the honour and blessedness of being his child, and an heir of eternal life? Let him give God all the glory; who alone makes him to differ from the worst of men in this world, or the most mis-

erable of the damned in hell. . . . Is any man eminent in
holiness, and abundant in good works, let him take nothing of the glory of it to himself, but ascribe it unto him
whose "workmanship we are, created in Christ Jesus unto
good works."[1]

The thought of man's complete dependence on a free omnipotent God controlled Edwards's whole religious outlook, and
acted as the guiding principle of his entire theology.

To Edwards, therefore, true religion was much more than either orthodoxy, or ethics, or the two put together. Edwards held
no brief for believism, or moralism, or formalism of any sort. True
piety was to him a supernatural gift, dynamic in character and intensely experimental in its outworking. It was, in fact, a realized
communion with God through Christ, brought into being by the
Holy Spirit and expressed in responsive affections and activities.

The root of piety, Edwards maintained, is a hearty conviction
(in his phrase, a "cordial sense") of the reality and glory of the divine and heavenly things spoken of in the gospel. Such a conviction is more than an intellectual grasp of theological ideas, or a
taking Christian truth for granted under the constraining pres-
sure of community opinion; it is, rather, the result of direct divine
illumination accompanying the written or spoken word of God,
as Edwards explained in 1734 in his second published sermon,
on Matthew 16:17, entitled "A divine and supernatural light, immediately imparted to the soul by the Spirit of God, shown to be
both a Scriptural and rational doctrine."

The divine enlightenment issues in conversion.

This light is such as effectually influences the inclination,
and changes the nature of the soul. It assimilates our nature to the divine Nature. . . . This knowledge will wean
from the world, and raise the inclination to heavenly
things. It will turn the heart to God as the fountain of good,
and to choose him for the only portion. This light, and this
only, will bring the soul to a saving close with Christ. It con-
forms the heart to the gospel, mortifies its enmity and op-

position against the scheme of salvation therein revealed: it causes the heart to embrace the joyful tidings, and entirely to adhere to, and acquiesce in, the revelation of Christ as our Saviour: it causes the whole soul to accord and symphonize with it . . . cleaving to it with full inclination and affection; and it effectually disposes the soul to give up itself entirely to Christ. . . . As it reaches the bottom of the heart, and changes the nature, so it will effectually dispose to a universal obedience. It shows God as worthy to be obeyed and served. It draws forth the heart in a sincere love to God . . . and it convinces of the reality of those glorious rewards that God has promised to them that obey him.[2]

From this renewal of the heart by vivifying light from God issue good works and holy affections. The skepticism of rationalists, and the delusions of "enthusiasts," about characteristically Christian affections forced Edwards to devote special attention to this subject: and in his *Treatise concerning Religious Affections* (published in 1746, originally preached as a course of sermons in 1742–43) he gave the world the fruit of his study. He begins by arguing that, inasmuch as the affections are the fundamental functions of the will, the fount of action, it follows of necessity that "true religion, in great part, consists in holy affections." "As the affections not only necessarily belong to the human nature, but are a very great part of it," Edwards explains; "so (inasmuch as by regeneration persons are renewed in the whole man) holy affections not only necessarily belong to true religion, but are a very great part of such religion. And as true religion is practical, and God hath so constituted the human nature, that the affections are very much the springs of men's actions, this also shows, that true religion must consist very much in the affections."[3] Having established this, Edwards proceeds to characterize "truly gracious and holy affections."

In all this, what Edwards is doing is clarifying and vindicating the Puritan conception of experimental religion against the cold moralism of the school of Tillotson. It is as the spiritual heir of Shepard, Flavel, and Stoddard, all of whom he constantly cites in his footnotes (the former especially), that Edwards is writing. With them, he is concerned to insist that true and vital Christianity is a religion of the heart as well as of the head, and to show as accurately as possible how the heart should be engaged in it. This is a peculiarly Puritan interest, and Edwards shows his oneness with the Puritan outlook by pursuing it.

Fourth, Edwards was a true Puritan in his *approach to preaching*. Like his seventeenth-century predecessors, he preached with a threefold aim: to make men understand, feel, and respond to gospel truth. Like them, he set out the matter of his sermons according to the threefold "method" of proposition, proof, and application—"doctrine, reason, and use," as the Puritans called it. Like them, he studied plainness of style, concealing his learning beneath a deliberately bald clarity of statement. It is sometimes imagined that, because in the pulpit he read a manuscript in a steady, quiet, even tone, and avoided looking at his congregation as he spoke, he did not share the Puritan concern to preach with directness, authority, and felt power—the concern which Baxter voiced when he spoke of his desire to be "a plain and pressing downright preacher," one who

> preached as never sure to preach again,
> And as a dying man to dying men.

But this is a mistake. Edwards knew very well that "the main benefit obtained by preaching is by impression made upon the mind at the time, and not by an effect that arises afterwards by a remembrance of what was delivered."[4] And when the earnestness and vehemence of Whitefield and the Tennents during the revival of 1740 came under fire from the Latitudinarians, who saw it as a regrettable lapse into "enthusiasm," Edwards ran to their defense:

> I think an exceeding affectionate way of preaching about the great things of religion, has in itself no tendency to beget false apprehensions of them; but on the contrary, a much greater tendency to beget true apprehensions of

them, than a moderate, dull, indifferent way of speaking
of them. . . . If the subject be in its own nature worthy of
very great affection, then speaking of it with great affection is most agreeable to the nature of that subject . . . and
therefore has most of a tendency to beget true ideas of it.
. . . I should think myself in the way of my duty, to raise
the affections of my hearers as high as possibly I can, provided that they are affected with nothing but truth. . . . I
know it has long been fashionable to despise a very
earnest and pathetical way of preaching; and they only
have been valued as preachers, who have shown the greatest extent of learning, strength of reason, and correctness
of method and language. But I humbly conceive it has
been for want of understanding or duly considering human nature, that such preaching has been thought to
have the greatest tendency to answer the ends of preaching. . . . An increase in speculative knowledge in divinity
is not what is so much needed by our people as something
else. Men may abound in this sort of light, and have no
heat. . . . Our people do not so much need to have their
heads stored, as to have their hearts touched; and they
stand in the greatest need of that sort of preaching, which
has the greatest tendency to do this.[5]

In fact, Edwards's own preaching was powerful in a high degree. Humanly speaking, he had a unique gift for making ideas
live by the luminous precision with which he expounded them.
He uncoils a length of reasoning with a slow, smooth exactness
that is almost hypnotic in its power to rivet attention on the
successive folds of truth sliding out into view. Had Edwards
been no more than a pagan don teaching economics, he would
without doubt have been a performer of Ancient Mariner quality in the lecture room. To this compelling expository power
was added in the pulpit a terrible solemnity, expressive of the
awe of God that was constantly on his spirit; and the result was
preaching that congregations could neither resist nor forget.
Edwards could make two hours seem like twenty minutes as he

bore down on his listeners' consciences with the plain old truths of sin and salvation, and the calm majesty of his inexorable analysis was no less used of God to make men feel the force of truth than was the rhapsodic vehemence of George Whitefield.

One of his hearers, asked whether Edwards was an eloquent preacher, replied: "If you mean by eloquence, what is usually intended by it in our cities; he had no pretensions to it. He had no studied varieties of voice, and no strong emphasis. He scarcely gestured or even moved; and he made no attempt, by the eloquence of his style, or the beauty of his pictures, to gratify the taste, and fascinate the imagination. But, if you mean by eloquence the power of presenting an important truth before an audience, with overwhelming weight of argument, and with such intenseness of feeling that the whole soul of the speaker is thrown into every part of the conception and delivery, so that the solemn attention of the whole audience is riveted, from the beginning to the close, and impressions are left that cannot be effaced, Mr. Edwards was the most eloquent man I ever heard speak."[6]

"His words," wrote his first biographer, Samuel Hopkins, "often discovered a great deal of inward fervour, without much noise or external emotion, and fell with great weight on the minds of his hearers; and he spake so as to reveal the strong emotions of his own heart, which tended, in the most natural and effectual manner, to move and affect others."[7] Such a feeling communication of felt truth was, in fact, precisely what the Puritans had had in mind when they spoke of "powerful" preaching.

As a Bible lover, a Calvinist, a teacher of heart-religion, a gospel preacher of unction and power, and, above all, a man who loved Christ, hated sin, feared God, Edwards was a pure Puritan; indeed, one of the greatest of all the Puritans. American historians of culture have recently rediscovered Edwards as a major contributor to the American philosophical and literary heritage. It is to be wished that evangelical Christians today might themselves rediscover the important contribution that this latter-day Puritan made to the elucidation of the biblical faith.

Last-century evangelicals, on the whole, admired Edwards,

but nonetheless they did him a threefold disservice. First, they accused him of being unreadable. But one has only to make the experiment to find that this is not so at all. The levelling of this charge was in fact a case of the mote and the beam. It is true that Edwards does not go in for the flowery padding which the nineteenth century regarded as essential to good style, but this is to his credit rather than otherwise. He is today far more palatable as a writer than are many of his older critics. The most one can say against him is that on occasion his desire for a clinical precision of language leads him to write sentences that are too long and complex for easy assimilation on first reading. But this is his only stylistic fault, and that not a common one; most of the time he is admirably clear, exact, and pointed.

Then, in the second place, the last century treated Edwards as an essentially philosophical theologian, chiefly on the strength of *The Freedom of the Will*. Now, it is true that Edwards had a genius for abstract reasoning, and that he indulged it to the full in this particular treatise. But we need to remember what sort of a treatise *The Freedom of the Will* is. It is not a work of biblical theology, but an elaborate polemical essay directed against what is, as Edwards truly saw, an essentially speculative and philosophical position—that of rationalistic Arminianism, which builds everything on the axiom that divine control of human action is incompatible with man's moral responsibility, and cannot therefore be a fact. Edwards chose the most obviously crushing way to deal with this position—to turn its own weapons against itself; to give it points and a beating, so to speak, on its own home ground. But *The Freedom of the Will* was an occasional performance, and is not characteristic of the rest of Edwards's work.

It is clear from his private notes and memoranda that metaphysical speculation fascinated him and was, indeed, his hobby, but he never let philosophy teach him his faith, or lead him away from the Bible. He philosophized from faith, not to it; he did not regard speculation as necessary to salvation, and no hint of his philosophical interests intrudes into his sermons. He took his convictions and concerns from the Bible, and it is as a scriptural theologian that his true stature is to be measured.

Finally—and this was the worst disservice of all—Edwards's last century admirers quite overlooked Edwards's most original contribution to theology: namely, his pioneer elucidation of biblical teaching on the subject of revival. This oversight is, perhaps, pardonable, since Edwards's thoughts on this subject were put out piecemeal in five early works which he composed in his thirties—*A Narrative of a Surprising Work of God in the Conversion of many hundred souls in Northampton and the neighbouring Towns and Villages* (1735); *A History of the Work of Redemption* (sermons preached in 1739, published in 1744); *The Distinguishing Marks of a Work of the Spirit of God* (1741); *Thoughts on the Revival of Religion in New England in 1740* (1742); and the *Treatise on the Religious Affections* (preached, 1742–43; published, 1746). All these save the second are concerned, in one way or another, to vindicate the two revivals which Edwards had himself seen against the current charge that they were mere outbreaks of fanaticism. This immediate aim might seem to limit their interest for later generations of readers. Embedded in them, however, is a fairly complete account of revival as a work of God—in other words, a theology of revival—which is fuller than any produced before Edwards's time, and is of lasting value. It is, perhaps, the most important single contribution that Edwards has to make to evangelical thinking today.

It is a notable fact that interest in the subject of revival is increasing at the present time: witness the growth of revival fellowships of various kinds within the Protestant denominations. More and more the conviction is spreading that only a visitation from on high can touch the needs of the churches today. But most of us find ourselves uncertain as to what exactly revival is, and what might be expected to happen if revival came. And there are in particular two types of mistake at this point to which we are all prone.

The first is the *antiquarian fallacy*. We fall victim to this mistake when we form a conception of revival from the history of a particular revival in the past, and then set up our conception, thus formed, as a norm and yardstick for any movement of revival in the future. To do this is to expose ourselves to a double danger.

On the one hand, we predispose ourselves to be too hasty in identifying with revival outbreaks of religious excitement which exhibit certain outward features that marked some revival of the past—prostrations, visions, spontaneous singing, or whatever the features are that have impressed us. We have to remember that the devil can produce the outward forms of religious excitement, as well as the Spirit of God, and that in fact Satan has often wrought havoc in the church through movements of self-deceived fanaticism which announced themselves, doubtless in all good faith, as movements of the Holy Spirit in revival. We need a criterion for telling the two apart; otherwise Satan will be free to fool us as he pleases by gratifying our hunger for revival with his own particular brand of "enthusiastic" delusions. And precedent—"former observation," as Edwards calls it—is not of itself a sufficient criterion for this purpose. In Edwards's words, "what the church has been used to, is not a rule by which we are to judge" in such cases, one way or the other.[8] We need a better touchstone than this for telling the spurious from the true.

Then, on the other hand, by conceiving of revival wholly in terms of some particular past revival, we make it harder for ourselves to recognize any future revival that God may send. For it is not God's habit to repeat Himself. There is no ground for supposing that the externals of the next revival will be just like the externals of the last one, any more than there would be for expecting two people to pass through exactly the same sequence of experiences in their conversion. Those who will only allow that God is at work when they see Him repeating exactly something that He has done before, Edwards tells us, "limit God, where he has not limited himself. And this is especially unreasonable in this case (i.e., that of revival)," he continues; "for whosoever has well weighed the wonderful and mysterious methods of divine wisdom in carrying on the work of the new creation—or in the progress of the work of redemption, from the first promise to the seed of the woman to this time—may easily observe that it has all along been God's manner to open new scenes, and to bring forth to view things new and wonderful . . . to the astonishment of heaven and earth. . . ."[9]

The second mistake that threatens us is *the romantic fallacy*. We fall into this when we let ourselves imagine that revival, once it came, would function as the last chapter in a detective story functions—solving all our problems, clearing up all the difficulties that have arisen in the church, and leaving us in a state of idyllic peace and contentment, with no troubles to perplex us any more.

A study of Jonathan Edwards on revival forewarns us against both these mistakes. In the first place, Edwards shields us from the antiquarian fallacy, by teaching us the biblical principles for determining whether an outbreak of religious excitement is an outpouring of God's Spirit or not. "We have a rule near at hand," he claims, "a sacred book that God himself has put into our hands, with clear and infallible marks, sufficient to resolve us in things of this nature."[10] And he labors to show us in thorough detail just what these marks are.

Then, in the second place, Edwards shields us from the romantic fallacy by constantly directing our attention to the problems which revival brings in its train. Revival means renewal of life, and life means energy. It is true that revival delivers the church from the problems created by apathy and deadness, but it is equally true that revival plunges the church into a welter of new problems created by the torrential overflow of disordered and undisciplined spiritual vitality.

In a revival, the saints are suddenly roused from a state of torpor and lethargy by a new and overwhelming awareness of the reality of spiritual things, and of God. They are like sleepers shaken awake and now half blinded by the unaccustomed glare of the sun. They hardly know for the moment where they are; in one sense, they now see everything, as they never saw it before, yet in another sense, because of the very brightness of the light, they can hardly see anything. They are swept off their feet; they lose their sense of proportion. They fall into pride, delusions, unbalance, censorious modes of speech, extravagant forms of action.

Unconverted persons are caught up in what is going on; they feel the power of truth, though their hearts remain unrenewed; they become "enthusiasts," harsh and bitter, fierce and vainglorious, cranky and fanatical. Then, perhaps, they fall into spectacular sin, and apostatize altogether; or else remain in the church to scandalize the rest of men by maintaining, on dogmatic perfectionist grounds, that while what they do would be sin in others, it is not sin in them. Satan (who, as Edwards somewhere observes, was "trained in the best divinity school in the universe") keeps step with God, actively perverting and caricaturing all that the Creator is doing. A revival, accordingly, is always a *disfigured* work of God, and the more powerful the revival, the more scandalizing disfigurements we may expect to see.

Hence we cannot wonder if the revival comes to be bitterly opposed by respectable church members of limited spiritual insight, on account of the excesses linked with it; nor can we be surprised to find—as we regularly do—that many ministers stand aloof from the revival, and even preach against it and try to suppress it, on the grounds that it is not a spiritual phenomenon at all. Edwards had had to face all this in his own experience, and he makes us face it too. "A work of God without stumbling-blocks is never to be expected," he wrote grimly in 1741; ". . . we shall probably see more instances of apostasy and gross iniquity among professors. . . ."[11] No; revival, though in itself a purging and purifying work of God, is never free from attendant disfigurements. We need not read beyond the New Testament to appreciate that. Yet this must not blind us to the fact that revival is a real and glorious work of God, and a blessing much to be desired when the church's vitality is low. We proceed now to examine Edwards's theological account of it.

We shall expound his teaching under three main heads.

Principles Concerning the Nature of Revival

Here there are three propositions to consider, of which the first is the most important and fundamental, and will occupy us the longest.

1. *Revival is an extraordinary work of God the Holy Ghost reinvigorating and propagating Christian piety in a community.*

Revival is an *extraordinary* work, because it marks the abrupt reversal of an established trend and state of things among those who profess to be God's people. To envisage God *reviving* His church is to presuppose that the church has previously grown moribund and gone to sleep. To speak of God *pouring out His Spirit* in an *awakening,* as Edwards, following Scripture, does, is to imply that God does something sudden and decisive to change a state of affairs in which the Spirit's quickening influence, and a lively sense of spiritual realities, were conspicuous by their absence.

Revival is a work of *reinvigorating and propagating Christian piety.* Though it is through the knowledge of Bible truth that the Spirit effects His reviving work, revival is not merely, nor even primarily, a restoring of orthodoxy. It is essentially a restoring of *religion.* We have seen what Edwards conceived Christian religion to be: an experimental acquaintance with, and a hearty, practical response to, the divine things set forth in the gospel. It is this that languishes during the time of sleep and barrenness before revival comes, and it is this that the outpouring of the Spirit renews. Hence the "distinguishing marks of a work of the Spirit of God," i.e. of a revival, all have to do with the deepening of experimental piety. We may quote at length from Edwards's exposition of these marks, in the little treatise on 1 John 4:1 which bears the phrase quoted as its title. All that is said is germane to our subject, and the passage as a whole is a fine example of Edwards's expository style.

I shall confine myself wholly to those marks which are given us by the apostle in the chapter wherein is my text, where this matter is particularly handled, and more plainly and fully than any where else in the Bible. And in speaking to these marks, I shall take them in the order in which I find them in the chapter.

1. When the operation is such as to raise their esteem of that Jesus who was born of the Virgin, and was crucified without the gates of Jerusalem; and seems more to confirm and establish their minds in the truth of what the gospel declares to us of his being the Son of God, and

the Saviour of men; it is a sure sign that it is from the Spirit of God. This sign the apostle gives us in the 2d. and 3d verses . . . (which speak of) a confessing not only that there was such a person who appeared in Palestine, and did and suffered those things that are recorded of him, but that he was Christ, i.e. the Son of God, anointed to be the Lord and Saviour, as the name Jesus Christ implies . . . .

The devil has the most bitter and implacable enmity against that person, especially in his character of the Saviour of men; he mortally hates the story and doctrine of his redemption; he would never go about to beget in men more honourable thoughts of him. . . .

2. When the Spirit that is at work operates against the interests of Satan's kingdom, which lies in encouraging and establishing sin, and cherishing men's worldly lusts; this is a sure sign that it is a true, and not a false, spirit. This sign we have given us in the 4th and 5th verses . . . by the *world* . . . the apostle evidently means everything that appertains to the interest of sin, and comprehends all the corruptions and lusts of men, and all those acts and objects by which they are gratified.

So that we may safely determine, from what the apostle says, that the spirit that is at work among a people, after such a manner, as to lessen men's esteem of the pleasures, profits, and honours of the world, and to take off their hearts from an eager pursuit after these things; and to engage them in a deep concern about a future state and eternal happiness . . . and the spirit that convinces them of the dreadfulness of sin, the guilt it brings, and the misery to which it exposes; must needs be the spirit of God.

It is not to be supposed that Satan would convince men of sin, and awaken the conscience. . . .

3. The spirit that operates in such a manner, as to cause in men a greater regard to the Holy Scriptures, and establishes them more in their truth and divinity, is certainly the Spirit of God. This rule the apostle gives us in the 6th verse . . . *We are of God;* that is, "We the apostles are sent forth of God, and appointed by him to teach the world, and to deliver those doctrines and instructions, which are to be their rule; *he that knoweth God, heareth us,"* etc. The apostle's argument here equally reaches all that in the same sense are *of God;* that is, all those that God has appointed and inspired to deliver to his church its rule of faith and practice; all the prophets and apostles . . . in a word, all the penmen of the Holy Scriptures. The devil never would attempt to beget in persons a regard to that divine word. . . . A spirit of delusion will not incline persons to seek direction at the mouth of God. . . . Would the spirit of error, in order to deceive men, beget in them a high opinion of the infallible rule, and incline them to think much of it, and be very conservant with it? Would the prince of darkness, in order to promote his kingdom of darkness, lead men to the sun?

4. Another rule to judge of spirits may be drawn from . . . the 6th verse . . . if by observing the manner of operation of a spirit that is at work among a people, we see that it operates as a spirit of truth, leading persons to truth, convincing them of those things that are true . . for instance if we observe that the spirit at work makes men more sensible than they used to be, that there is a God, and that he is a great and sin-hating God; that life is short, and very uncertain; and that there is another world; that they have immortal souls, and must give account of themselves to God; that they are exceeding sinful by nature and practice; that they are helpless in themselves; and confirms them in other things that are agreeable to some sound doctrine; the spirit that works thus, operates as a spirit of truth; he represents things as they truly are. . . . And therefore we

may conclude, that it is not the spirit of darkness that doth thus discover and make manifest the truth. . . .

5. If the spirit that is at work among a people operates as a spirit of love to God and man, it is a sure sign that it is the Spirit of God. This sign the apostle insists upon from the 6th verse to the end of the chapter . . . and speaks expressly of both love to God and men; of *love to men* in the 7th, 11th, and 12th verses; and of *love to God* in the 17th, 18th, and 19th verses; and of both together, in the last two verses. . . . The spirit that . . . works in them an admiring, delightful sense of the excellency of Jesus Christ . . . winning and drawing the heart with those motives and incitements to love, of which the apostle speaks . . . viz. the wonderful free love of God in giving his only-begotten Son to die for us, and the wonderful dying love of Christ to us, who had no love to him, but were his enemies; must needs be the Spirit of God. . . . The spirit that . . . makes the attributes of God as revealed in the gospel, and manifested in Christ, delightful objects of contemplation; and makes the soul to long after God and Christ—after Their presence and communion, acquaintance with Them, and conformity to Them—and to live so as to please and honour Them; the spirit that quells contentions among men, and gives a spirit of peace and good will, excites to acts of outward kindness, and earnest desires of the salvation of souls . . . there is the highest kind of evidence of the influence of a true and divine spirit.[12]

Edwards's case is that wherever these fruits are appearing, there the Spirit of God is at work; and, therefore, that these are the signs which infallibly indicate whether an outbreak of religious excitement, disorderly and in some ways distressing as it may be, is a work of revival or not. The criterion of revival is not the excitement and hullabaloo of the meetings, but the fruit of the Spirit—faith in, and love to, the Father and the Son, and the Scriptures and their teaching, and good works to benefit other men. Where these fruits suddenly begin to appear in a church or community, after a time of barrenness, there revival, in some degree, has begun, whatever attendant disfigurements may appear at the same time.

The substance of religion, as Edwards conceived it (and he was a true Puritan to stress this) is conscious communion with God, and under the intense influence of the outpoured Spirit in a time of revival the individual's sense of God's presence, and absorption in the knowledge of Him, and joy in the assurance of His love, might be raised to very remarkable heights. Edwards saw a good deal of this among his people, but no case seemed to him more outstanding than that of his own wife, whose experience he described at length (without saying whose it was) in *Thoughts on the Revival* (in a section headed simply: "The nature of the work in a particular instance"). The description should be read in full; we have space to quote only a few sentences. Sarah Edwards's experience, writes her husband, included the following elements:

> A very frequent dwelling for some considerable time together, in views of the glory of the divine perfections and Christ's excellencies; so that the soul has been as it were perfectly overwhelmed, and swallowed up with light and love, a sweet solace, and a rest and joy of soul altogether unspeakable. . . . This great rejoicing has been with trembling, i.e. attended with a deep and lively sense of the greatness and majesty of God, and the person's own exceeding littleness and vileness. . . . The things already mentioned have been attended with . . . an extraordinary sense of the awful majesty, greatness, and holiness of God. . . . The strength of the body was very often taken away with a deep mourning for sin, as committed against so holy and good a God. . . . There has been a very great sense of the certain truth of the great things revealed in the gospel; an overwhelming sense of the glory of the work of redemption, and the way of salvation by Jesus Christ. . . . The person felt a great delight in singing praises to God and Jesus Christ, and longing that this present life may be, as it were,

one continued song of praise to God. There was a longing,
as the person expressed it, to sit and sing this life away; and
an overcoming pleasure in the thoughts of spending an
eternity in that exercise. . . .[13]

Such is the inward heart of the realized communion with God,
the true, pure Christian piety, into which all the saints of God are
led, more or less deeply, by the reviving work of the Holy Ghost.
"If such things are enthusiasm, and the fruits of a distempered
brain," writes Edwards with fine irony, "let my brain be evermore
possessed of that happy distemper!" Such experiences as these,
he held (and, surely, with justice) were proof positive that the
Holy Spirit of God was at work in the religious movements out of
which the experiences came.

   It should be stressed, finally, under this head, that to Edwards
revival meant the restoring of Christian piety *in a community*. The
object of revival was the church, and the effect of the blessing was
to spread the faith to the unconverted outside the church. Revival is a corporate affair. It was upon the company of disciples
that the Spirit was poured out at Pentecost; it is the church to
which God brings awakening (cf. Isa. 51:17; 52:1). This is not, of
course, to deny that an individual Christian may be spiritually vi-
talized while the church around remains dead, but simply to assert that the characteristic work of God which we are discussing
at present is a work which in some sense has the church, and not
just an individual Christian, as its object.

   2. *Revivals have a central place in the revealed purposes of God.*

   "The end of God's creating the world," declares Edwards,
"was to prepare a kingdom for his Son (for he was appointed heir
of the world)."[14] This end is to be realized, first through Christ's
accomplishing of redemption on Calvary, and then through the
triumphs of His kingdom. "All the dispensations of God's providence henceforward (since Christ's ascension), even to the final
consummation of all things, are to give Christ his reward, and fulfil his end in what he did and suffered upon earth."[15] A universal
dominion is pledged to Christ, and in the interim before the final consummation the Father implements this pledge in part by

successive outpourings of the Spirit, which prove the reality of
Christ's kingdom to a skeptical world and serve to extend its
bounds among Christ's erstwhile enemies.

> When God manifests himself with such glorious power, in
> a work of this nature (sc., such as the New England re-
> vival), he appears especially determined to put honour
> upon his Son, and to fulfil his oath that he has sworn to
> him, that he would make every knee to bow . . . to him.
> God hath had it much on his heart, from all eternity, to
> glorify his dear and only-begotten Son; and there are
> some special seasons that he appoints to that end,
> wherein he comes forth with omnipotent power to fulfil
> his promise . . . to him. Now these are times of remarkable
> pouring out of his Spirit, to advance his kingdom; such is
> a day of his power. . . .[16]

And Edwards goes further. "From the fall of man, to our day,"
he claims, "the work of redemption in its effect has mainly been
carried on by remarkable communications of the Spirit of God.
Though there be a more constant influence of God's Spirit always
in some degree attending his ordinances; yet the way in which the
greatest things have been done towards carrying on this work, always have been by remarkable effusions, at special seasons of
mercy. . . ."[17] On the assumption that every recorded renewal of
vital piety among God's people indicates an outpouring of the
Spirit, Edwards seeks to show that generalization holds with regard to Bible history, and that we have no reason to doubt that it
holds still. Edwards, as a postmillennialist, looked forward to the
conversion of the world; and he confidently predicted that this
would be the direct consequence of a mighty revival throughout
the whole church, leading to an unprecedented missionary offensive to every quarter of the globe.

Accordingly, when the church's life is ebbing out and God's
judgments are falling on it, and missionary work is in decline, the
Christian should hope for an outpouring of the Spirit that will reverse this state of affairs. And he has warrant for entertaining

such a hope, and expressing it in his prayers: warrant, not in any worthiness on the church's part, but in the Father's eternal resolve to glorify the Son in His kingdom.

3. *Revivals are the most glorious of all God's works in the world.*

Edwards insists on this, to shame those who professed no interest in the divine awakening that had come to New England, and insinuated by their attitude that a Christian's mind could more profitably be occupied with other matters.

> Such a work is, in its nature and kind, the most glorious of any work of God whatsoever (Edwards protests). It is the work of redemption (the great end of all the other works of God, and of which the work of creation was but a shadow) . . . it is the work of new creation, which is infinitely more glorious than the old. I am bold to say, that the work of God in the conversion of one soul . . . is a more glorious work of God than the creation of the whole material universe. . . .[18]

It follows, therefore, Edwards implies, that the theme of revival will be sweet and absorbing to the right-minded Christian man, whose heart rejoices when he sees the glory of God, and that the professed believer who can raise no interest in the subject must be spiritually in a very poor state.

Principles Concerning the Outward Form of Revival

We can be brief here, for we have already indicated how Edwards viewed this matter. He himself expounds all the points that fall under this head with particular application to the New England awakening, but we shall state them in a more generalized form.

Revival, Edwards tells us, is a *mixed* work. At each point Satan's tares intrude among God's wheat. From one standpoint, this makes the glory of God's work more apparent. "The glory of divine power and grace are set off with the greater lustre by what appears at the same time of the weakness of the earthen vessel. It is God's pleasure to manifest the weakness and unworthiness of the subject, at the same time that he displays the excellency of his power and the riches of his grace."[19] God is content to allow human weakness and sin to obtrude itself in times of revival, in order to make it evident beyond all peradventure that the spiritual fruits of the movement spring, not from any goodness in the persons concerned, but solely from His own work of grace. So Edwards writes again:

> It is very analogous to the manner of God's dealing with his people, to permit a great deal of error, and suffer the infirmity of his people to appear, in the beginning of a glorious work of his grace, for their felicity, to teach them what they are, to humble them, and fit them for that glorious prosperity to which he is about to advance them, and the more to secure to himself the honour of such a glorious work. For, by man's exceeding weakness appearing in the beginning of it, it is evident that God does not lay the foundation of it in man's strength or wisdom.[20]

Accordingly, Satan is not restrained from working in times of revival. And Satan has a characteristic strategy which he employs at such times. "When he finds that he can keep men quiet and secure no longer, then he drives them to excesses and extravagances. He holds them back as long as he can; but when he can do it no longer, then he will push them on, and, if possible, run them upon their heads."[21] Thus, he seeks to carry away revived believers by exploiting the strength of their feelings, tempting them to pride, censoriousness, impatience of all established order in the church, and belief that the Spirit has more freedom to work when Christians leave themselves in a state of disorganization, and when ministers preach without bothering to prepare their sermons. Satan seeks to delude revived believers by immediate suggestions and inspirations, inviting them to conclude that all the thoughts and texts which come into their mind unbidden must be messages from God. He seeks to lead them into imprudences of all sorts in the heat of their zeal. Such is his regular mode of procedure when a revival is in progress. Edwards delineates it very fully in the fourth part of his *Thoughts on the Revival.*

It is for this reason, Edwards insists, that it is so vitally important to judge spiritual movements, not by their immediate phenomena or by-products, but by their ultimate effects in the lives of those involved in them. If you concentrate on the phenomena, you can always find a great deal that is spurious, and ill-considered, and wrong-headed, and wild, and fanatical; and then you will be tempted to conclude that there is nothing of God in the movement at all. But, as we saw, the right way to assess what is happening is to see whether amid all the tumult and disorder, the "distinguishing marks of a work of the Spirit of God" are appearing. If they are, then we may know that it is God at work.

We shall be wise not to conclude too hastily that what Edwards is saying here has no message for us. We should be foolish to imagine that if God poured out His Spirit we should be able straightaway to recognize what was happening. Revival has always come in unexpected ways, through unexpected and often unwelcome people. We should not rule out the possibility that one day we shall ourselves stand nonplussed before an ebuillient and uproarious spiritual movement, wondering whether it is of God, and finding ourselves strongly impelled by our instinctive distaste for its surface crudities and stupidities, to look no further, but write it off at once. At such times, we shall need to bear in mind what Edwards has told us about the mixed character of revivals, and the principles of judgment that should be applied in such a case.

Prayer for Revival

It is God's will, wrote Edwards,

> through his wonderful grace, that the prayers of his saints should be one great and principal means of carrying on the designs of Christ's kingdom in the world. When God has something very great to accomplish for his church, it

is his will that there should precede it the extraordinary prayers of his people; as is manifest by Ezek. 36:37, "I will yet, for this, be enquired of by the house of Israel, to do it for them" (see the context). And it is revealed that, when God is about to accomplish great things for his church, he will begin by remarkably pouring out the spirit of grace and supplications, Zech. 12:10.[22]

This being so, Christians who desire revival have a strong incentive to pray for it. Nor is this all; Christians have a positive duty to pray for it. Edwards sought to prove this in *A Humble Attempt to Promote Explicit Agreement and Visible Union of God's People in Extraordinary Prayer for the Revival of Religion,* a treatise which he wrote in support of a Memorial circulated throughout English-speaking Christendom in 1746 by certain Scottish ministers, calling for special prayer on Saturday evenings, Sunday mornings, and the first Tuesday of each quarter, over a period of seven years, for the conversion of the world. Edwards argued the duty of making such prayers from the biblical predictions and promises of the extension of the church which showed it to accord with God's will that men should pray for world-wide revival, from the terms of the Lord's prayer, and also from the undoubted need of revival in the world church of Edwards's own day. (The New England awakening had petered out in 1742.) We quote two thought-provoking passages:

> If we look through the whole Bible, and observe all the examples of prayer that we find there recorded, we shall not find so many prayers for any other mercy, as for the deliverance, restoration, and prosperity of the church, and the advancement of God's glory and kingdom of grace in the world . . . the greatest part of the book of Psalms is made up of prayers for this mercy, prophecies of it, and prophetical praises for it. . . .

> The Scripture does not only abundantly manifest it to be the duty of God's people to be much in prayer for this great mercy, but it also abounds with manifold considera-

tions to encourage them in it. . . . There is perhaps no one thing that the Bible so much promises, in order to encourage the faith, hope, and prayers of the saints, as this; which affords to God's people the clearest evidence that it is their duty to be much in prayer for this mercy. For, undoubtedly, that which God abundantly makes the subject of his promises, God's people should abundantly make the subject of their prayers. . . .[23]

Here, then, is a task for all God's people in every age: to pray that God will build up Zion, and cause His glory to appear in her, by revival blessing. We shall do well to take Edwards's words to heart, and with them his closing remarks in this treatise, with which we close our own paper:

And I hope, that such as are convinced it is their duty to comply with and encourage this design, will remember we ought not only to go speedily to pray before the Lord, and to seek his mercy, but also to go constantly. We should unite in our practice these two things, which our Saviour unites in his precept, PRAYING and NOT FAINTING. If we should continue some years, and nothing remarkable in providence should appear as though God heard and answered, we should act very unbecoming believers, if we should therefore begin to be disheartened, and grow dull and slack in seeking of God so great a mercy. It is very apparent from the word of God, that he is wont often to try the faith and patience of his people, when crying to him for some great and important mercy, by withholding the mercy sought, for a season; and not only so, but at first to cause an increase of dark appearances. And yet he, without fail, at last succeeds those who continue instant in prayer, with all perseverance, and "will not let him go except he blesses. . . ." Whatever our hopes may be, we must be content to be ignorant of the times and seasons, which the Father hath put in his power: and must be willing that God should answer prayer, and fulfil his own glorious promises, in His own time.[24]

3

JOHN KNOX AND THE
SCOTTISH REFORMATION

G. N. M. Collins

It would be difficult to find, in the whole range of Scottish history, a more controversial figure than John Knox. The estimates formed of him are so widely divergent that, at one extreme, he is reckoned an inspired prophet, oracular in pronouncement, infallible in judgment; and, at the other, an unscrupulous self-seeker, a boorish demagogue, whose malign influence upon the Scottish Church is even yet, after four centuries, bedevilling the ecumenical movement. Even his old church of St. Giles speaks of him with divided voice. Dr. Charles Warr describes him as "violent, aggressive and domineering, coarse in apprehension and devoid of aesthetic appreciation." Worse still, according to Warr, "there ran in his complex character a yellow streak of enervating cowardice." But Dr. Harry Whitley regards him as "the haunting ghost of our past betrayals and present disloyalties and complacencies. . . . He is the uneasy conscience of modern Scotland." And Elizabeth

Whitley, whose graceful pen has recently given us such a sympathetic picture of the Reformer, regards him as " 'a burning and a shining light'; a preacher whose voice, serving the Word of God, became the trumpet call to which his own people rallied."

There are qualities in Knox, however, that even his fiercest detractors feel bound to acknowledge; and, on the whole, he emerges from the fires of criticism with scarcely "the smell of fire" upon his coat. Andrew Lang, certainly no admirer of Knox, admits in the end that he was "a great man, a disinterested man, in his regard for the poor a truly Christian man; as a shepherd of Calvinistic souls a man fervent and considerate; of pure life; in friendship loyal; by jealousy untainted; in private life genial and amiable." And, as for the alleged "yellow streak" in him, the Regent Morton, notwithstanding that he came, more than once, under the stinging lash of the Reformer's reproof—or perhaps because of it—spoke over his open grave by the grey walls of St. Giles, the oft-quoted eulogium. "There lies he who never feared nor flattered flesh."

Knox in Exile

The picture of Knox's early life is not particularly clear. He was born at Giffordsgate, near Haddington, which was then one of the strongest centers of the Roman Catholic Church in the Lowlands of Scotland. His father, William Knox, was a farmer. Of his mother, a Sinclair by name, we know nothing. The year 1505 has been commonly accepted as the date of his birth, but several notable historians argue for a later date, 1514, or perhaps 1515. He was educated at St. Andrews and, possibly, at Glasgow, and the date of his ordination to the priesthood is given as 1531. But it is not until 1546 that he emerges in the clear light of history. At that time he was serving as tutor to the sons of two East Lothian gentlemen of Protestant sympathies; and he had become attached to George Wishart who had spent some time in the vicinity, preaching the Reformed faith which he had learned while on the Continent. In all probability, Wishart was Knox's spiritual father, and the attachment between them was extremely strong. But East Lothian was a dangerous place for people of Protestant sympathies, for it was in close proximity to St. Andrews, the Roman Catholic citadel in Scotland, and the hierarchy had already shown, by putting Patrick Hamilton to a martyr's death, their complete intolerance of reform. So John Knox comes clearly into the story of the Scottish Church as Wishart's bodyguard, carrying a two-handed sword. But it was with the sword of the Spirit that Knox was to do his best work for the cause of Christ.

His call to leadership came in dramatic circumstances. After the assassination of the notoriously profligate Cardinal Beaton, the Castle of St. Andrews, where he had dwelt in voluptuous luxury and where he had callously watched George Wishart perish in the flames, passed into the hands of certain Scottish nobles who were sympathetic to the Reformation cause and who hoped, not only that Scottish Protestants would rally to them, but also that help from England against the French would be speedily forthcoming. Knox cast in his lot with them, bringing with him his schoolboy charges whose parents had to flee from home in order to avoid arrest for their Protestant leanings. While he continued his tutoring in the Castle, Knox also gave lectures on the Gospel of John—that Gospel in the fourteenth chapter of which, as he said, he "first cast his anchor." His outstanding gifts as expositor and apologist attracted the attention of the reforming party and they urged him to become their minister. But, dreading "lest he should run where God had not called him," Knox declined until, one day, John Rough in the course of an address on the election of ministers, pounced suddenly upon him, calling him, in the name of the congregation, to assume pastoral charge of them. The congregation signified their assent, but the astounded Knox burst into tears and fled to his room.

Deeming the call to be from God, however, he entered upon his duties with a sense of vocation that never left him. From the beginning he used great plainness of speech. With him there could be no half-measures. Laodiceanism was foreign to his nature. "Others," they said, "sned (lopped) the branches of the Papistry; he strikes at the root." His friends feared for his safety.

What had Hamilton and Wishart said of Rome and her doctrines in comparison with this bold Reformer? If the Church had slain those men, would she spare Knox?

Knox's ministry to the St. Andrews garrison was terminated by the arrival of the French fleet in July 1547. The Castle walls were breached by the attackers, and the garrison were forced to surrender. For nineteen weary months thereafter Knox toiled as a galley-slave, and to the end of his life he suffered from the effects of that terrible experience.

But the shaping of God's hand is discernible in the happenings of that period, for they led to Knox's coming to England after his release, by English intervention, in 1549, and to his time of service with reforming brethren south of the Border. The reformed Church of England was already divided into two sections, one of which desired to hold on to the old ritual and ceremony of pre-Reformation times, while the other wished to extend the purification of the Church much further than anything that had, as yet, been achieved. In this Puritan section, Knox became an acknowledged leader, and it was due to his influence that a rubric was inserted in the English Communion Office expressly disallowing the worship of the consecrated elements in the Lord's Supper. For he was the "runagate Scot" to whom Dean Weston refers as having taken away "the adoration or worshipping of Christ in the sacrament . . . so much prevailed that one man's authority at that time."

Ecclesiastical preferment might have been his, but he declined the offers made, partly from disagreement with the policy of Reform in England, and partly because he felt, as he put it, that "the time would not be long that England would give me bread." In 1553, with many of the Reformed persuasion, he fled to the Continent from the persecution which had broken out under Mary Tudor on her succession to the throne. Some of his detractors charged him with cowardice on this account, and, for a time, he tended to reproach himself for having fled. But when he asks, "Why did I flee?" he answers, "Assuredly, I cannot tell; but one thing I am sure; the fear of death was not the chief cause of my fleeing."

Today, we can see the hand of God very clearly in this period of exile, for it was thus that Knox made contact, not only with the reforming movement in Germany, but—what was much more important for the Scottish Reformation—with the Reformed Church of Geneva.

It was Knox's reputation as a Puritan that led to his being called to take charge of the English refugees at Frankfurt. But the peace of the congregation was soon disturbed by the arrival of a new party of English refugees who adhered to the less reformed party. The ensuing trouble led to Knox's leaving Frankfurt and removing to Geneva. There, the English congregation to which he ministered was of the Puritan persuasion, and they continued to be his principal pastoral interest for the remainder of his exile. But even after his return to Scotland, his link with English Puritanism continued strong and, although he never returned to minister in England, he still had many contacts with English Protestantism through which his influence operated.

Knox had interrupted his ministry in Geneva for a few months in 1555–56 in order to visit Scotland, where the Queen-Regent was following, for political reasons, a more conciliatory policy towards the Reformed party. The result was that a spirit of compromise began to manifest itself among the nobility, insomuch, indeed, that they resumed attending the Mass, believing that reform would come gradually without any major trouble. Knox thought otherwise, and denounced this temporizing policy, calling upon those who were following it to break with a practice that would inevitably retard the reforming movement. Wherever he went, and the opportunity presented itself, he ministered the sacrament of the Lord's Supper in its New Testament simplicity.

His crusade bore fruit. In 1557, many of the Scottish nobility signed what is known as the First Covenant, pledging themselves to "maintain, set forward, and advance the most blessed Word of God and His congregation" and to resist tyranny at the risk of their very lives.

When, two years later, Knox returned finally to Scotland and assumed the leadership of the Reformed party, "the time to favour Sion, yea, the set time," was come. The quality of his leadership was immediately tested, and he came through the test triumphantly. "I assure you," wrote Randolph to Cecil; "the voice of that one man is able in one hour to put more life in us than five hundred trumpets continually blustering in our ears." He had his objective, and incessantly he stormed heaven with his importunate cries that he might attain it. Scotland was the burden of his prayer. And the Scotland he desired from the Lord, and for the Lord, was a land liberated spiritually from the corrupting thraldom of Rome and politically from her ensnaring alliance with Papist France.

Knox and the Church of Scotland

Without attempting to follow out, even in the briefest outline the story of the Scottish Reformation, let us consider the contribution made by Knox to the well-being of the Scottish Church and nation.

1. He recalled the Scottish Church to its original allegiance— to Christ the Church's Head, not to the Bishop of Rome. The attempts by Augustine of Canterbury, a millennium earlier to bring the Celtic Church into communion with Rome had completely failed. The Celtic Church clung tenaciously to her independence, and despite the deterioration which set in at, and subsequent to, the Synod of Whitby in 664, it was not until Malcolm Canmore married his English Princess, Margaret, in 1068 or 1070, that the Scottish Church surrendered her independence entirely to Rome. Margaret, whose great ambition had been to become a nun, came to believe that she had been called by God to serve Him in the Court instead of in the cloister, and her supreme aim now was to bring her husband's realm into the Roman fold. She built and endowed churches, introduced vestments and the use of the crucifix, and brought in a number of clergy from south of the Border to help with the Romanizing of the Kirk. The victory of the Church of Rome in Scotland was achieved by the enforcement of royal authority.

But Knox's *First Book of Discipline* broke the tyranny thus established. In it, Christ alone was recognized as Head of the Church, and the principle was established, in accordance with the scriptural authority adduced, that "it appertaineth to the people, and to every several congregation, to elect their own minister."

2. Knox recalled the church to the teaching of Holy Scripture, as the supreme authority and the final court of appeal. This estimate of the Holy Scriptures was, indeed, characteristic of all the Reformers and of their precursors in the evangelical succession. "When Luther turned his back on Rome," writes Dr. J. A. Wylie, "he turned his face toward the Bible." But this statement is more accurate in inverted form; for it was when Luther turned his face to the Bible that he turned his back on Rome. It was to the teaching of the Bible that he appealed in his famous Theses.

It has to be admitted, of course, that Luther's doctrine of inspiration lacked the consistent clarity that we find in the pronouncements of Calvin, Zwingli, and Knox on the same subject. But the strength of his challenge to the papal chair lay in his conviction of the supreme authority of Holy Scripture. "The Scriptures," he declares, "although they were written by men are not from men but from God." And again, "We must make a great difference between God's Word and the word of man. A man's word is a little sound that flies into the air and soon vanishes; but the Word of God is greater than heaven and earth, yea, greater than death and hell, for it forms part of the power of God, and endures everlastingly; we should therefore diligently study God's Word, and know, and assuredly believe that God Himself speaks unto us."

It was this tremendous conviction that expressed itself in his memorable words at the Diet of Worms, when to the demand that he should recant, he replied: "Having been conquered by the Scriptures referred to, and my conscience taken captive by the Word of God, I cannot and will not revoke anything, for it is neither safe nor right to act against one's conscience. Here I stand; I can do no other. So help me God."

Calvinism, it is true, became the dominant strain in Scottish Protestantism, but the fact that there were other strains ought not to be forgotten. Lollardism had affected Scotland before John Knox was born. The form of Protestantism for which Patrick

Hamilton died was mainly Lutheran. And the faith of George
Wishart was probably Zwinglian. But whatever difference in emphases may be traced in these systems, they were at one in making the Word of God supreme in all matters of faith and doctrine.

It fell to John Calvin, who succeeded Zwingli in the leadership of the Reformed Church in Switzerland, to provide the first
systematic statement of revealed theology from the Reformed
viewpoint, viz. *The Institutes of the Christian Religion.* There, in the
clearest possible terms, he claims the submission of all believers
to the doctrine of Holy Scripture as the Divinely inspired, and
therefore infallible, Word of God. "The Scriptures," he declares,
"are the only records in which God has been pleased to consign
His truth to perpetual remembrance," and therefore "the full authority which they ought to possess with the faithful is not recognized, unless they are believed to have come from heaven, as directly as if God had been heard giving utterance to them."

Knox's association with Calvin during the Scot's years of exile
in Geneva had its good effect upon Scotland in the years that followed. And yet Knox's appeal was never to the authority of
Calvin, but to the authority to which Calvin himself appealed, the
Holy Scriptures. Referring to the reforming activities of Knox
and his Scottish associates, John Row the historian declares,
"They took not their pattern from any Kirk in the world; no, not
from Geneva itself; but laying God's Word before them, they
made reformation according thereunto, both in doctrine first,
and then in discipline."

Their own anxiety to be thoroughly biblical in all their theological interpretations comes out in their preface to the *Scots Confession,* where they request, "If any man will note in this our Confession any article or sentence repugnant to God's Holy Word,
that it would please him of his gentleness, and for Christian charity's sake, to admonish us of the same in writing; and we, upon
our honour and fidelity, do promise him satisfaction from the
Holy Scriptures, or due reformation of that which he shall prove
to be amiss."

Their broad principle of interpretation was finely expressed
by Knox in one of his memorable interviews with Queen Mary of

Scotland. The discussion had got on to theological lines. "Ye interpret the Scriptures in one manner, and other interpret in another. Who am I to believe? and who shall judge?" said the Queen.

"Madam," replied Knox, "ye shall believe God, that plainly speaketh in His Word, and further than the Word teacheth you ye shall believe neither the one nor the other. The Word of God is plain in itself; and if there appears any obscurity in one place, the Holy Ghost, which is never contrarious to himself, explains the same more clearly in other places."

Modern ecumenical leaders who, like the elusive Erasmus, have no stomach for "assertions," and yet who would like to serve themselves heirs of the Reformers, have been saying of late that the view of inspiration favored by Calvin and his school was not the high doctrine of plenary, verbal inspiration which later Reformers taught. And this they support by the miserable subterfuge of isolating certain comments from their context and attaching to certain words a meaning that was utterly foreign to the theological vocabulary of four centuries ago. Professor John Murray, in his *Calvin on Scripture and Divine Sovereignty*, says well in this connection (and his words are as closely applicable to Knox as they are to Calvin himself), "In Calvin we have a mass of perspicuous statement and of lengthened argument to the effect that Scripture is impregnable and inviolable, and it would be the resort of desperation to take a few random comments, wrench them from the total effect of Calvin's teaching, and build upon them a thesis which would run counter to his own repeated assertions respecting the inviolable character of Scripture as the oracles of God and as having nothing human mixed with it."

It was foreign to the usage of these men to "present the dictates of the Holy Ghost as a series of debatable propositions"—to quote Professor B. B. Warfield—and even Brunner, who claims for the theology of his own school that it "returns to the inner spirit of the reformation," admits that Calvin "in the dogmatic formulation of the authority of the Bible, was already entirely under the sway of the orthodox view of literal divine inspiration"— an admission which alone suffices to put the exponents of the Crisis theology out of the true Reformed succession.

That then was the ground which Knox and his associates took in reforming the Scottish Church. Nothing could be admitted to the doctrine and worship of the Church for which clear sanction could not be adduced from Holy Scriptures. Everything had to be "according to the pattern" which God Himself had given in His Word.

Another part of the contribution that Knox made to the Scottish Reformation was that he called the Church to the Great Commission of "preaching the Gospel to every creature." The recall was urgently needed, for the preaching of the Word had long been neglected. Where, indeed, it was continued the practice was frowned upon by the hierarchy. The case of Thomas Forret, the Vicar of Dollar, is indicative of the spirit of the times. Hearing that Forret was preaching to his people every Lord's Day, Bishop Crichton of Dunkeld remonstrated with him over his excessive zeal on the ground that if he continued his practice the people might begin to think that the Bishops ought to preach also! But, in a conciliatory way, the Bishop advised him to preach only occasionally, when he found "any good Epistle or any good Gospel"! But when Forret sought the Bishop's guidance as to which were the good, and which the bad, Epistles and Gospels, Crichton raised his hands, saying, "I thank God that I never knew what the Old and New Testament was . . . I will know nothing but my portuise and my pontifical."

The prevalency of Protestant preaching, and the interest awakened among the people thereby, did indeed prompt some of the clergy to preach also, but often with ludicrous results. Many of them were so ignorant that they could scarcely read, and even Gavin Dunbar, Bishop of Glasgow, when he attempted to preach at Ayr, to counteract the influence of George Wishart, found that the effort was beyond him. After stammering a few sentences, he apologized to the people that he was not able to do better, adding. "But have us still for your bishop, and we shall provide better for the next time."

But better provision was already being made for Scotland, and God honored the faithful preaching of His Word by adding unto the Church daily those who were being saved.

Knox's leadership was largely influential also in recalling the Church, and particularly its office-bearers, to the purity of life that is requisite in those who bear the vessels of the Lord. Probably in no country affected by the Reformation had the corruption of the Church touched such depths as it did in Scotland. One has only to read Dr. Hay Fleming's carefully documented booklet *The Church from which the Reformation Delivered Us* to learn how thoroughly bad things were. The celibate clergy had their concubines everywhere, and their numerous offspring were a sore drain on the Church's treasury. And reformation of this scandalous evil could not be expected with David Beaton—the "carnal Cardinal"—as Knox with full justification calls him, at the head of the hierarchy. "Priests and doos mak' foul houses," said the common people in one of the by-words which arose from the evils of the time. And immorality was accompanied by overmastering avarice. Everything was available for money, and nothing without.

Knox's message to Scotland was also a call to the duties implied in the priesthood of all believers upon which he and the other Reformers laid such stress. A man had a responsibility for his own soul that no priest or presbyter could take over from him. Heads of households had responsibilities for the religious instruction and upbringing of their charges. Writing to the Commons, Knox declares, "Ye are in your own houses Bishops and Kings . . . let there be worship of God morning and evening . . . and let no day slip over without some comfort received of the Word of God." As Elizabeth Whitley so neatly shows in her *Plain Mr. Knox*, although Robert Burns was no admirer of Knox, it is Knox's work that he is really extolling in *The Cottar's Saturday Night* where he depicts "the priest-like father," though a peasant, leading his family in the worship of God.

Knox and Scotland

It was Knox, too, who, under God, delivered Scotland from the despotism of the ruling house. This rugged Scot was a democrat to the very core of his being. He has been severely criticized for his attitude to the Sovereign powers of his time, and he had to stand a trial for treason in his native land; this, at the instigation of Queen Mary. But Knox's pronouncements with regard to the Throne will bear investigation—even his *Blast against the Monstrous Regiment of Women.* To understand the *Blast,* one has to begin by translating the title into present-day speech, in the process of which it loses its offensiveness. For "monstrous" simply means "unnatural," and "regiment" means "rule"; so that what Knox is protesting against is "the unnatural rule of women."

Knox took a more extreme attitude in this connection than did any of the Reformers. But it has to be remembered that he, more than any, had suffered from the "monstrous regiment of women." Mary of Guise, the Scottish Queen-Regent, had been his chief opponent in his work of reforming the Church. Mary Tudor had stained her hands with martyr blood, and had sent multitudes of her best subjects into exile; Knox among them. And Mary of Scotland had come to her Scottish throne with the avowed intention of destroying the Reformed Church in Scotland, no matter what that might cost. And yet, however "monstrous" he may regard the "regiment" of women to be, he is no rebel against it where it exists, so long as it is restricted to the recognized sphere of civil power and government, as witness his letter to Elizabeth of England in July 1559: "It apperteineth to you therefore to ground the justice of your authority, not upon that law which from year to year doth change, but upon the eternal providence of Him Who, contrary to nature, and without your deserving, hath thus exalted your head. If thus, in God's presence, ye humble yourself, as in my heart I glorify God for that rest granted to His afflicted flock within England, under you, a weak instrument, so will I with tongue and pen justify the same in Deborah, that blessed Mother in Israel." Knox expressed himself similarly in one of his interviews with Mary of Scotland, praying that she might be "as blessed within the commonwealth of Scotland as ever Deborah was in the commonwealth of Israel."

In those interviews Mary Stuart and John Knox were representatives of principles that were diametrically opposed. Mary believed in the Divine Right of kings, even to the extent of holding, as some one has put it, that "kings had a Divine right to govern wrong." Her son, James VI and I, in his treatise *The True Law of Free Monarchies*, expresses the view, which doubtless his mother had held before him, that the king is free to do as he pleases with his subjects, who, he says, "are not permitted to make any resistance but by flight, as we may see by the example of brute beasts, and unreasonable creatures, among the vipers." In his *Basilicon Doron* he further maintains "that the office of a king is partly civil and partly ecclesiastical," and that "a principal part of his function consists in ruling the Church."

Now, as against this, Knox held that "all power is founded on a compact expressed, or understood, between the rulers and the ruled, and no one has a right to govern save in accordance with the will of the people and the law of God."

That Knox should propagate such views was, in Mary's judgment, the very quintessence of disloyalty. "Think you," she demanded, "that subjects, having the power, may resist their princes?"

"If princes exceed their power, Madam," came the reply, "no doubt they may be resisted even by power. For no greater honour is to be given to kings than God has commanded to be given to father and mother. But the father may be struck with a frenzy, in which he would slay his children. Now, Madam, if the children arise, join together, apprehend the father, take the sword from him, bind his hands, and keep him in prison till the frenzy is over, think you, Madam, that the children do any wrong? Even so, Madam, it is with princes that would murder the children of God that are subject to them."

A clear assertion of his democratic rights comes out in Knox's answer to the Queen when she remonstrated with him over a public reference he had made to her plans for re-marriage. "What are ye within this commonwealth?" she demanded with disdain. "A subject born within the same" was the prompt answer, "And albeit I neither be Earl, Lord, nor Baron within it, yet has God made me, (however abject that ever I be in your eyes) a profitable member within the same."

"Modern democracy came into being in that answer," is Principal T. M. Lindsay's comment on the Reformer's rejoinder. We indeed give John Knox less than his due if we fail to recognize him, not only as, in the main, the liberator of the Scottish people from the thraldom of the Papal hierarchy, but also as the champion of their democratic rights. "Before God, there is no respect of persons," declares the *First Book of Discipline*, and "that equality before God," says Professor Croft Dickenson, "branching out from a sturdy independence well-rooted in the past, gave to the Scot that 'divine right of manhood' which has sometimes been mistaken for pride."

What Knox and his associates did for the causes of education and poor relief is by no means the measure of what they planned to do. If the schools and colleges for which they planned in the *First Book of Discipline* did not immediately arise, it was due, not to lack of zeal on their part, but solely to the greed of the nobles who made unlawful inroads upon the Church's patrimony for their own enrichment. To the same cause must be attributed, in the main, the failure of the poor-relief plans. Professor A. F. Mitchell rightly declares that "the history of the world, the history of the Christian Church, has few passages more noble than this, where these poor ministers, not yet assured of decent provision for their own maintenance, boldly undertake the patronage of the peasantry, and say that they would rather suffer themselves than ask that teinds should be exacted from those who had been so long ground down."

But if the plans of the Reformers in these departments did not reach immediate fulfillment, they at least provided the ideal to which they themselves unyieldingly struggled, and which was brought to realization in better days, when the leaven of Reformed teaching had more fully permeated the nation.

Conclusion

That Scotland has been slow in recognizing her indebtedness to her great Reformer was foreseen by Knox himself. "What I have been to my country," he says, "albeit this unthankful age will not know, yet the ages to come will be compelled to bear witness to the truth." Grudgingly, the intervening ages have borne their witness to his greatness. To be frank about his failing is only to make the picture more lifelike. But let us judge him in the light of the age to which he belonged, and of the situation in which he served. No sycophant he, this rugged son of the Lothians. Of the arts of diplomacy he was completely innocent; the shifts of compromise his soul hated. "Men delighting to swim betwixt two waters," he writes, "have often complained upon my severity; fearing, as it seemed, that the same should trouble the quietness of brethren. But I do fear that that which men term lenity and dulceness doth bring upon themselves and others, more fearful destruction than yet hath ensued the vehemency of any preacher within this realm." But when the critics have had their say, and the necessary adjustments have been made, the ultimate result comes out in some such assessment as Robert Barbour made some eighty years ago: "if . . . religion be allowed to have been hitherto the largest factor in our national life, and this little country, in virtue of it, be admitted to have given lessons to the great world; then we owe this, under God, first of all to one man, and that man was JOHN KNOX."

In his latter days Knox had the heartbreak of seeing much of his work marred by men with whom self-interest came before principle. But his faith never faltered. "Whatsoever shall become of us, and of our mortal carcasses," he declared, "I doubt not but that this cause, in despite of Satan, shall prevail in the realm of Scotland. For as it is the eternal truth of the eternal God, so shall it once, and for all, prevail, howsoever for a time it be impugned."

In Scotland we have, of late, been celebrating the four-hundredth anniversary of the Scottish Reformation; but, in the final summary of events, nothing has appeared to give rise to high optimism regarding the future of the Reformed witness among us. To garnish the tombs of the prophets is not enough. Writing to John Fenwick amidst the struggles of the Second Reformation, Samuel Rutherford said, "It is true, in great part, what ye write of this Kirk, that the letter of religion only is Reformed, and scarce that.

I do not believe our Lord will build His Zion in this land on this skin of Reformation."

And that is our conviction today. God will build His Zion on nothing less than the eternal verities of His infallible Word. Let the words of Scotland's Reformer ring in our ears to admonish and inspire us wherever we may be exercising our ministry: "As it is the eternal truth of the eternal God, so shall it once, and for all, prevail, howsoever for a time it be impugned."

4

THE PURITAN DOCTRINE
OF APOSTASY

W. H. Davies

Apostasy—the very word sounds ugly; yet the most casual observer of the progress of the Christian faith cannot help noticing the constant recurrence, in both communities and individuals, of serious defections from Christian doctrine and practice.

The New Testament often addresses itself to this problem. The Epistle of James, for instance, as Thomas Goodwin reminds us, "is but a continued character and discovery of unsound professors."[1] The Puritans who themselves saw much active apostasy in their own days, gave serious thought to this phenomenon. The theological problems to which it gave rise could not but intrigue them. The relation of this falling away to the principles of gospel truth was a subject which exercised them considerably, and we find them carefully examining apostasy in the light of divine sovereignty, of the saints' perseverance, and of the state in which the reprobates stood before they lapsed. Most of the Puritan writers who deal with this subject do so in the course of other studies, as, for example, Thomas Goodwin in his *Discourse of Election*; it was left to John Owen to give us a thoroughgoing discussion in a formal treatise. This work, written with his customary exhaustiveness and prolixity, was published in 1676, seven years before his death. The book's full title is *The Nature of Apostasy from the Profession of the Gospel and the Punishment of Apostates declared, in an Exposition of Hebrews 6:4–6; with an Enquiry into the causes and reasons of the decay of the Power of Religion in the world, or the present general defection from the Truth, Holiness, and Worship of the gospel; also, of the proneness of Churches and Persons of all sorts unto Apostasy. With Remedies and Means of Prevention.* This being the fullest and best Puritan treatment of our theme, we shall use it as our main source.

The Nature of Apostasy

Apostasy in general denotes defection from the tenets of some religious community. For our purpose, Christian apostasy (if so improper a phrase may be allowed) is to be defined in broad terms as defection from the truth, holiness, and worship of the gospel. (The definition is Owen's own.)

Owen founds his analysis of apostasy on Hebrews 6:4-6, the classical passage. He does not hide the fact that it presents considerable problems to the expositor. "Many have the difficulties been about its interpretation," he notes; "for both doctrinally and practically, sundry have miscarried."[2] His own examination of it is meticulous, but too long to reproduce here; we must content ourselves with summarizing his conclusions. Before we do so, however, we must call attention to the two fundamental principles which govern Owen's whole understanding of both the passage and the subject with which it deals.

The first principle is that *distinction must be drawn between the various operations of the Holy Spirit.* There are gifts and graces; there are workings ordinary and extraordinary; and as the Spirit's workings differ in kind, so they may differ also in their consequences. All experiences of the Holy Spirit are not saving experiences, neither do all such experiences carry with them any certainty of saving grace. Owen writes of the people to whom the words of this passage were written:

1. They were such as not long were converted from Judaism unto Christianity, upon the evidence of the truth of its doctrine, and the miraculous operations wherewith its dispensation was accompanied.

2. He intends not the common sort of them, but such as had obtained especial privileges among them; for they had received extraordinary gifts of the Holy Ghost, as speaking with tongues or working of miracles.

3. And they had found in themselves and others convincing evidence that the kingdom of God and the Messiah, which they called "the world to come," was come unto them, and had the satisfaction and glories of it.

4. Such persons as these, as they have a work of light on their minds, so, according unto the efficacy of their convictions, they may have such a change wrought upon their affection and their conversation as that they may be of great esteem among professors; and such these here intended might be. . . .

But, he adds, "the least grace is a better security for heaven than the greatest gifts or privileges whatsoever."[3]

The second principle is that *enlightenment by the Holy Spirit is not necessarily a saving operation.* The passage speaks of persons who were "once enlightened," i.e. were given light and knowledge through teaching, were instructed in Christian truth, and were enabled by the Spirit to apprehend and know "the doctrines of the gospel concerning the person of Christ."[4] Owen is at pains to show how great a privilege and mercy it is to be thus enlightened and given actual spiritual knowledge by the Spirit;

but he is equally at pains to show that it is a privilege that may be lost, and that in such cases its only outcome is to aggravate the sin of those who were made partakers of it, and increase their condemnation.

There is, says Owen, a knowledge that is "purely natural and disciplinary, attainable and attained without any especial aid or assistance of the Holy Ghost." But "the illumination intended (in Heb. 6:4), being a gift of the Holy Ghost, differs from and is exalted above this knowledge that is purely natural; for it makes nearer approaches unto the light of spiritual things in their own nature than the other doth." "This spiritual illumination gives the mind some satisfaction, with delight and joy in the things that are known."[5] In this sense, those who were "enlightened" enjoyed a real experience of the Holy Spirit: they "tasted" delight and pleasure in hearing, and a certain inward change of feeling and attitude took place in them. But that was all; and it was not enough. "Tasting" is at best a beginning. It should lead on to feasting and nourishing. But in the case envisaged it did not.

Here are Owen's conclusions from this survey of the passage, in his own words:

I. All the gifts of God under the gospel are particularly heavenly.

II. The Holy Ghost, for the revelation of the mysteries of the gospel, and the institution of the ordinances of spiritual worship, is the great gift of God under the New Testament.

III. There is a goodness and excellency in this heavenly gift which may be tasted or experienced in some measure by such as never receive them in their life, power, and efficacy.

IV. A rejection of the gospel, its truth and worship, after some experience had of their worth and excellency, is a high aggravation of sin, and a certain presage of destruction.

Owen concludes that the people mentioned in the text are not true believers, for there is no mention of faith nor of anything else that is peculiar to believers in virtue of their saving relationship to God in Christ. And this is confirmed by the way in which those whom the writer regards as true believers are distinguished from such people in verses 9ff. The "falling away" of those who were "enlightened" Owen sees as "a total renunciation of all the constituent principles and doctrines of Christianity, whence it is denominated." "For the completing of this falling away, it is required that the renunciation be avowed and professed . . . which cannot be without casting the highest reproach and contumely imaginable upon the person of Christ himself, as is afterwards expressed." Such apostates cannot be renewed unto repentance; against them the greatest severity of God will come.

Total and Partial Apostasy

Owen now proceeds to distinguish total from partial apostasy. Total apostasy has already been described. Partial apostasy he defines thus:

> When any important principle of evangelical truth is forsaken and renounced, especially when many of them are so; when the rule of obedience which the gospel prescribeth is habitually neglected; when men believe otherwise than it teacheth, and live otherwise than it requireth, there is a partial apostasy from it, whose guilt and danger answers the degrees and measures which in each kind it proceeds unto. . . . Men are apt to please themselves, to approve of their own state and condition. . . . Churches content themselves with their outward order and administration, and contend fiercely that all is well, and the gospel sufficiently complied withal, whilst their outward constitution is preserved and their laws of order kept inviolate . . . and it is known that the judgment of Christ concerning churches . . . is oft-times very distant from

their own concerning themselves. . . . Only a few remain
who fruitlessly complain that, under all these conflicts,
the glory, power, and purity of the Christian religion are
lost in the world.

In a pregnant phrase in his preface, Owen declares: "Religion is
the same that ever it was, only it suffers by them that make profession of it. Whatever disadvantage it falls under in the world,
they must at length answer for in whose misbelief and practice it
is corrupted." Note that Owen says *mis*belief, not *un*belief; not refusing to believe, but believing wrongly. We might distinguish
partial from total apostasy by saying that, while the latter is apostasy *from* the truth, the former is apostasy *in* the truth, since it
does not involve a complete departure from all the fundamentals
of the gospel. Partial apostasy, says Owen, is widespread (it was
then; is it less so now?); and it is no less dangerous than it is dis-
honoring to God.

Partial Apostasy: Its Causes and Character

Owen distinguishes three spheres of submission to the
gospel, in each of which apostasy may take place. Men may lapse
from the *truth* of the gospel (its doctrines), the *holiness* of the
gospel (the matter of Christian obedience), and the *worship* of
the gospel (which Owen regards as "the trial of our faith and obedience, as to their profession" in public). Owen proceeds to review the nature and causes of apostasy in each sphere.

Apostasy from the Truth of the Gospel
This, he says, is the fundamental sphere of apostasy, for God's
truth is the foundation of all gospel precepts and institutions.
"Without the real belief of it no man can be obedient as he
ought."[6] Yet men have always been prone to forsake the truth.
Owen illustrates this from the record of church history, from the
apostolic age to his own day, and then considers the reasons for
this condition of things.

First, he lists *enmity* against God and His word. The tendency of gospel truth is to renovate the mind and will, and engage and re-order the whole soul. But fallen man's natural enmity against God's word seeks to arrest its incoming and to inhibit its transforming work. There is something in every man that seeks to expel the word, and in apostates this principle has its way. "Hence spiritual truths are first neglected, then despised, and at last, on easy terms parted withal. For men, by conviction, and on rational grounds and motives, whether natural or spiritual, may receive that truth, and give an assent unto it, which, when it should be reduced to practice, the will and affections will not comply withal."[7] "For in such posture of mind, men's corruptions will prevail against their convictions. First they will stifle the truth as to its operation, and then reject it as to its profession."[8] Truth has invaded the head, but sin stops it from reaching the heart, and finally routs it out of its bridgehead in the mind and expels it entirely.

Next, Owen mentions *spiritual darkness and ignorance*, "which abides in the minds of men under the profession of the truth." The truth of the gospel, spiritually understood, creates certainty and provides a double support against the overthrow of faith by revealing the stability of God's purpose to preserve His elect, and the means whereby this preservation is accomplished. Those who lapse, however, were evidently not enlightened to understand these things. "We may be assured concerning them all, that they never had that intuition into nor comprehension of spiritual things which alone could secure their stability. No man who forsakes the truth ever saw the glory of it, or had experience of its power." God's truth must be received as God's truth, and God's elect do so receive it. But men may profess the truth without any enjoyment of this evidence; and this is the state of darkness of mind which leads to apostasy.

The third cause listed is the *pride and vanity* of men's minds, which prompts them to exalt their own imaginations and make themselves the sole judge of divine matters. When the gospel requires us, as it does, to believe things which are above human reason, as finite, and contrary to it, as depraved, pride of intellect prompts men to despise and reject the gospel on this very account; and there is great danger of apostasy along these lines, Owen insists, all the greater because it is so grievously underestimated.

Careless security and groundless confidence is the next factor mentioned. Owen shows how this presumptuous spirit disposes men to apostasy by prompting them to sinful negligence, indifference to the truth of the gospel, and vain confidence in their own ability to stand fast.

Love of this present world is a further factor.

The influence of Satan, whose aim is to keep men from knowing the gospel, and to turn aside those who have received it, must also be remembered.

God is no unconcerned spectator of apostasy from His truth, Owen adds; the action of those who lapse brings down from Him direct judicial consequences. "God will by one means or another, deprive them of the light and means of the knowledge of his truth, so that ignorance and darkness shall cover them and irresistibly increase upon them." Thus, the marks of the apostate will be: ignorance of his need of Jesus Christ; want of experience of the power of the Spirit of Christ; want of submission to the sovereignty of God; want of evidence within oneself of the divine authority of the Scriptures.

Apostasy from the Holiness of the Gospel

The doctrine of the gospel is to Owen a doctrine of holiness. This internal holiness, Owen insists, differs from anything which other systems of teaching demand. *Romanism*, with its legalism, externality, and non-requirement of faith in Christ, *moralism*, with its reliance on natural light and ability, and non-requirement of regeneration, and *perfectionism*, with its non-requirement of constant conflict with sin, represent three forms of apostasy from Christian holiness.

The practice of gospel holiness is ungratifying to the flesh: for "that holiness which the gospel requireth will not be kept up or maintained, either in the hearts or lives of men, without a continual conflict, warring, contending; and that with all diligence, care, watchfulness, perseverance therein." Also, evangelical holiness will not allow of, or consist with, the habitual omission of any one duty, or satisfaction of any one lust; and "indulgence of one sin will make way in the minds and consciences of men for the admission of other sins also, and divert the soul from the use of those means whereby all other sins should be resisted." Thus one permitted sin sets a man's feet on the highroad of apostasy straight away.

A worse form of apostasy from gospel holiness is an open lapse into profane and sensual living; and "the first occasion hereof in all ages," Owen declares, "has been given by or taken from the public teachers or leaders of the people in the matter of religion."[9] Hence he takes occasion to remark that "the well being of the Church depends on the right discharge of the office of the ministry"[10] and to charge ministers, first, that they "keep pure and uncorrupted the doctrine of the gospel, especially that concerning the holiness enjoined in it";[11] second, that they diligently teach this doctrine; third, that they give a true representation of both their doctrine and their Lord in their lives. Owen also takes occasion to give warning against the evil effects of contending for truth in a manner inconsistent with gospel holiness; he speaks of the offence taken "at the divisions that have been among them (professing Christians), and continue so to be, with the management of them in an evil contentious frame of spirit."[12]

Apostasy from the Worship of the Gospel

This Owen treats with brevity, and so must we. He distinguishes two ways of lapsing in this sphere:

1. By neglecting, and refusing to observe, the appointments of Christ;

2. By adding to what Christ has appointed in a way inconsistent with and so destructive of it. The causes of such lapses are also two in number: (a) those who have already lapsed from gospel truth find gospel ordinances "no way suited unto, nor indeed consistent with, that faith and obedience which they have betaken themselves unto"; (b) "want of spiritual light to see through the veils of outward institutions, and of the wisdom of faith to obtain communion with God in Christ by them" leads

men to multiply externals in worship, and to be exclusively occupied with them.

Remedies and Safeguards

We conclude by summarizing Owen's final chapter, "Directions to avoid the power of a prevailing apostasy." Here are his pieces of advice:

1. Labor for a true sense of the way in which God's glory is involved in the situation; learn to mourn the declension which robs Him of His glory, and pray for its removal; and meanwhile remain constant in professing the truth openly, at whatever cost, and adorning your profession with exemplary holiness.

2. Watch over your heart, keeping it alive and awake to its own deceitfulness, constant and confident in looking to Christ for upholding grace, and "attentive unto its own frames, its progress or decays in holiness."

3. Take care not to rest and trust merely in the outward privileges of the Church, or the possession of spiritual gifts, or as many do, in the gifts of others and the satisfaction they receive thereby."[13] Ask yourself constantly whether these privileges are having the effect of making your heart better and humbler, your faith stronger and your apprehension of spiritual things more vivid, your diligence greater, and your readiness to suffer for Christ more wholehearted. If they are not having this effect, you are neglecting to profit from them, and are in danger.

4. Take heed of being infected by national vices, so that you unthinkingly follow the crowd down the primrose paths of sin. "For commonness will take off a sense of their guilt, and countenance will insensibly take away shame."

5. "Carefully avoid all those miscarriages of professors which alienate the minds of men from the gospel, and countenance them in the contempt of the profession of it." There are three classes of such miscarriages that are found in, or charged upon, Christians: "(a) want of love and unity among themselves. (b) Want of usefulness and kindness towards all. (c) Spiritual pride

and censoriousness, or rash judging of other men." "For that judging, or condemning of others, wherewith they are so provoked," Owen concludes, "there is but one way whereby it may be done, . . . and this is in our lives. The practice of holiness judgeth all unholy persons in their own breasts."

Owen wrote his treatise with the spiritual decline of post-Restoration days in his view; but the character of apostasy, like that of other spiritual conditions, does not change with the passage of time, and in our own day apostasy from the gospel, in all those spheres that Owen specifies, remains a fact to be reckoned with, a problem to be handled, and a temptation which besets us all. Owen's teaching is thus exceedingly relevant, and we shall do well to ponder it and take it to heart.

5

KNOWLEDGE— FALSE AND TRUE

D. Martyn Lloyd-Jones

As we come to the end of our conference, it is essential that we should attempt to apply what we have been considering together, and perhaps not only that, but to take a general view of what we have been doing and to comment on it. There is no need to apologize for doing this. It is something the Puritans themselves invariably did; they were first and foremost pastoral, and therefore we must of necessity be pastoral. If the Conference ends without this pastoral note, which means the application of what we have been considering together, it will have failed in its purpose. The very title and name of our Conference demands our doing it. But that is not our only reason for doing so. It is not a sufficient reason; indeed, as I am hoping to show you, it can even be a dangerous one. I have very much stronger reasons for doing this than a mere desire to perpetuate what the Puritans did in their day and generation.

What are these stronger reasons? The first is, that it would be extremely dangerous for us not to do this. That is much more important than simply the desire to be Puritan in our method and scheme of things. We are compelled to do this because of the terrible danger of not doing it. Another reason we might adduce would be this: that there could be nothing quite so ridiculous as to turn the teaching of the Puritans, of all people, into a kind of new scholasticism and to spend our time in merely quoting texts, repeating phrases, and displaying our theoretical knowledge. That would be to do what the great opponents of the Puritans did. I mean the Caroline Divines, and people like them, whose sermons consisted very largely of strings of classical allusions.

Here then are our main reasons for spending our time together in this way at the end of the Conference.

The dangers confronting Christian people are not uniform and always the same. There are different types of personality and different emphases in the life of the Christian Church and in the Gospel. We who gather here, for example, are very well aware of the particular dangers that confront the activist—that type of person who is so common among us in evangelical circles—the man who lives on his energy and on what he does, who is always busy, organizing meetings and attending them, etc., and who says that you must always be "doing" something. We have realized very clearly the terrible danger that is inherent in that kind of activism, and we are never tired of protesting against it and of showing the danger of an almost exclusive emphasis on life, living, and activity at the expense of doctrine, understanding, and a growth in knowledge. But while we see that so clearly, there is a real possibility of our being unaware of the entirely different type of danger that confronts us, and which is something that applies to a different kind of individual. The first thing we always have to do is to know ourselves, to note the particular group to which we belong, and to realize that there are dangers inherent in every type and in every group. To come immediately to the point, there can be no question at all, it seems to me, that the peculiar danger that threatens those of us who meet annually in this Conference, is the danger of pride of intellect and pride of knowledge.

I have put that quite bluntly. I am not saying that we are actually guilty of it. My whole object is to show that there is a very real danger of it. I do not say that my discernment and diagnostic capacity, such as it is, is able actually to detect the presence of this disease. But, if I may be allowed to use a medical illustration, I am not at all sure that I have not noticed some of its prodromal symptoms. Let me expound my illustration. In the field of medicine and diseases of the body, there are what are known as infectious fevers. For instance, take a condition like measles. You think of this, do you not, in terms of a little child covered with a rash, who also has a cough, and is feverish, etc. Those are certainly manifestations of measles. But, and this is the interesting thing, the rash in measles, if I remember rightly, does not come out until about the fourth day of the disease. Before that you have an ill and a sick child who is feverish, complains of headaches, is off its food, may vomit, and so on. In addition, on the inside of the cheeks there may be white spots. Now what are these? They are quite clearly symptoms. Yes, but they are not actually those of measles as such; they are what are called "prodromal" symptoms, and the really good physician is a man who can recognize them and does not have to wait until the rash appears. He is so experienced, and he has so cultivated the art of medicine, that when he recognizes a certain group or complex of prodromal symptoms he says, "It looks to me as if this child is sickening for measles."

That is what is meant by prodromal symptoms, and I am suggesting that while I cannot make a true or a full diagnosis of this horrible condition of pride of intellect and of knowledge, I think that I have occasionally, in certain instances, seen certain of the prodromal symptoms. I propose, therefore, to consider this whole subject with you, and I do so in terms of what we find in 1 Corinthians 8:1–3: "Now as touching things offered unto idols, we know that we all have knowledge. Knowledge puffeth up, but charity edifieth. And if any man think that he knoweth anything, he knoweth nothing yet as he ought to know. But if any man love God, the same is known of Him." I want to consider this with you in order that we may apply it to ourselves. We need take no time in dealing with the particular context and the state of affairs in the church at Corinth. The apostle is dealing here with the question of the meats offered to idols because it was a cause of division in the church. There were the more enlightened, the stronger brethren, and there were the weak brethren. They did not see alike on this matter. The strong brother said there was no such thing as another God, that there was but one God. Everybody should know that, any man who knows anything at all knows that; therefore the idea that you should not eat meat offered to idols was just nonsense, and was virtually a going back to idolatry. A Christian was free to eat any meat he liked. Some of them went so far as to say that if asked he could even go to the heathen festivals. "Why not," they asked, "as 'these gods' are really non-existent?" So they went. And thus they were becoming a stumbling block to the weaker brethren, whom they despised of course, because of their weakness of intellect and grasp and understanding. There was grievous trouble in the church of Corinth because of this conflict between the enlightened men of knowledge, and those who were weaker and lacking in knowledge.

The exact context is most interesting. But we are concerned with the way, the most interesting way, in which the apostle deals with it. As is his custom he does not deal with the thing just in and of itself and directly; he lifts it up; he finds a great principle. And the principle he finds is this whole question of knowledge. The real trouble in Corinth, in a sense, was not at all the question of meats offered to idols, but simply men's view of their own knowledge. So he discusses the matter primarily in terms of their attitude toward knowledge. Our theme therefore, and the principle which we extract from our text, is the danger of a false view of knowledge.

To be accurate in our exegesis let me indicate that the "knowledge" Paul speaks of here is not the same as that referred to in 1 Timothy 6:20, where he talks about some who have gone astray and made shipwreck of the faith because of—as it is translated there—"science falsely so-called." "Science" there means knowledge, "knowledge falsely so-called." But that is not the same "knowledge" as we have here in 1 Corinthians 8. There, the problem has reference to a kind of mystical knowledge, and to people claiming that they were receiving some direct knowledge by inspiration; it was the danger of a false mysticism. But here, it is "knowledge" in the sense in which we normally use the term and in which, certainly, it applies to us who are members of this Conference.

There is no need, of course, to emphasize the fact that knowledge is all-important. We can never know too much. Knowledge is essential, doctrine is vital. The Bible is full of doctrine, and the New Testament particularly so. The epistles are mighty, glorious expositions of doctrine and of truth. The apostles not only preached the truth, but they emphasized the all-importance of a knowledge of the truth. Ultimately most of the troubles in the Church, according to the teaching of the epistles, stem somewhere or another from a lack of knowledge and of understanding. Knowledge, therefore, is in and of itself absolutely essential; indeed we must give it priority, and see to it that it always comes first. We were reminded of that in the paper which gave an exposition of Dr. John Owen's teaching on the question of apostasy. Truth came first, you remember, then godliness, and then worship. We are all agreed about that. It is no problem to us. But—and this is where our theme comes in—it is possible for us to develop a false notion of knowledge. It is possible for this gift of knowledge and understanding, which is in many ways God's most precious gift to us next to the gift of His Son and our salvation, to become a snare to us and very real danger in our spiritual life. Such was the position in Corinth. It is good for us therefore at the end of this Conference, in which we have been spending so many hours in the pursuit of knowledge and of understanding—it is good for us that we should face this possible danger which may be confronting us. I suggest the following treatment of the subject.

Causes of a False View of Knowledge

First, we must consider *the causes of this false view of knowledge*. We cannot go into these in detail, but we may divide them into *general* and *particular*. Obviously at the back of everything is the adversary. The devil having failed to keep us out of the faith and in a state of ignorance and darkness of the mind, and having seen that we have discovered the danger of a busy activism that may be nothing but a man revolving around himself, suddenly completely changes his tactics. Transforming himself into an angel of light, he drives us to such an extreme in this matter of knowledge as eventually to ensnare us quite as successfully as he ensnares the activist. In other words we are back to a phenomenon with which we are all so familiar—the danger of going violently from one extreme to the other, the danger of over-correction. It seems to be the besetting sin of mankind and one of the most terrible results of the Fall, that there is nothing so difficult as to maintain a balance. In correcting one thing we go to such an extreme as to find ourselves in an equally dangerous position. We are always confronted by the devil, who is ever ready to take the best things and turn them into his own instruments of unrighteousness and to produce the shipwreck of our souls.

A second general cause is, as a well-known proverb reminds us, "a little learning." "A little learning is a dangerous thing." That does not mean, of course, that there is no danger in much knowledge. There is. But I am not sure that in this respect there is not a greater danger in a little, because it always means that the element of the tyro or novice who imagines that his little knowledge is all knowledge comes in. Is it not notorious that first year students always know much more than final year students? I leave it at that—the danger that arises from a little learning.

But we must give more attention to the third cause which may be a little more controversial. To me, there is a very special danger at this point and in this matter which we are discussing, in reading as against preaching. Perhaps in the age in which we live this is one of the greatest dangers of all. I am asserting that reading is much more dangerous than listening to preaching, and I suggest that a very real danger arises in this connection if a man just spends his time reading and does not come under the power of preaching. What do I mean? I mean something like this. While a man is reading a book there is a sense in which he is in entire control. It depends partly on the book, I know, but speaking generally that is true. He can pick it up and put it down, and if it is beginning to make him feel uncomfortable he can shut it up and go for a walk and—he can do many things. But you cannot do all that when listening to preaching. Of course, you may be rude enough to get up and go out, and some people do so, but on the whole that is not the custom.

Preaching in a sense, therefore, safeguards us from these peculiar dangers that arise from reading only, provided of course that it is true preaching. For when a man is listening to true preaching, he comes under the "power" of the truth in a way that he does not when he is only reading. You may or may not like Phillips Brooks's definition of preaching as "truth mediated through personality," but there is a great deal to be said for it; and the Scriptures give us many illustrations of that. God does use the human personality. Not only that, a preacher not only expounds but also applies the Scriptures, and thereby makes sure that application takes place. When a man reads a book, however, he may never come to application. He can decide to shut the book and stop whenever he likes; there is no insistence upon the application. I fear that in this present age, when people are tending to listen less and less to preaching, and preaching becomes shorter and shorter, and our reliance upon reading becomes correspondingly greater, we are therefore more exposed to the danger than our forefathers were. I am not of course denouncing reading, and saying that there should be a ban on all publications! Of course not! I am simply trying to show the dangerous tendency that arises, and asserting the priority and primacy, and the superiority, of preaching. We need to be brought under the *power* of the truth. We do not like that, but it is the business of the preacher to do that, and if he fails to do so he is a very poor preacher. We always try to evade these conclusions and applications, but the preacher brings them home. He holds us, and makes us face them, and therefore he safeguards us against certain dangers. An age which attaches greater importance to reading than to the preaching of the Word is already in a dangerous position.

But let us pass to particular causes. One is, to take a purely theoretical and academic interest in truth and knowledge, to make knowledge an end in and of itself—the purely theoretical and academic approach. This is an obvious and well-known danger. I therefore take the general principle for granted, and mention only certain particular illustrations of it here.

I have always felt that it is wrong to hold examinations on scriptural knowledge, for the reason that it tends to develop this theoretical interest in it. It makes a subject of it, something which you have to learn in order to pass your examination or to get a certain number of marks. It may not happen, I grant, but I am suggesting that the moment you have an examination you have already started this tendency to regard biblical knowledge as a subject in and of itself, like any other subject. I remember lecturing at a certain conference in America in 1932. The conference had been started by a saintly bishop in 1874 for religious people, but it had degenerated, not so much in numbers but in its theology and approach to truth. I found there that the great claim for this conference (and this is how it was advertised) was that it taught any subject in which anybody could be conceivably interested. I also found that item number sixteen on the list of advertised subjects was "Religion." There is an example of this purely academic and theoretical interest in truth—you take it up as a subject: chemistry, history, art, religion, theology—knowledge about these matters. And if you have an examination in addition, the whole thing is greatly aggravated.

It is also, and I say this with very real regret, one of the dangers inherent in a study of religious history. I have known three men who have been expert historians on the history of Christianity, the history of the Church, and the history of its great men and movements. They had given their whole lives to this, and all three were particularly interested in the eighteenth century. But what has always amazed me is that though they spent their lives in reading about those glorious revivals of religion and those mighty men of God, it had not touched them at all. To them it was just a subject, a matter of academic and historical interest. They knew all the details, but as for the spirit of the thing, it was as if they had never read about it at all. That, I suggest, is a danger that is always inherent in the historical approach, and is an illustration of this purely theoretical approach.

The same thing can apply also even in the process of studying theology. It can become just a subject set for an examination, or a subject essential to obtaining a certain degree or diploma. And the very fact that this is the system may result in a man viewing the knowledge of God entirely in this way. But even without examinations this is still a possibility. A man can take a purely academic and theoretical interest in theology. I have known many such men. They happen to have had that as their hobby, whereas others turned to crossword puzzles. It was essentially the same approach—there was no question about that at all. It was purely theoretical, and thus it had become this false type of "knowledge." Are we entirely free from this danger?

The second particular cause is that we approach truth purely in terms of intellect—intellect only. There is nothing so dangerous as to isolate the intellect. We are all agreed about the priority of intellect. But there is all the difference in the world between our asserting its priority and talking only about intellect and regarding man as if he were nothing but an intellect. There is nothing that is so calculated to lead a man directly to this "false knowledge," about which the apostle is speaking, as a purely intellectual interest in truth, in which the heart is never engaged at all and the power of the truth is not felt, indeed in which feeling does not enter at all. The man is merely concerned to absorb knowledge with his mind. And it is precisely the same when the will is not engaged. If the interest does not lead to any action, or "move" the will, it is equally bad. We need not stay with this. The text for all this is, of course, Romans 6:17: "But God be thanked," says the apostle, "that ye have obeyed"—will!—"from the heart"—heart!—"the form of sound doctrine delivered to you"—to the mind. There you have them together. If you isolate the intellect and leave out the heart and the will, it is certain that you will end in this position of having a false view of knowledge, and indeed as I want to show, with false "knowledge" also.

To vary the expression, this danger is one of knowing "about" a subject rather than knowing it. "Knowing about!" What a vital distinction this is. What a difference there is between preaching about the Gospel and preaching the Gospel! It is possible to preach around the Gospel and say things about it without ever presenting it. That is quite useless—indeed it can be very dangerous. It may be true of us that we know "about" these things, but do not really know them. And this, of course, becomes all-important when we realize that the whole end and object of theology is to know God! A Person! Not a collection of abstract truths, or a number of philosophical propositions, but God! A Person! To know Him!—"the only true God, and Jesus Christ, Whom Thou has sent"!

There we have what I would regard as the main causes of this trouble. I would add just one further practical one for the preacher—the preacher only. This is very germane to the matter under consideration in this kind of conference. There are men who seem to me to be using the Puritans and their writings as a substitute for thought. Let me expound that. A man once came to me after listening to an attempt of mine to preach a sermon in which, as I am doing now, I had made a detailed analysis of a certain condition and had given the reply to it in a number of propositions. He was a preacher himself and he asked me, "Did you find that list of questions and answers in one of the Puritans?" He revealed to me thereby that that was what he did himself! I must confess that I was rather amazed and alarmed at the thing, but I can see the possibility. Now if you do that, you are using the Puritans as a substitute for thought. You are not working the thing out yourself and putting yourself through the process and discipline of thought, but you are just taking ready-made divisions and thoughts. The moment you do that you are undoubtedly guilty of having this "false knowledge." It is something purely for the mind. God deliver us from this danger of "preaching the Puritans" or of using them as a substitute for honest thinking and travail of soul. This applies equally, of course, to the misuse of any other writers.

Indications of a False View of Knowledge

We come now to the second general heading, *signs and indications of this condition.* There are certain general signs of this possession of a false knowledge and a false view of knowledge. For instance in such cases there is always a lack of balance. It is the bit of knowledge that the man happens to have that he is always interested in, and he knows nothing else. So there is lack of balance at once. He has been suddenly attracted by a type or aspect of knowledge, and goes after it. He acquaints himself with this; but he knows nothing else and is lopsided and lacking in balance. That in turn expresses itself in the use of slogans, clichés, tabloid expressions, and phrases which always characterizes this condition. These phrases keep tripping off the tongue; the same catch phrases and slogans always. That is unfailingly indicative of a little knowledge, a lack of true knowledge, and above all of this lack of balance of knowledge.

The apostle uses the term "puffed up"—"knowledge puffeth up." What an expression! What does he mean? He is describing a proud man, is he not? Here is a man who thinks he really "knows it all"; he is not like those other people, he knows; he is a man of knowledge and understanding. He knows it all! He is not like those others who never read; he is a great reader. And, of course, as the result of this he has arrived, and he is proud of it. "Puffed up!" How do we know that he is proud of his knowledge? Well, he is always parading it. The heavy, important, Puritan gait! The way of speaking and so on! That is a part of the parading that is inevitably one of the manifestations of being "puffed up." How difficult it is to stand erect with all this great weight of knowledge!

It manifests itself also in an impatience of any restraint and any correction; and still more in an impatience with any opposing view. It is intolerant of anything else. It "knows," and nothing else must even be suggested. No opposing view has a right to exist, and must not even be considered. In other words it is a part of this being "puffed up." It means "arrogance." The apostle James knew certain people of this type, so he says, "Be not many masters, my brethren" (James 3:1). What a terrible thing it must be to have a church with nothing but masters in it. All are authorities, all know everything and "all about it." "Be not many masters, my brethren." But there is always this tendency to feel that you do know, and understand, and, of course, to let it be known. So men arrogate unto themselves positions—and thereby betray themselves.

But still more serious is the way in which this manifests itself in its attitude to others. That was the trouble in the church at Corinth where these men who were enlightened said, "We have knowledge, we know." The apostle's reply was, "We know that we all have knowledge." Now he was there, according to some of the commentators, repeating their own phrase, "We have knowledge." The result was that their attitude to others was one of superiority. They tended to despise others, they were like the Pharisees. They did not boast so much of the good works they did as of their knowledge and their understanding. These others who did not understand, who were not clear about idols—why, they were almost beneath contempt. So they looked down upon them, were inconsiderate toward them, and said they were hardly worthy to be considered at all. It may show itself like that. Or it may show itself by just ignoring these others altogether. You ignore them to such an extent that you do not even feel contemptuous toward them, because in a sense they are not there at all! You are so much up in the air and in the clouds yourself that you do not even see them. It is as if they were not there.

Then another way in which it manifests itself is in feeling that these other people who are so slow to learn are a hindrance to us. Why should the preacher still be dealing with such simple matters? These men who know so much would like to go on to the great things, but the preacher is always staying there with some preliminaries. There he is, preaching evangelistic sermons every Sunday night, and on Sunday mornings he seems to be thinking that he has many people in his congregation to whom everything has to be explained in great detail. Because of that they are being held back and cannot go on to the great heights. They have long scaled the Alps, why does not the preacher take them to Mount Everest? These other people are just a nuisance and a hindrance with their slowness. Now that was the case in Corinth, and it is the case in many churches today. These men of knowledge want to go on, but they are being held back by these others whom they therefore despise. There it is, displayed in the attitude toward others.

The last sign that I am going to mention, in order that I may pass on to something else, is that in some cases this wrong view of knowledge, and this possession of what is not true knowledge, manifests itself by its victim just doing nothing at all; he simply enjoys his "knowledge." He does not seem to be aware of the fact that there is a lost soul anywhere in the world. He spends the whole of his time in reading, and if he meets people, in letting them know what he has been reading and in having discussions about Truth. There are sections of the Church today, with the world as it is, which never have any contact with the world at all. You never hear of their having a single convert; they do not seem to be aware of the existence of the problems of mankind and the ravages of sin. Why not? Because they spend the whole of their time within that circle of theirs, dotting their i's and crossing the t's, arguing about their great knowledge, and displaying it to one another. They are thus completely useless and entirely cut off from any kind of activity. We may not know this in its extreme form; but I would ask everyone present to examine himself or herself. Have you not found that it is a very easy thing indeed to spend the whole of your time in just reading and adding to your knowledge and building up your understanding, and forgetting all about the sinful world in which you live? It is the peculiar temptation that comes to people of intellect and ability who have realized the importance of knowledge. You can spend the whole of your life in merely adding to your own knowledge or in comparing notes with others who are like yourself.

The Uselessness of False Knowledge

But let us come to the third section which is *the uselessness of such supposed knowledge.* Look at the way in which the apostle puts it in the second verse: "If any man think that he knoweth anything." Well, he says, there is only one thing to say about him— "he knoweth nothing yet as he ought to know"; which means partly, that this man who is proud of the knowledge that he thinks is his has not really got any knowledge at all. Is this not obvious?

The argument is that if this man had a true knowledge of God, he simply could not be like that. So the apostle says, this man who thinks he knows, in fact "knows nothing yet as he ought to know," because if he did know as he ought to know he could not possibly be behaving as he is. This does not need any demonstration; it is a sheer impossibility; he has no true knowledge. He thinks that he has a knowledge of God, but all he has is some kind of knowledge "about" God; it is not a knowledge of God, otherwise he could not possibly be what he is.

Let me put this in the words of the great George Whitefield. He is talking about the Bible:

> This is my rock, this is my foundation. It is now about thirty-five years since I have begun to read the Bible upon my pillow. I love to read this Book, but the Book is nothing but an account of the promises which it contains, and almost every word from the beginning to the end of it, speaks of a spiritual dispensation, and the Holy Ghost that unites our souls to God and helps a believer to say, "My Lord and my God." If you content yourselves with that—(now he means by that the Bible itself remember)—if you content yourselves with that the devil will let you talk of doctrines enough.—(Now listen to Whitefield)—You shall turn from Arminianism to Calvinism; you shall be orthodox enough, if you will be content to live without Christ's living in you.[1]

Note what Whitefield says. If you just go in for that sort of theoretical intellectual knowledge, the devil will let you talk of doctrine enough, you will turn from Arminianism to Calvinism, you shall be orthodox enough, if you will be content to live without Christ's living in you. The devil does not care at all whether you change from being an Arminian to being a Calvinist if you do not know Christ and if you do not know God. One is as bad as the other. A theoretical Calvinism is of no more value than a theoretical Arminianism—not the slightest. That is what Whitefield is saying. He therefore warns against this because he is concerned about our having the Spirit. And he goes on to say, "Now when you have got the Spirit, then you may say 'God is mine.' " His point is that any knowledge which falls short of that does not interest the devil at all, because it is not really this true knowledge which is going to make a difference to you. That is how Whitefield puts it, who was himself a Calvinist and one of the greatest evangelists the world has ever known.

But let me adduce another reason. Why is this such a ridiculous position to be in—this feeling that we really do know and that we have knowledge, this pride in ourselves and this despising of those activists, those busy people who do not know any theology or doctrine, those people of whom we speak in a derogatory manner and whom we more or less dismiss? Why is this so utterly ridiculous? And why is it not a real knowledge at all? The answer is—because of the vastness of the knowledge!

What do I mean? The knowledge about which we are speaking is *a knowledge of God!* All these doctrines are about God! The moment you realize that you see how impossible it is that a man should be proud of his knowledge. The moment he realizes the endlessness, the vastness of the knowledge, he is bound to realize that he is but a pigmy, a mere beginner, a little child paddling at the edge of the ocean. He thought he was out in the great depths. Great depths! He knows nothing about them, he has been thinking in purely theoretical terms. But when you realize that all this knowledge, everything in the Bible, is meant to bring us to know God, the Everlasting and the Eternal, in the Glory and the Majesty and the Holiness of His Being—how can a man be proud of his knowledge when he realizes that that is the knowledge about which we are speaking?

Or take the way the apostle puts it in writing to the Ephesians. He is praying for these Ephesians and he "bows his knees unto God the Father." What for? Well this, he says: "That they, together with all other saints, may come to know the breadth, and the length, and the depth, and the height; and to know the love of God, which PASSETH knowledge" (Eph. 3:18–19).

Think of a little man strutting about because he knows so much, because he has read the Puritans, and has read theology and is not like these other people who are ignorant. "Puffed up!" Poor fool, who is not aware of ignorance—"he knoweth nothing yet as he ought to know." If he really had a true knowledge of God, he could not be like that. The thing is a sheer impossibility. The endlessness, the vastness of it all!

Men with True Knowledge

In order to emphasize this great truth I felt I could do nothing better than remind you of the experiences of certain men who knew just a little about this knowledge of which I am speaking. Let me start with Charles Haddon Spurgeon, who puts it like this:

> All ye that think that you know and have a knowledge of the truth, may the Holy Spirit grant that we may not say a word which is not strictly verified by our experience. But I hope we can say we have had converse with the Divine Father. We have not seen Him at any time, nor have we beheld His shape. It has not been given to us, like Moses, to be put in the cleft of the rock and to see the back parts or the train of the invisible Jehovah. But yet we have spoken to Him, we have said "Abba, Father." We have saluted Him in that title which came from our very heart, "Our Father, which art in Heaven." We have had access to Him in such a way that we cannot have been deceived. We have found Him, and through the precious blood of Christ we have come even to His feet. We have ordered our cause before Him, and we have filled our mouth with arguments. Nor has the speaking been all on our side, for He has been pleased to shed abroad by His Spirit His love in our hearts. While we have felt the Spirit of adoption He, on the other hand, has showed to us the loving-kindness of a tender Father. We have felt, though no sound was heard; we have known, though no angelic messenger gave us witness, that His Spirit did bear witness with our spirit

that we were born of God. We were embraced of Him—
no more at a distance. We were brought nigh by the blood
of Christ.[2]

That is real true knowledge of God! Well, there is one example.
But let us come to some others.

Issac Watts tells us that when John Howe, the Puritan, died, it
was found that he had written the following on the blank leaf of
his own Bible:

> But what I sensibly felt through the admirable bounty of
> my God and the most pleasant, comforting influence of
> His Spirit on October 22nd 1704, far surpassed the most
> expressive words my thought can suggest. I then experi-
> enced an inexpressibly pleasant melting of heart, tears
> gushing out of mine eyes for joy that God had shed
> abroad His love abundantly through the hearts of men;
> and that, for this very purpose, mine own heart should be
> so signally possessed of and by His blessed Spirit.[3]

Watts also quotes the case of John Flavel. Flavel was on a jour-
ney when suddenly God began to deal with him in this intimate
manner:

> There going on his way his thoughts began to swell and
> rise higher and higher like the waters in Ezekiel's vision,
> till at last they became an overwhelming flood. Such was
> the intention of his mind, such the ravishing tastes of
> heavenly joys, and such the full assurance of his interest
> therein, that he utterly lost all sight and sense of the world
> and all the concerns thereof, and for some hours he knew
> no more where he was than if he had been in a deep sleep
> upon his bed. Arriving in great exhaustion at a certain
> spring he sat down and washed, earnestly desiring, if it
> was God's good pleasure, that this might be his parting
> place from the world. Death had the most amiable face in
> his eye that ever he beheld, except the face of Jesus Christ

which made it so, and he does not remember, though he believed himself dying, that he even thought of his dear wife and children or any earthly concernment. On reaching his inn the influence still continued banishing sleep—still, still the joy of the Lord overflowed him and he seemed to be an inhabitant of the other world. He many years after called that day one of the days of heaven, and professed that he understood more of the life of heaven by it than by all the books he ever read or discourses he ever entertained about it.[4]

That is the great John Flavel bearing his testimony. But let Jonathan Edwards also speak to us about this:

As I rode out into the woods for my health in 1737, having alighted from my horse in a retired place as my manner commonly has been, to walk for divine contemplation and prayer, I had a view that was for me extraordinary of the glory of the Son of God as Mediator between God and men, and His wonderful, great, full, pure and sweet grace and love and meek and gentle condescension. The grace that appeared so calm and sweet appeared also great above the heavens. The Person of Christ appeared ineffably excellent, with an excellency great enough to swallow up all thoughts and conceptions, which continued, as near as I can judge, about an hour, which kept me a greater part of the time in a flood of tears and weeping aloud. I felt an ardency of soul to be what I know not otherwise how to express, emptied and annihilated, to lie in the dust and be full of Christ alone, to love Him with a holy and pure love, to trust in Him, to live upon Him, and to be perfectly sanctified and made pure with a divine and heavenly purity.[5]

Let me give one more. It is from a book published in 1635 by Robert Bolton, a Puritan, in which he relates the experience of a man named John Holland. This is what he says:

Hear how another blessed saint of God ended his days. Having the day before he died continued his meditation and exposition upon Romans 8 for the space of two hours or more, on the sudden he said, "Oh stay your reading! What brightness is this I see? Have you lit up my candles?" To which I answered, "No, it is the sunshine" for it was about five o'clock in a clear summer's evening. "Sunshine" said he, "Nay, my Saviour-shine!" "Now farewell world, welcome heaven! The day star from on High hath visited my heart. Oh speak it when I am gone and preach it at my funeral, God dealeth familiarly with men." (That is what he wanted them to preach after his death, "God dealeth familiarly with men.") "I feel His mercies, I see His majesty; whether in the body or out of the body I cannot tell, God He knoweth, but I see things that are unutterable." So, ravished in spirit he roamed towards heaven with a cheerful look and soft sweet voice, but what he said we could not conceive. With the sun in the morning following, raising himself as Jacob did upon his staff, he shut up his blessed life with these blessed words: "Oh, what a happy change shall I make; from night to day, from darkness to light, from death to life, from sorrow to consolation, from a factious world to a heavenly being. And oh my dear brethren, sisters and friends, it pitieth me to leave you behind, yet remember my death when I am gone and what I now feel I hope you shall find ere you die, that God dealeth familiarly with men. And now thou fiery chariot that came down to fetch up Elijah carry me to my happy Home, and all ye blessed angels who attended the soul of Lazarus to bring it up into heaven, bear me, O bear me, into the bosom of my Best Beloved. Amen. Amen. Come Lord Jesus, Come quickly." And so he fell asleep.[6]

That is true knowledge. That is what we should understand by knowledge. My argument is this, that when we realize that that is the knowledge to which the Bible is meant to bring us and that that is the whole end of theology and the whole purpose of all teaching concerning these matters—when we realize that that is "knowledge," can we possibly feel that we have knowledge and be "puffed up" and boast of "our knowledge" and "our learning" in these matters? The thing is a sheer impossibility.

Tests of True Knowledge

But let us consider the tests which show whether we have this true knowledge. First and foremost, obviously, is love of God. As the apostle puts it in verse 3 (1 Cor. 8:3): "If any man love God." That, he says in effect, "is knowledge." In other words, here is the argument. To know God, of necessity, is to love Him. You cannot know God without loving Him. It is impossible. Why? Because God is love, because of the glory of His Being, because God is Who and What He is. If any man really knows God he will be "lost in wonder, love and praise"; he will love God. True knowledge always leads to a love of God. If therefore we cannot say that we love God, have we any right to claim any knowledge of God? We can have a great deal of knowledge about Him and concerning Him, we can even apprehend with our minds the full scheme of salvation, but we still may be ignorant of "knowledge of God." "This is life eternal, that they might know Thee, the only true God, and Jesus Christ Whom Thou hast sent." That knowledge has been defined in the above quotations from the writings of godly men.

Second, another way to test knowledge is by the character it produces. "Knowledge puffeth up," says the apostle, "but charity edifieth"—builds up. What kind of character does it build up? It is described perfectly in 1 Corinthians 13: "Charity suffereth long, and is kind; charity envieth not, charity vaunteth not itself, is not puffed up, doth not behave itself unseemly, seeketh not her own, is not easily provoked, thinketh no evil; rejoiceth not in iniquity, but rejoiceth in the truth; beareth all things, believeth all things, hopeth all things, endureth all things. Love never faileth: but whether there be prophecies, they shall fail; whether there be tongues, they shall cease; whether there be knowledge, it shall vanish away. For we know in part, and we prophesy in part. But when that which is perfect is come, then that which is in part shall be done away." That is the character. What are its characteristics? First and foremost, humility. Look at those men in the Bible who have had a glimpse of God. They fall down as "dead." They say with Isaiah, "Woe is me, for I am undone!" Proud of their knowledge and their learning and their superiority? No!—they feel that they are unclean and not fit to be there at all, that they are not in a position to criticize anybody because they are so aware of their utter unworthiness. True knowledge invariably leads to humility, and also to holiness and godliness.

What about the attitude to the neighbor? It has been stated perfectly there in 1 Corinthians 13—we will love our neighbor. Our Lord Himself said that it is the second great commandment: "Love thy neighbour as thyself." And, of course, especially so if he is weak and ignorant. What if he is an Arminian? What if he does not understand the doctrines of grace? How are we to treat him? Are we to despise him, are we to dismiss him as a fool, or as a nonentity, or as a man who knows nothing—is that to be the attitude? Let me again quote Whitefield to you: "Believers consider Christ's property in them. He says 'My sheep.' Oh, blessed be God for that little, dear, great word 'My!' We are His by eternal election, 'the sheep which Thou hast given Me' says Christ. They were given by God the Father to Christ Jesus in the covenant made between the Father and the Son from all eternity." What a noble, wonderful statement of the great doctrine of election, one of the doctrines of grace! But Whitefield goes on: "They that are not led to see this, I wish them better heads, though I believe numbers that are against it have got better hearts. The Lord help us to bear with one another where there is an honest heart!"

There is nothing to be added to that. It is the right way to look at it. "I wish they had better heads," says Whitefield, and, of course, we must say that with him. We believe these people are wrong and that they are mistaken; but the trouble is in their heads. They have not seen it. Do not despise or deride them, do not dismiss them, do not walk on the other side of the street when you see them coming, do not feel that they are not fit to have converse with you or that you would be wasting your time if

you even discussed anything with them. No, no! Let us rather say
with Whitefield, that their hearts are better than their heads. And
as long as a man's heart is right, though his head may be wrong,
let us be patient with him, let us try to help him. We should not
spend our time just proving that we are right and everybody else
is wrong. If you believe that you are right and the other wrong,
well, it is your bounden duty to try to put him right, and you do
so by loving him, by being patient with him, by understanding.
You do not browbeat him, you do not knock him down; still less
do you dismiss him. You try to understand him and put things to
him, and reason with him. You do not hurl slogans at him; you
expound the Scriptures in as loving a manner as you can, and try
thus to lead him to a better understanding with his head. Oh yes,
when a man has this true knowledge he must "love his neighbor
as himself."

Results of True Knowledge

In other words, to sum it up, what is the result of true knowledge? First: it is that we rejoice in the Lord. My friends, we do not
only believe in the Lord when we know Him, we rejoice in Him.
"Rejoice in the Lord alway: and again I say, rejoice." The happi-
est people in the Church ought to be those who know the doctrines of grace. They should not be "puffed up" with their little
knowledge, they should be men filled with joy because they know
God and something about His love.

Likewise they should have a holy zeal for God's Name, and re-
sulting from that they should be filled with compassion for the
lost. The greatest evangelists the world has ever known have been
men who have held the doctrines of grace. Why? Because they
have had the greatest knowledge of God. Did you know that this
was a fact, that every single person who was involved in the beginning of the great missionary enterprise in the seventeen-
nineties was what is called a Calvinist? I dislike the use of these la-
bels and extra-biblical terms, but that is a simple fact of history.
There is a notion abroad today that a man who holds these doc-

trines of grace is a man who does nothing and that he does not believe in evangelism. Why is that notion abroad? Why have people got that notion? Is there something in it? If there is, it means this, that the knowledge we think we have is no knowledge at all. We have got this theoretical useless knowledge, and it is not a knowledge of God. If a man knows God, he will above all others have a zeal for the glory of God and the Name of God. He will want the whole world to come to God, he will be the most active preacher and evangelist of all. He *must* be because his knowledge of God is greater and his compassion for the lost is greater. And, as we know, there was no man in the eighteenth century who was so active, none who labored so indefatigably as that great George Whitefield from whom I have been quoting.

The man who has true knowledge will be full of compassion for the lost and of zeal for the glory of God. There is no need to prove this, the thing demonstrates itself. If only we knew Him! That is why the Son came from heaven, to let the world know something about the glory of the Father. He even came into the world and died to do this. And we should know Them—God the Father, God the Son, and God the Holy Spirit. And as we do, we shall in our little measure produce our Lord's life and shall be patient, as He was patient: "A bruised reed shall He not break, and the smoking flax shall He not quench." God have mercy upon us for the intolerance that often results from our false knowledge, and for the arrogance which is so often displayed. "Let this mind be in you, which was also in Christ Jesus." The lowly Jesus! Let us show that we know God by not only loving God but by loving our neighbor, and especially the lost and those who are weak and feeble and who have fallen by the way, the children in the faith, the beginners, and those who are slow to learn. Let us be patient with them, even as He has been patient with us.

My last word—how are we to get this knowledge? I give you but the bare headings. Bible study. Obviously you start there. But in addition, self-examination. How vital that is! Reading the Bible is not enough. And, may I add, even reading a few short notes on it is not enough. Self-examination! How do you examine yourself? If you read your Bible correctly, you will soon discover. Ask yourself questions, apply what you are reading to yourself. Say: "This was spoken to a Pharisee, is it true of me?"—and so on. But if you want further help as regards self-examination, read the diaries of men who have truly known God. Jonathan Edwards drew up a list of questions for people to ask themselves. John Fletcher of Madeley did exactly the same thing. You can use them if you like. But however you do it, be sure that you do it. Examine yourself!

Then another thing—and I want to emphasize this—balanced reading. I am concerned about this. I know of nothing that has such a tendency to produce false knowledge and to make men victims of this false knowledge as reading which lacks balance. If a man reads nothing but theology, he is exposing himself to this danger. I would therefore advise that we should always balance our reading as we balance our material diet. You should not eat only one kind of food. If you eat nothing but proteins you will soon be ill. You should always have a balanced diet. That principle is equally essential here. "What do you mean?" asks someone. Well, if I may say so with humility, the thing that has been of the greatest help to me has been to balance theological reading with the reading of biographies. That is the best advice I can give. I have always done this; I have always done it on holiday and I have tried to do it day by day. But on holiday in particular I used always to give my mornings to reading some theological work, but I was also careful to read some biography at night.

It worked like this. Having read for three or four hours in the morning, I felt before lunch that I was quite a considerable man, and that I had a great deal of knowledge which I would be able to display to others. There I was! But I remember very well when I first "stumbled"—and I am speaking the truth literally—when I first stumbled across Jonathan Edwards in 1928. I had never heard of him before, but I began to read him and I soon discovered that you cannot read a page of Jonathan Edwards without feeling very small indeed. It completely corrected what had been happening in the morning. The best antidote to the poison of false knowledge is to read a biography like that of Jonathan Edwards or Whitefield or Fletcher of Madeley.

I have generally tried to do the same thing on Sunday night. Sunday is a very dangerous day for a preacher. If you want to keep yourself in order, when you get home on Sunday night and have had a cup of tea or a very light meal, pick up one of these men—Whitefield, Edwards, etc. or one of those great Puritans and their experiences. I don't care which of them it is. And if you have gone home foolishly thinking that you had had a wonderful day and that you were a great preacher and had preached mighty sermons, you will not have read them for long without being brought back to earth. Indeed you will soon begin to feel that you have never preached in your life. Have we, I wonder, have we ever really preached? How many times? How often have we had Whitefield's experiences? There he is on one occasion preaching, when suddenly he stops and says to the congregation, "Oh, I would that you were feeling now what I feel!" What about it, preachers? How monstrous, how ridiculous, how foolish it is to think that we know these things, that we have a knowledge of God simply because we have garnered a certain amount of intellectual and theoretical and academic information! "Grow in grace and in the knowledge of the Lord." Can we say with Spurgeon that we know what it is to be "embraced" by Him? Have we ever really been there in His presence in a "sensible" way—using the term "sensible" as the Puritans used it?

To "know and feel" that God is near! What is the value of all the knowledge we may have if we are ignorant of that? "Though I have the gift of prophecy, and understand all mysteries, and all knowledge; and though I have all faith so that I could remove mountains, and have not charity, I am nothing" (1 Cor. 13:2). May God preserve us from this "false knowledge" which is not knowledge but a counterfeit, and which is finally useless.

Part 2

Press toward the Mark

❧

1961

6

THE PURITAN IDEA
OF COMMUNION WITH GOD

J. I. Packer

The thought of communion with God takes us to the very heart of Puritan theology and religion. This becomes clear as soon as we see how this subject stands related to other themes which stood in the forefront of Puritan interest. We all know, for instance, that the Puritans were deeply concerned with the many-sided problem of man—man's nature and place in the world, man's powers and possibilities for good and evil, man in the "fourfold state" of innocence, of sin, of grace, and of glory. And to their minds the whole end and purpose of man's existence was that he should have communion with God. "Man's chief end is to glorify God, and to enjoy him for ever."[1] Again: we all know that the Puritans were deeply and constantly concerned with the doctrine of *the covenant of grace*—its nature, its terms, its blessings, the modes of its dispensation, its seals and ordinances. The covenant of grace has been called the characteristic Puritan doctrine, as justification by faith was the characteristic doctrine of Luther. And to the minds of the Puritans the end and purpose of the covenant of grace was to bring men into union and communion with God. Or again: the Puritans never tired of dwelling on *the mediation of Christ* in the covenant of grace—His humiliation and exaltation, His satisfaction and intercession, and all His gracious relations—as Shepherd, Husband, Friend, and the rest—to His own covenant people. And the Puritan view of the end and purpose of the mediation of Christ is made plain to us by John Owen when he speaks of Christ's "great undertaking, in his life, death, resurrection, ascension, being a mediator between God and us . . . to bring us to an enjoyment of God."[2] Thus, to the Puritans, communion between God and man is the end to which both creation and redemption are the means; it is the goal to which both theology and preaching must ever point; it is the essence of true religion; it is, indeed, the definition of Christianity. The present paper is an attempt to plumb the Puritan understanding of this communion, and to gain some idea of the kind of religion to which this understanding gave rise.

The present-day value of such a study needs no stressing. For all who know anything of Puritan Christianity know that at its best it had a vigor, a manliness, and a depth, which modern evangelical piety largely lacks. This is because Puritanism was essentially an experimental faith, a religion of "heart-work," a sustained practice of seeking the face of God, in a way that our own Christianity too often is not. The Puritans were manlier Christians just because they were godlier Christians. It is worth noting two particular points of contrast between them and ourselves.

First, we cannot but conclude that whereas to the Puritans communion with God was a *great* thing, to evangelicals today it is a comparatively *small* thing. The Puritans were concerned about communion with God in a way that we are not. The measure of our unconcern is the little that we say about it. When Christians meet, they talk to each other about their Christian work and Christian interests, their Christian acquaintances, the state of the churches, and the problems of theology—but rarely about their daily experience of God. Modern Christian books and magazines contain much about Christian doctrine, Christian standards, problems of Christian conduct, techniques of Christian service— but little about the inner realities of fellowship with God. Our sermons contain much sound doctrine—but little relating to the converse between the soul and God. We do not spend much time, alone or together, in dwelling on the wonder of the fact that God and sinners have communion at all; no, we just take that for granted, and give our minds to other matters. Thus we make it plain that communion with God is a small thing to us. But how different were the Puritans! The whole aim of their "practical and experimental" preaching and writing was to explore the reaches of the doctrine and practice of man's communion with God. In private they talked freely of their experiences of God, for they had deep experiences to talk about, like the "three or four poor women sitting at a door in the sun" whom Bunyan met at Bedford:

> their talk was about a new birth, the work of God on their hearts, also how they were convinced of their miserable state by nature; they talked how God had visited their souls with his love in the Lord Jesus, and with what words and promises they had been refreshed, comforted, and supported against the temptations of the devil. Moreover, they reasoned of the suggestions and temptations of Satan in particular; and told to each other by which they had been afflicted, and how they were borne up under his assaults. . . . And methought they spake as if joy did make them speak. . . .[3]

And the Puritans never ceased to feel a sense of awe and wonder that access to God in peace and friendship was possible for them at all. "Truly for sinners to have fellowship with God, the infinitely holy God, is an astonishing dispensation," wrote Owen;[4] and Puritan hearts thrilled again and again at the wonder of God's "astonishing" grace. To them it was the most wonderful thing in the world. Yet we in our day take it for granted! Surely something is wrong here.

Then, second, we observe that whereas the experimental

piety of the Puritans was *natural and unselfconscious*, because it was so utterly God-centered, our own (such as it is) is too often *artificial and boastful*, because it is so largely concerned with ourselves. We are interested in religious experience, as such, and in man's quest for God, whereas the Puritans were concerned with the God of whom men have experience, and in the manner of his dealing with those whom He draws to Himself. The difference of interest comes out clearly when we compare Puritan spiritual autobiography—*Grace Abounding*, say, or Baxter's autobiography, or the Memoirs of Fraser of Brea—with similar works of our own day. In modern spiritual autobiography, the hero and chief actor is usually the writer himself; he is the center of interest, and God comes in only as a part of his story. His theme is in effect "*I*—and God." But in Puritan autobiography, God is at the center throughout. He, not the writer, is the focus of interest; the subject of the book is in effect "*God*—and me." The pervasive God-centeredness of Puritan accounts of spiritual experience is a proof of their authenticity, and a source of their power to present God to the modern reader. But when experience of God is told in a dramatized and self-glorifying way, it is a sure sign that the experience itself, however poignant, lacked depth, if, indeed, it was genuine at all.

These two contrasts show clearly enough how urgently Christians today need to learn what the Puritans have to teach on the subject of communion with God.

A word, now, about source material. Our main source will be John Owen's great work, *Of Communion with God the Father, Son, and Holy Ghost, each person distinctly, in love, grace, and consolation; or, the Saints' Fellowship with the Father, Son, and Holy Ghost, unfolded.* This treatise, first published in 1657, was reprinted in 1674 with a prefatory epistle by Daniel Burgess, who called it "the only (treatise) extant, upon its great and necessary subject." This was true only from a formal standpoint, and with reference to Owen's Trinitarian analysis of communion with God; the substance of what Owen says is found in less systematic form in very many Puritan expositions. One of the richest of these is Thomas Goodwin's *The Object and Acts of Justifying Faith*. This study will draw mainly on these two representative volumes. Other relevant sources would be Puritan expositions of the Song of Solomon (Sibbes, Collinges, Durham, and others) and of the favorite Puritan theme of "walking with God" (Bolton, Baxter, Thomas Gouge, etc.), but we shall not need to tap any of these save Baxter's treatment of "Walking with God" in *The Divine Life*.

A Relationship between God and Man

The Puritan analysis of communion with God can be set out in seven propositions.

1. *Communion with God is a relationship of mutual interchange between God and man.*

Such is the idea which the New Testament word *koinonia* (translated in the English Bible as "fellowship" and "communion") expresses. In general, *koinonia* denotes a joint participation in something by two or more parties, an active sharing in which the parties give to and receive from each other. "Communion consists in giving and receiving."[5] Such a relationship naturally implies the existence of some prior bond between the parties concerned. Accordingly, Owen defines *koinonia* between God and men as follows: "our communion . . . with God consisteth in his communication of himself unto us, with our returnal unto him of that which he requireth and accepteth, flowing from that union which in Jesus Christ we have with him"—a "mutual communication in giving and receiving, after a most holy and spiritual manner, which is between God and the saints, while they walk together in a covenant of peace, ratified by the blood of Jesus."[6]

2. *Communion with God is a relationship in which the initiative and power is with God.*

Note how Owen defines it as beginning with "*his* communication of himself to *us*," with "our returnal unto him of that which he requireth" coming in only on the basis of this. Communion with God is a relationship which God Himself creates by giving Himself to us; only so can we know Him, and respond to Him. In the narrow sense of our communing with God, communion is a

Christian duty; in the broader and more fundamental sense of
God's communicating Himself to us, whether to prompt our communing or to reward it, communion is a divine gift. Thus conceived, the idea of communion with God is broader than in our
common present-day usage. We tend always to think of communion
with God *subjectively* and *anthropocentrically*; we limit it to our conscious experience of God, our deliberate approach to Him and
His felt dealings with us. But the Puritans thought of communion
with God *objectively* and *theocentrically*, taking the idea to cover, first,
God's approach to us in grace, pardoning, regenerating, and making us alive to Himself; next, all His subsequent self-giving to us;
and only then extending it to our own conscious seeking after,
and tasting of, His gracious presence. They were not less concerned about experimental acquaintance with God than we are—
rather, indeed, the reverse—but they did not isolate this concern
in their minds from their broader theological concern about the
doctrine of divine grace. Thus they were saved from the point of
false mysticism, which has polluted much Christian devotion in recent times. The context and cause of our experienced communion with God, said the Puritans, is God's effective, life-giving
communion with us; the former is always to be thought of as a
consequence and, indeed, an aspect of the latter. The idea of communion with God thus covers the whole of the grace-and-faith-
relationship with God in which we stand, a relationship which
God Himself initiates and in which at each stage the initiative remains in His hands. The Barthians of our day proclaim that God
is the active subject in all human relationships with Him as if this
were a new discovery, but the Puritans knew this long ago.

3. *Communion with God is a relationship in which Christians receive
from, and respond to, all three Persons of the Trinity.*

The Puritans constantly insisted that the doctrine of the Trinity was the foundation of Christian faith, and that if it falls, everything falls. The reason for this insistence was that they saw that
the Christian salvation is a Trinitarian salvation, in which the economic relations of the three divine Persons as they work out salvation together mirror their essential and eternal relations in the
glorious life of the Godhead. The first Person, the Father, is re-

vealed as the One who initiates, who chooses a people to save and
His Son to save them, and plans a way of salvation that is consistent with His holy character. The second Person is revealed as
Son and Word in relation to the Father, imaging and embodying
in Himself the Father's nature and mind and coming forth from
the Father to do His will by dying to redeem sinners. The third
Person proceeds from the first two as their executive, conveying
to God's chosen the salvation which the Son secured for them.
All three are active in fulfilling a common purpose of love to
unlovely men; all three give distinct gifts of their bounty to the
chosen people, and all three, therefore, should be distinctly acknowledged in faith, and in an appropriate response, by Christian believers. This is the theme which John Owen expounds in
his treatise *Of Communion*.

Consider first the Father, says Owen. His special gift to us may
be described as an attitude and exercise of fatherly *love:* "free, un-
deserved, and eternal. . . . This the Father peculiarly fixes upon
the saints: this they are immediately to eye in him, to receive of
him, and to make such returns thereof, as he is delighted withal."[7]
Owen points out that in the New Testament love is singled out as
the special characteristic of the Father in His relation to us
(1 John 4:8; 2 Cor. 13:14; John 3:16; 14:27; Rom. 5:5; Titus 3:4).

The way to receive the Father's love is by *faith*; that is, in this
case, by believing and acknowledging that Christ comes to us,
not of His own initiative, but as the gift to us of a loving Heavenly Father.

> It is true, there is not an immediate acting of faith upon
> the Father, but by the Son. He is "the way, the truth, and
> the life: no man cometh unto the Father, but by" him
> (John 14:6). . . . But this is that I say: When by and
> through Christ, we have an access unto the Father, we
> then . . . see his love that he peculiarly bears unto us, and
> act faith thereon. We are then, I say, to eye it, to believe it,
> to receive it, as in him; the issues and fruits thereof being
> made out unto us through Christ alone. Though there be
> no light for us but in the beams, yet we may by the beams

see the sun, which is the fountain of it. Though all our refreshment actually lie in the streams, yet by them we are
led up to the fountain. Jesus Christ, in respect of the love
of the Father, is but the beam, the stream, wherein
though actually all our light, our refreshment lies, yet by
him we are led to the fountain, the sun of eternal love itself. Would believers exercise themselves herein, they
would find it a matter of no small spiritual improvement
in their walking with God. . . . The soul being thus by faith
through Christ . . . brought unto the bosom of God, into
a comfortable persuasion, and spiritual perception and
sense of his love, there reposes and rests itself. . . .[8]

How should we respond to the Father's love? By *love* in return: that is, says Owen, "by a peculiar delight and acquiescing in
the Father revealed effectually as love unto the soul."[9] He goes on
to analyze this love which we owe Him as consisting of four elements—rest, delight, reverence, and obedience, in combination
together.

Next, Owen says, consider the Son. His special gift to us is
grace—communicated free favor, and all the spiritual benefits
which flow from it. All grace is found in Him, and is received by
receiving Him.

There is no man whatever that hath any want in reference
unto the things of God, but Christ will be unto him that
which he wants. . . . Is he dead? Christ is life. Is he weak?
Christ is the power of God, and the wisdom of God. Hath
he the sense of guilt upon him? Christ is complete righteousness. . . . Many poor creatures are sensible of their
wants, but know not where their remedy lies. Indeed,
whether it be life or light, power or joy, all is wrapped up
in him.[10]

All this, says Owen, is in the mind of Paul when he speaks of "the
grace of our Lord Jesus Christ" (2 Cor. 13:14), and of John when
he says, "of his fullness have we all received, and grace for grace"

(John 1:16). In expounding the meaning of Christ's grace, Owen makes much of the "conjugal relationship" between Christ and His people, and offers a detailed Christological exegesis of the Song of Songs 2:1–7 and chapter 5.

The way in which men receive Christ's love is by *faith*; that is, in this case,

> free, willing consent to receive, embrace and submit unto the Lord Jesus, as their husband, Lord and Saviour, to abide with him, subject their souls unto him, and to be ruled by him for ever. . . . When the soul consents to take Christ on his own terms, to save him in his own way, and says, Lord . . . I am now willing to receive thee and to be saved in thy way, merely by grace; and though I would have walked according to my own mind, yet now I wholly give up myself to be ruled by thy Spirit, for in thee have I righteousness and strength, in thee am I justified and do glory; then doth it carry on communion with Christ. . . . Let believers exercise their hearts abundantly unto this thing. This is choice communion with the Son Jesus Christ. Let us receive him in all his excellencies as he bestows himself upon us. Be frequent in thoughts of faith, comparing him with other beloveds . . . preferring him before them, counting them all loss and dung in comparison of him . . . and let our hearts give up themselves unto him; let us tell him, that we will be for him and not for another; let him know it from us, He delights to hear it . . . and we shall not fail in the issue of sweet refreshment with him.[11]

How should we respond to the conjugal affection and loyalty of Christ toward us? By maintaining marital chastity toward Him, says Owen: that is, by refusing to trust or hanker after any but he for our acceptance with God; by cherishing His Spirit, sent to us for our eternal benefit; and by maintaining His worship undefiled, according to the Scripture pattern. This necessitates a daily deliberate submission to Him as our gracious

Lord. Daily we should rejoice before Him in the knowledge of His perfection as a Savior from sin; daily we should take the sins and infirmities of that day to His cross to receive forgiveness ("this is every day's work; I know not how any peace can be maintained with God without it");[12] daily we should look to Christ, and wait on Him, for the supply of His Spirit to purify our hearts and work holiness in us. Holiness, according to the Puritans, cannot be attained without the exercise of faith, any more than it can be perfected without the effort of fighting sin. The saints, say Owen,

> look upon him (Christ) as . . . the only dispenser of the Spirit, and of all grace of sanctification and holiness. . . . He is to sprinkle that blood upon their souls, he is to create the holiness in them that they long after. . . . In this state they look to Jesus; here faith fixes itself, in expectation of his giving out the Spirit for all these ends and purposes; mixing the promises with faith, and so becoming actual partaker of all this grace. This is . . . their communion with Christ; this is the life of faith as to grace and holiness. Blessed is the soul that is exercised therein.[13]

Finally, says Owen, consider the Spirit. He is called the Comforter, and *comfort*—strength and encouragement of heart, and assurance and joy—is His special gift to us. This comfort is conveyed in and through the understanding which He gives us of the love of God in Christ, and of our share in God's salvation (John 14:26–27; 16:14; Rom. 5:5; 8:16). The Spirit's ministry as our Comforter consists in

> his bringing the promises of Christ to remembrance, glorifying him in our hearts, shedding abroad the love of God in us, witnessing with us, as to our spiritual state and condition, sealing us to the day of redemption; being the earnest of our inheritance, anointing us with . . . consolation, confirming our adoption, and being present with us

in our supplications. Here is the wisdom of faith; to find out, and meet with the Comforter in all these things; not to lose their sweetness, by lying in the dark as to their author, nor coming short of the returns which are required of us.[14]

How are we to respond to the comforting work of the Spirit? By taking care not to *grieve* Him by negligence or sin (Eph. 4:30), or to *quench* Him by opposing or hindering His work (1 Thess. 5:19), or to *resist* Him by refusing His word (Acts 7:51), but to give Him constant thanks, and to pray to Him for a continuance of His peace and goodness. (Owen finds in Rev. 1:4 a precedent for such prayer to the Spirit.)

This, then, according to Owen, should be the pattern of our regular communion with the three Persons of the Godhead, in meditation, prayer, and a duly ordered life. We should dwell on the special mercy and ministry of each Person toward us, and make our proper response of love and submission distinctly to each. Thus we are to maintain a full-orbed communion with God.

Goodwin propounds a similar conception, with less concern for verbal precision but greater exuberance and warmth than we find in what Moffat called "the dark grey pool of Owen's ratiocination." Owen has shown us intercourse with the Truine God as a part of Christian duty; in the following passage, Goodwin sets it before us as a part of God's gift of assurance. Apropos of 1 John 1:3 and John 14:17–23, Goodwin writes:

> There is communion and fellowship with all the persons, Father, Son, and Holy Ghost, and their love, severally and distinctly . . . Christ putteth you upon labouring after a distinct knowing of, and communion with all three persons . . . rest not until all three persons manifest their love to thee . . . in assurance, sometimes a man's communion and converse is with the one, sometimes with the other; sometimes with the Father, then with the Son, and then with the Holy Ghost; sometimes his heart is drawn out to consider the Father's love in choosing, and then the love

of Christ in redeeming, and so the love of the Holy Ghost, that searcheth the deep things of God, and revealeth them to us, and taketh all the pains with us: and so a man goes from one witness to another distinctly, which I say, is the communion that John would have us to have. . . . And this assurance it is not a knowledge by way of argumentation or deduction, whereby we infer that if one loveth me then the other loveth me, but it is intuitively, as I may so express it, and we should never be satisfied till we have attained it, and till all three persons lie level in us, and all make their abode with us, and we sit as it were in the midst of them, while they all manifest their love to us . . . this is the highest that ever Christ promised in this life (in his last sermon, John 14).[15]

Friendship between God and Man

4. *Communion with God is a relation of friendship between God and man.*

This thought brings into perspective at once John Owen's complex analysis. Communion with God means simply behaving as a *friend* of the God who has called you His *friend*. Thomas Goodwin dwells on the love of Christ, who, when we had fallen into sin and enmity against God, died to make us His friends again—though "he could have created new ones cheaper"[16]— and develops powerfully the thought that friendship is not a means to an end, but an end in itself, and that true friendship is expressed in the cultivation of our friend's company for its own sake:

Mutual communion is the soul of all true friendship; and a familiar converse with a friend hath the greatest sweetness in it . . . (so) besides the common tribute of daily worship you owe to (God), take occasion to come into his presence on purpose to have communion with him. This is truly friendly, for friendship is most maintained and kept up by visits; and these, the more free and less occasioned by urgent business . . . they are, the more friendly they are. . . . We use to check our friends with this upbraiding. You still (always) come when you have some business, but when will you come to *see me?* . . . When thou comest into his presence, be telling him still how well thou lovest him; labour to abound in expressions of that kind, than which . . . there is nothing more taking with the heart of any friend. . . . "[17]

This whole section of Goodwin's exposition deserves study, but we cannot stay with it now.

5. *Communion with God is the life of heaven begun on earth.*

Frequently the Puritan writers make the point that though there are two ways of communing with God, by faith here and by sight hereafter (2 Cor. 5:7; 1 Cor. 13:12), the relationship itself remains the same in both. Communion with God by sight, in heaven, "is by a more high and elevated way, but it is of the same nature, and hath still the same object" as communion with God by faith, here below.[18] Fellowship with God is a true foretaste of heaven, and to enjoy it is to enter into faith's victory over death. So John Preston, when dying, answered the question, did he find himself afraid? with the whispered words: "no; I shall change my place, but I shall not change my company." And Bunyan's Mr. Stand-fast, as he stood in the river, was able to declare, "I am going now to see that Head that was Crowned with Thorns, and that Face that was spit upon, for me. I have formerly lived by Hear-say, and Faith, but now I go where I shall live by sight, and shall be with him, in whose Company I delight myself." It is in this connection that we should note the Puritan insistence that communion with God, our present entry into the life of heaven, brings into our hearts the joy of heaven—the "glorified joy" of 1 Peter 1:8, the joy of the Lord which is joy in the Lord and is found in God's presence alone.

6. *Communion with God in Christ is enjoyed in a special way at the Lord's Table.*

Not that there is any special grace conveyed to the faithful communicant which he could not otherwise have; the Puritans all agreed with Robert Bruce that "we get no other thing in the Sacrament, than we get in the Word."[19] But there is a special exercise of faith proper to the Lord's Table, where Christ's supreme act of love is set before us with unique vividness in the sacramental sign; and from this should spring a specially close communion with God. Let Richard Baxter expound this.

> Also in the sacrament of the body and blood of Christ, we are called to a familiar converse with God. He there appeareth to us by a wonderful condescension in the representing, communicating signs of the flesh and blood of his Son, in which he hath most conspicuously revealed his love and goodness to believers: there Christ himself with his covenant gifts are all delivered to us by these investing signs of his own institution. . . . No where is God so near to man as in Jesus Christ; and no where is Christ so familiarly represented to us, as in this holy sacrament. Here we are called to sit with him at his table, as his invited, welcome guests; to commemorate his sacrifice, to feed upon his very flesh and blood; that is, with our mouths upon his representative flesh and blood, and with our applying faith upon his real flesh and blood, by such a feeding as belongs to faith. The marriage covenant betwixt God incarnate and his espoused ones, is there publicly sealed, celebrated and solemnized. There we are entertained by God as friends . . . and that at the most precious costly feast. If ever a believer may on earth expect his kindest entertainment, and near access, and a humble intimacy with his Lord, it is in the participation of this sacrifice feast, which is called The Communion, because it is appointed as well for our special communion with Christ as with one another. It is here that we have the fullest intimation, expression, and communication of the wondrous love of God; and therefore it is here that we have the loudest call, and best assistance, to make a large return of love; and where there is most of this love between God and man, there is most communion, and most of heaven, that can be had on earth.[20]

Public Worship and Private Meditation

7. Communion with God requires that we discipline ourselves to public worship and private meditation.

"Order and method" were not first heard of with Agatha Christie's Hercule Poirot; both were Puritan watchwords, and they express one fundamental aspect of the Puritan approach to life. Both one's outward conduct and one's inward thoughts, said the Puritans, must be ordered; if you would know deeper communion with God, you must see to it that you worship Him regularly, and think of Him constantly. We quote Baxter again:

> The assemblies of his saints that worship him in holy communion are places where he is likelier to be found than in an ale-house or a play-house. We must not be strange to him in our thoughts, but make him the object of our most serious meditations . . . we are far from him, when our thoughts are (ordinarily) far from him. I know that it is lawful and meet to think of the business of our callings, so far as is necessary to the prudent successful management of them; and that it is not requisite that our thoughts be always actually upon God: but he that doth manage his calling in holiness, doth all in obedience to God's commands . . . and he intendeth all to the glory of God, or the pleasing of his blessed will; and he often reneweth these actual intentions; and oft interposeth thoughts of the presence, or power, or love, or interest of him whom he is serving; he often lifteth up his soul in some holy desire or ejaculatory request to God; he oft taketh occasion from what he seeth, or heareth, or is doing, for some spiritual meditation or discourse. . . . All the day long our thoughts should be working either on God, or for God. . . . Our hearts must be taken up in contemplating and admiring him, in magnifying his name, his word, and works; and in pleasant, contentful thoughts of his benignity, and of his glory, and the glory which he conferreth on his saints. He that is unskillful or unable to manage his own thoughts with some activ-

ity, seriousness, and order, will be a stranger to much of the
holy converse that believers have with God. . . .[21]

The Christian must be diligent and tireless in doing God's
will in the world, but mere Christian activity is not enough.
Through it all, the Christian's heart and mind should ever be going out to God Himself, seeking communion with Him in it. To
rest complacently in the thought that one is doing what God
commanded, and not to be ever seeking to "keep up communion" with God Himself through all one's work in His cause, is a
Pharisaic snare. In the piercing words of Richard Alleine,

> Count not that thou hast lived that day, in which thou hast
> not lived with God.

> Keep close to God, by keeping close to duty. Keep close to
> duty, and keep close to God in duty. Call not that a duty,
> which thou canst not call communion with God. Make
> not duty to do the work of sin, to take God out of sight.
> Let not prayer, or hearing, or sacraments, be instead of a
> God to thee. Such praying and hearing there is amongst
> many but know not thou anything for religion, wherein
> thou meetest not with God.[22]

There was once a day when Jeremiah was sent of God to say to
Israel, "Stand ye in the ways and see, and ask for the old paths,
where is the good way, and walk therein, and ye shall find rest for
your souls" (Jer. 6:16). As we study the Puritan idea of communion
with God, may it be that God is speaking in similar terms to us?
These are "old paths," paths, indeed, as old as the Bible, and paths
which our Puritan forefathers found to be in truth "the good way."
We do well to ask ourselves whether we have yet learned to walk in
them, and, if not, to humble ourselves and seek for grace to begin
now. "And ye shall find rest for your souls."

7

THE PURITAN DOCTRINE
OF CHRISTIAN JOY

J. Gwyn-Thomas

It may come as a surprise to some to know that the Puritan pastors were great advocates of Christian joy. Contrast the following quotation from Sibbes's exposition of 2 Corinthians 1:24 with the common conception of a sour-faced, unsmiling, and tight-laced preacher who continually rebuked everything that would lead to joyfulness. Sibbes writes, "The end of the ministry is not to tyrannize over people's souls, to sting and to vex them, but to minister comfort, to be helpers of their joy; that is to help their salvation and happiness, which is here termed joy, because joy *is a principal part of happiness in this world and in the world to come.* This is the end, both of the word, and of the dispensation of the word, of the ordinances of salvation, of the sacraments, and all, *that our joy may be full*; as our blessed Saviour saith, 'These things have I spoken unto you, that your joy may be full' (John 15:11)." Or we may quote the godly Richard Baxter:

All Christ's ways of mercy tend to, and end in the Saints'
joys. He wept, suffered, sorrowed that they might rejoice; He sendeth the Spirit to be their comforter; He
multiplieth Promises, he discovers their future happiness, that their joy may be full; He aboundeth to them
in mercies of all sorts; He maketh them lie down in
green pastures, he leadeth them by the still waters, yea,
He openeth to them the Fountain of Living Waters, that
their joy may be full.

Let me immediately state that this joy here spoken of is joy in
God; the enjoyment of God arising from the soul's most intimate
communication with God.

But, since the Puritans, as watchful pastors, were aware that
they were often confronted with persons who were rejoicing without grounds for so doing, it was necessary for them to expose
false joy; and in so doing they threw much light upon the nature
of true joy. Therefore in this paper I will follow their lead and first
seek to deal with counterfeit joy. As in other aspects of Christian
experience, so in this, the devil is anxious and ready to deceive
and to pervert the unwary soul.

False Joy

So then, being well versed in the subtleties and deceptions of
human nature, these same godly men exposed this possibility
that joy in a Christian could be carnal and wrongly founded;
could be indeed, a merely natural emotion with a false veneer of
spirituality. They sharply distinguished carnal human delight
from that which had a holy origin. Baxter gave directions against
what he calls sinful mirth, and his searching examination clearly
separates that joyousness which is rightly founded from that
which is not. Mirth is sinful, says Baxter,

1. When men rejoice in that which is evil; as in the hurt of
others or men's sin or in the sufferings of God's servants,

or the afflictions of the church, or the success or prosperity of the enemies of the Church.

2. When it tendeth to the committing of sin, or is managed by sin.

3. When it is unseasonable or in an unmeet subject, e.g. as when an unsanctified miserable soul be taken up in mirth, that is in the power of sin and Satan and near to Hell.

4. When it is a hindrance to our duty.

5. Mirth is most horridly odious when it is blasphemous and profane.

Having thus ensured that the nature of sinful mirth should be clearly understood, Baxter directs as follows:

1. First see that thou be a fit person for mirth, and that thou be not a miserable slave of Satan in an unregenerate, unholy, unjustified state.

2. Yet do not destroy nature by over much heaviness, under pretence that thou hast no right to be merry.

3. (In direction 3 Baxter gives the true method of rejoicing, to which we shall return later.)

4. Mark well the usefulness and tendency of all thy mirth. A Christian that hath acquaintance with himself and with the work of holy watchfulness, may discern what his mirth is, by the tendency and effects, and know whether it doth him good or harm.

5. Take heed that the flesh defile not your mirth.

6. Consider what your mirth is like to prove to others, as well as yourselves.

7. Never leave out Reason and Godliness from any of your mirth. Abhor that mirth that maketh a man a fool, or playeth the fool.

8. Watch your tongues in all your mirth; for they are very apt to take liberty then to sin. Mirth is to the tongue as holidays and playdays to idle scholars; who are glad of them as time in which they think they have liberty to game and fight and do amiss.

Finally directions 9–12 contain warnings against mirth degenerating into levity or profaneness, or becoming immoderate in measure. The cure for this, Baxter suggests, is to remember the presence of God, and that death and judgment are at hand, and that our souls are yet under a great deal of sin, wants, and dangers, and that we have a great deal of serious work to do; to look on Jesus Christ and remember what an example He gave us upon earth; to think on the ordinary way to Heaven described in Scripture, which is through many tribulations, afflictions, fastings; to think of the lives of saints in the past, who went to Heaven through labor, watchings and fastings, and poverty and cruel persecutions, and not through carnal mirth and sport; and finally to think of the many calamitous objects of sorrow that are abroad in the world—the millions of heathen and other enemies or strangers to Christ; the obstinate Jews; the dark corrupted state of the unreformed churches, where religion is woefully obscured and dishonored by ignorance, error, superstition and profaneness; the Papal tyranny and usurpation; and the divided state of all the churches, together with "the profaneness, and persecution, and uncharitablesness, and contentions, and mutual reproaches and revilings which make havock for the Devil among the members of Christ."

False joy, then, is an irrational and frivolous emotion, unrelated to God and His salvation. By contrast, the road to true joy is to see that we have strong, reasonable, and spiritual grounds for rejoicing, and that such joy be always linked with its Source and Object.

The Reasonableness and Duty of Rejoicing

After this warning of the nature, unprofitableness, and danger of sinful merriment, it is necessary to emphasize that the same pastors who gave such fearful warnings against it, were also equally insistent upon proclaiming the duty of rejoicing from a right foundation. Joy in the Christian was not to them a matter of temperament, nor was it merely optional; joy was the divinely intended expression of a living faith, and so it was a constant duty to "labour to be of such a temper, as that we may glory and rejoice." Sibbes lays it down thus, "Joy is that frame and state of soul that all who have given their names to Christ either are in, or should labour to be in." From Christians God requires joy; to rejoice is a debt which they owe Him.

The saintly John Howe in his treatise on *The Blessedness of the Righteous* affirms as much in these solemn words: "Possess thy soul with the apprehension, that thou art not at liberty in this matter: but that there is a certain spiritual delectation, which is incumbent on thee as indispensable duty." "Settle this persuasion in your hearts, that the serious, rational, regular, seasonable exercise of delight and joy is a matter of duty, to be charged upon conscience, from the authority of God, and is an integral part in the religion of Christians." In another place Howe exclaims, "It is plain, that it is the common duty of all to delight in God."

When Sibbes wrote that God requires joy at the hands of Christians as a duty, he also wrote, "And he doth prepare and give them matter enough of joy." Consider, first, the ills Christians are freed from. They are freed from sin and the wrath of God, from eternal damnation, and from the sting of death. These are the greatest and most terrible ills that there are. Or consider the state that God brings them into by believing. Being in the favor of God, they enjoy the fruits of that favor, "peace and joy in the Holy Ghost." And then for the life to come, they are under "the hope of glory." "A Christian, which way so-ever he look, hath matter of joy. God the Father is his, Christ is his, the Holy Ghost is his comforter, the angels are his, all are his, life or death, things present or things to come, all are his; 1 Corinthians 3:22. Therefore, there is no question of this, that every one that hath given his name to Christ is in a state of joy, if he answer his calling, or he should labour to be in it, he wrongs his condition else."

Sibbes continues to stress this point, giving reasons why all Christians must labor to be in that state of joy. The first reason is that God, who gives them such matter of joy, may have glory from them. For what should the life of a Christian be, that is freed from the greatest ill, and advanced to the greatest good? His life should be a perpetual thanksgiving to God; and how can a man be thankful that is not joyful? Second, joy makes a man active in good, when he is anointed with the oil of gladness. Third, joy strengthens the Christian to meet suffering. We have many hard things to go through in this world. How shall a man suffer them joyfully, unless he labor to bring himself into this temper of joy? Fourth, a Christian's joy helps others. Every man should labor to encourage others. We are all fellow-passengers on the way to heaven. Therefore to bring others on more cheerfully, we ought to labor to be in a joyful state. Those who do not rejoice bring an ill report upon the way of God, as if it were a desolate, disconsolate way; just as the spies brought an ill report upon the land of Canaan, whereupon the people were disheartened from entering into it.

If a Christian does not rejoice, continues Sibbes, it is not because he is a Christian, but because he is not Christian enough, because he favors the worse principle in him, or indulges himself in some work of the flesh. God in the covenant of grace is all love and mercy. He would have us in our pilgrimage to heaven to "finish our course with joy."

It should be noted that in this matter of joy the Puritan pastors were being consistent to their basic principles of preaching. One of the controlling principles of their preaching was "the primacy of the intellect." Man is a rational being, and God moves man by addressing truth to his mind. As we consider the directions given by such men as Howe, Baxter, and Sibbes, we must observe their emphatic insistence that joy is the only rational state of the Christian in view of the truth about his spiritual condition. For Christians to lack joy is utterly irrational. The state of joy is a reasonable state: it has the best of foundations, for it ultimately rests on the gracious nature and being of God. John Howe devotes a whole treatise to this subject under the title *Of Delighting in God.*

Joy in God and from God

In turning to this holy exercise of delighting, or rejoicing, in God, we must remind ourselves that the Puritans always sought to be God-centered in their treatment of gospel themes. Let us heed this fact before we examine their directions for the practice of holy joy, for their method requires us first to consider the object of that joy—namely God Himself, whom Howe describes as "The delectable Object." "God," he says, "is in Himself, the best and most excellent Being; wherein we behold the concurrence of all perfections; the most amiable and beauteous excellencies." Baxter also exults in God Himself as he writes:

> Rightly understand, what delight in God it is that you must seek and exercise. It is not a mere sensitive delight, which is exercised about the objects of sense, or phantasie, and is common to beasts with men. Nor is it the delights of immediate intuition of God, such as the blessed have in heaven; nor is it an enthusiastic delight, consisting in irrational raptures, and joys which we can give no account of the reason of. Nor is it delight inconsistent with sorrow and fear, when they are duties. But it is the solid rational complacency of the soul in God and holiness, arising from the apprehensions of that in Him, which is justly delectable to us.

> Let your minds delight themselves in God considered
> in himself as the only object of highest delight. . . . Behold
> him in the infinite perfections of His Being; his Omnipo-
> tence, Omniscience, and his Goodness, his Holiness,
> Eternity and Immutability. And as your eye delighteth in
> excellent pictures of gardens or fields not because they
> are yours, but because they are delectable subjects to the
> eye; so let your minds delight themselves in God, consid-
> ered in Himself as the only object of highest delight.

Our joy in God may be *contemplative* when the soul solaces itself in the pleasant meditation of God, or it may be *sensitive* delight, whereby the soul "tastes" how gracious the Lord is. The
young Christian experiences more of the latter than of the former, as in the course of nature human creatures first exercise
sense, and by slower and more gradual process, come on to acts
of ratiocination afterwards. But in a mature believer contemplative and sensitive delight should go hand in hand.

Howe expounds at length God's communication of His Being
and attributes to man, which is the presupposition of our being
able to rejoice in Him whether contemplatively or sensitively.
This communication begins with, and thereafter flows from, the
new birth.

> God is to be enjoyed and delighted in by this delectable
> communication intervening by which he now frames the
> soul according to his own image, and gives a heart after
> his own heart, that is, such as is suitable to him, as he
> would have it be. And this way only is anyone in a possi-
> bility to delight in God, by having a good frame of spirit
> communicated to him and in-wrought in him. Now is he
> composed to delight and blessedness, being by the same
> workmanship created in Christ Jesus both to good works
> and the best enjoyments.

Here, then, is the foundation for right rejoicing. It is the fruit
of the new birth; God has wrought in man the nature which is ca-

pable of rejoicing in spiritual things. Not only is God the object of joy, He too is the One Who has made it possible for us to rejoice in Himself. This He has done by His regenerating activity and His gift of the Holy Spirit.

Directions

This is what Howe writes, "partly to direct, partly to excite, unto that delightful pleasant life":

1. *Fill your minds with the essential truths of the Christian faith.*

"Endeavour," says Howe, "to have a mind well instructed in the knowledge of such things as more directly concern the common practice of a religious man, as such. That is, to be thoroughly insighted into practical truths or into that truth which is after godliness." Howe maintains that such truths "are plain and but few," and cites as examples "repentance toward God and faith toward our Lord Jesus Christ," which two things, he says, comprehend the whole counsel of God. And the summary of our duties is in the Great Commandment of loving God with our whole being and our neighbor as ourselves.

2. *"Be principally intent to have your soul become habitually good and holy, by its own settled temper and complexion inclined, and made suitable to the way of righteousness and life."*

The paths of righteousness are agreeable and pleasant only to a restored, sound, and healthy soul; you must *be* good in order to *do* good with any enjoyment. "'Tis not to be hoped it can be delightful to act against inclination." Therefore, since heart-rectitude must be had, it must be sought earnestly and without rest. Often ought heaven to be visited with such sighs and longings as that of the psalmist, "O that my ways were directed to keep Thy righteous judgments. Let my heart be sound in Thy statutes, that I be not ashamed" (Psalm 119:80). In other words—seek the new birth, and make it your business to be holy, always and everywhere, until it becomes more natural to you than being unholy!

3. *Persevere in holiness and continually mortify all evil desires.*

"Your work is not done as soon as you begin to live," writes

Howe, "as care about an infant ceases not as soon as it is born. Let it be therefore your constant business to tend to your inward man; otherwise all things will soon be out of course. God hath coupled delight with the labour of a Christian, not with sloth and neglect of himself. Consider thy soul seriously. Wretched man! who tillest the field, but not thy soul; and lovest to see thy garden neat and flourishing, but lettest thy spirit lie as a neglected thing, and as if it were not thine." So Baxter says, "O leave your beastly and childish pleasures and come and feast your souls in God. Think not of joying both together."

4. *Be frequent in the actual exercise of gracious principles, and in practicing and doing as they direct.*

"Exercise yourself unto godliness. Turn the powers of your soul upon God. Act seasonably the several graces of the Spirit that terminate directly upon him. Let none grow out of use. At some times repentance, at others faith, now your love, then your fear: none of these are placed in you or sanctified in vain. Retire much with God, learn and habituate yourselves into secret converse with Him, contemplate his nature, attributes and works, for your excitation to holy adoration and praise." As gracious principles are more frequently exercised, they grow more lively and vigorous, and will thence act more strongly and pleasantly. Warning his readers against partiality in keeping the commandments, he concludes, "Pass thus, in your continual practice, through the whole circle of Christian duties and graces, with an equal respect to all God's commandments; not so partially addicting yourselves to one sort of exercise, as to disuse and neglect the rest; which kind of partiality is that which starves religion and stifles the delight of it."

There is no short cut, says Howe, to a holy life: to become holy we must live according to God's commands in all departments of life and in all its relationships, public and private.

5. *Understand that the Christian religion is intrinsically a delightful thing.*

"Be ye confirmed in the apprehension, that religion is in itself a delightful thing, even universally and in the whole nature of it."

As this may sound strange doctrine to some, I beg leave to quote Howe more fully. He contends that a double error will be avoided if this direction is obeyed:

> 1. The first error—that religion is in the whole nature of it such a thing to which delight must be alien and banished from it; as if nothing should belong to, or could consist with it, but sour severities, pensiveness, and sad thoughts.

> 2. The second error—That if any delight did belong to it at all, it must be found only in peculiar, and extraordinary assurances and persuasions of God's love; and be the attainment consequently of none but more eminent Christians.

The basis of Howe's claim, that Christianity is intrinsically delightful, is found in the gracious operation of the Holy Spirit in regeneration, whereby the Christian possesses a rectified heart. Acts even of self-abasement, self-denial, and self-devoting, proceeding from such a source—how can they but be pleasant? Or as Baxter would say—"Penitent sorrow is only a purge to cast out those corruptions which hinder you from relishing your spiritual delights. Delight in God is the health of your souls."

6. *Apply yourselves to the doing of all the acts of true religion for a higher reason, and with a greater design, than your own delight.*

Otherwise, says Howe, you destroy your own work and despoil your acts of their substantial moral goodness, and consequently of their joyfulness also. "That is not a morally good act, which is not referred to God, and done out (at least) of an habitual devotedness to Him, so as He be the supreme end thereof."

7. *Yet disallow not yourself to taste and enjoy the pleasure of well doing; yes, and (secondarily and in due subordination) to design and endeavor that you may do so.*

Note, says Howe "with great admiration of the Divine goodness that hath made and settled such a conjunction between the duty of the righteous and their delight; that hath laid such laws

upon them, as in the keeping whereof there is such a reward."
Baxter says, "Understand how much these holy delights are pleasing unto God, and how much he is for their pleasure."

8. *And because that disposedness of heart unto such a cause of holy
practice, may not be constantly actual, and equally sensible at all times,
you must take heed, that as to the distempers and indispositions you now
discern in your own spirit, you do neither indulge yourself nor despair;
but take the proper road of redress.*

Watch against sin, pray, and hope in God till joy and spiritual
vigor arise in you once more. I shall conclude these directions
with Howe's eloquent plea for diligence and thoughtfulness:

> You must expect to be dealt with as a sort of creature ca-
> pable of understanding your own concernments; not to be
> hewed and hammered as senseless stones that are ignorant
> of the artists' intent, but as living stones to be polished and
> fitted to the spiritual building, by a hand that reasonably
> expects your own compliance and co-operation to its
> known design. Therefore if ever you would know what a
> life of spiritual delight means, you must constantly strive
> against all your spiritual distempers that obstruct it, in the
> power of the Holy Ghost.

One might briefly summarize these directions in these
words—know the plan of salvation; make sanctification your life
work despite the opposition and wiles of the old nature; and constantly practice good works in all your ways and stations in life, re-
membering that your new nature is tuned to delight by the Hand
of the Master, to whom you must live, and realizing that He delights in your delight and to this end has sent His Spirit to enable
you to live joyfully to His glory.

The Danger and Sin of Failing to Rejoice

As we have heard the Puritans urging us to joy in God, we may
have already worked out our reasons or excuses for lacking this

joy. We may have pleaded to our self-justification, our temperament, extenuating circumstances, the cares of office, or even the state of mankind both politically and religiously. Yet I venture to suggest that before you acquiesce in your joyless condition any more, you should pay heed to what our Puritan mentors would say of the sin of failing to delight in God and the implications of failure so to do. Bear with me in this summary of Baxter's words to the joyless man:

1. Thou vilifiest and dishonourest him, if thou judge Him not the worthiest for Thy delight.

2. If thou delight not in him, thy thoughts of God will be seldom or unwelcome and unpleasant thoughts.

3. Thy speech of Him will be seldom. The worldling thinks and talketh of his wealth and business; the proud man in his dignities and honour; the voluptuous beast in his lusts and sports and meats and drinks, because they most delight in these. And so must the Christian think and talk of his God . . . as being his delight.

4. Lack of joy will keep you away from holy duties, in which you should have communion with God.

5. It will corrupt your judgments, and draw you to think that a little is enough. A man that hath no delight in God and godliness is easily drawn to think that little and seldom and cold and formal and heartless, lifeless preaching and praying may serve the turn; and any lip service is acceptable to God. And hence he will be further drawn to reproach those that go beyond him, to quiet his own conscience.

6. If you delight not . . . you will do that which you do without a heart, with backwardness and weariness.

7. Lack of joy makes men apt to quarrel with the word, and every weakness in the minister offendeth them, as sick stomacks that have some fault or other still to find with their meat.

8. It greatly inclineth men to carnal and forbidden pleasures, because they taste not the higher and more excellent meats.

9. The want of delight in God and holiness, doth leave the soul a prey to sorrows, every affliction that assaulteth it may do its worst, and hath its full blow at the naked and unfortified heart.

10. The want of a delight in God and holiness is the way to Apostasy itself. Few men will hold on in a way that they have no delight in, when all other delights must be forsaken for it.

In considering the effects upon the soul of the lack of joy, let us remember that the Puritans taught that joy and sorrow, delights and afflictions were not contrary conditions but complementary. Indeed Baxter urges that we should use afflictions as a great advantage "for your purest and unmixed delight in God." "When all friends have forsaken us save only one, that one is sweeter to us than ever." We cannot be excused from joyfulness while our God reigns and is "the same, yesterday, today and forever"!

Joy and the Word and Ministry

Again, spiritual responsibilities should not take away our joyfulness, else we misconceive our office. Ministers are to be "helpers of our joy," for they constantly utter and propound matter and grounds of joy from the Word of God. To the objection that ministers make God's people to sorrow and often vex and trouble them, the saintly Sibbes replies, "Indeed, carnal men think so and they cannot brook the sight of them as men opposite to their delights and carnal course. Those who judge ministers so are not true believers, for they (i.e. true believers) account ministers as helpers of their joy." He analyzes how ministers help forward the joy of God's people as follows:

1. "By acquainting people with the ill estate they are in. For all sound comfort comes from the knowledge of our grief and freedom from it. They must plough before they sow, and the law must go before the Gospel."

2. By showing the remedy for sin, which is in Jesus Christ. "Joy comes from reconciliation with God in Christ, joy comes from peace. Now ministers are messengers of reconciliation and messengers of peace, and messengers of joy."

3. By advising in cases of conscience what people should do.

4. By forcing joy as a duty upon them.

5. In death itself, ministers help God's people in a joyful departure hence, to give them a good and comfortable departure out of this world, drawing comfort out of the Word for this purpose.

Here is Sibbes's answer to the complaint that faithful preaching makes against joy by arousing pangs of conscience:

A physician comes, and he gives sharp and bitter purges; saith the patient, I had thought you had come to make me better, and I am sicker now than I was before. But he bids him be content, all this is for your health and strength and for your joyfulness of spirit after, you will be the better for it. So in confidence of that, he drinks down many a bitter portion. So it is in those who sit under the ministry of the word of God, though it be sharp and severe, and cross their corruptions, yet it is medicinal physic

for their souls, and all will lend to the health of the soul,
in joy afterwards.

Others will object that the Word of God is for doctrine—"to
teach and instruct"—and not particularly for joy. No Puritan
would contend against the value of the Word of God for all teaching and exhortation and all reproof—but they would add, surely,
that all these tend to comfort. "Doctrine," says Sibbes, "is for comfort; for what is comfort but a strengthening of the affections
from some sound grounds of doctrine imprinted upon the understanding, whereof it is convinced before?" Comfort is but doctrine applied to a particular comfortable use. "It is a kind of joy
to the soul to have it stablished in sound doctrine, that is the
ground of comfort. So that notwithstanding anything that can be
objected, the end of the word of God, especially in the dispensation of it, is to joy and comfort."
     Not that the minister has it in his own power to give joy; only
the Holy Spirit can do that. The minister is only the helper, not
the author, of joy. Sibbes writes, "The Spirit of God can only comfort, because he knows all the discomforts of our hearts, he knows
all our griefs, all the corners of our hearts, that the minister cannot do. The Spirit strikes the nail and seals the comfort to the
soul: we are but helpers." Therefore we must beware lest we exalt
any means of grace—whether the ministry, reading, or any outward task or person—above the Spirit, and look to it for comfort
rather than to Him.

Joy and the Troubled Conscience

The Puritans held that the testimony of a good conscience is
a ground of both comfort and joy. Heaven is begun in a good
conscience, they said, even as hell is begun in an evil conscience.
Sibbes puts it in this way: "Now when the conscience witnesseth
aright, it witnesseth with God, and God is always clothed with joy."
     However, these pastors often had to deal with Christians who
were inclined to over-introspection and who lived exact lives, yet

were troubled in conscience. They had to face the problem—why was this? and how can this condition be put right?

First, what is conscience? Sibbes says, "Conscience is in fact a court set up in man by God": for conscience acts as a registrar of our actions, a witness to our conduct, an accuser of our faults, a judge, passing sentence, and an executioner.

There is, however, a way to a good conscience: namely to follow the directions given earlier in this paper, which should lead to a state of joy. But if a good conscience still does not breed joy, this, says Sibbes, is because of (1) the imperfection of our state in this world. It is possible for our conscience to be misled by faulty reasoning or ignorance. Or (2) conscience may look to feelings and not to faith. In such a case the reason is "distempered by melancholy and reasons falsely." Or (3) conscience may be looking only at that which is still left of the old nature. Sibbes graphically corrects this by saying that God's children should have two eyes, one to look on that which is good, that God may have glory and they comfort, "instead of the eye fixed wholly on the remainders of their rebellious lusts." Or (4) conscience may fail to enjoy comfort because the sinner is slow to accept the full truth of his inward corruptions and to rest only on the work of Christ. On this, "God will bring us to comfort," says Sibbes, "but it must be by the sense of our own unworthiness. He will forgive our sins, but it must be by the sight and sense of our sins. He will bring us to life but it must be by death. He will bring us to glory but it must be by shame. God works by contraries; therefore in contraries believe contraries."

So if we would have joy in the testimony of conscience, we must not deprive ourselves of joy because we are not perfect in grace; "but rejoice that God hath wrought any measure of grace in such unclean and polluted hearts as ours are. For the least measure of grace is a pledge of perfection in the world to come."

We shall, however, infallibly forfeit true joy if we indulge ourselves in any sin. Knowing how readily we all grasp at excuses for sin, I close this section with a quotation from Manton:

> Sin taketh away joy and peace: the whole strength of men
> and angels, cannot make the conscience of a sinner to re-

joice. Yes, the children of God must take heed, that they do
not violate peace of conscience by allowing the least sin;
you are to walk so that you may be in a condition capable
of joy; none walk sweetly, but they that walk strictly . . . Acts
9:31, "They walked in the fear of the Lord and in the comfort of the Holy Ghost," and that is a sweet couple.

Joy and Faith

Without faith joy cannot be maintained. Thomas Manton in
his exposition of John 17:13 commenting on the words of our
Lord "that they might have my joy fulfilled in themselves," writes
of faith:

> It is a help to joy, it represents the excellency, truth and
> reality of spiritual things. That which we rejoice in, must
> be good, true, present. All joy ariseth from the presence
> of some good, either in actual possession, or in firm ex-
> pectation. It is the nature of faith to make things absent,
> present, it giveth being to hope, it sets up a stage in the
> heart of a believer, where God is represented acting what-
> ever he hath promised.

Baxter echoes these thoughts in his tenth direction on how to
delight ourselves in God. He writes:

> It is only a life of faith that will be a life of holy heavenly
> joy. Exercise yourselves therefore in believing contempla-
> tions of things unseen. It must not be now and then a
> glance of the eye of the soul towards God . . . but a walk-
> ing with him, and frequent addresses of the soul unto
> Him, which must help you to the delight which believers
> find in their communion with him.

Manton exquisitely summarizes the means by which joy is
maintained through the divinely appointed graces and ordi-

nances. Faith he says, giveth the title, hope the sight, obedience the evidence. The Word is the fuel for faith and hope. Prayer brings us nearer to Him, thus nearer to the Fountain of Joys. . . . The sacraments lead us into sweeter experiences—"it is as when a man hath a good lease confirmed to him. It is not the bread and the wine which rejoiceth the heart, but the renewing of the Covenant." Lastly, meditation refreshes the soul and feeds joy. "Hereby we have a Pisgah-sight, it giveth us a foretaste of heaven, and filleth our souls with joy and blessedness."

Joy and Service

We have already seen that joy in God ought to make the believer a more willing and more active servant. In fact, however, almost the only thing that we have heard about joy in our generation is of the joy of winning souls. I trust that the difference in emphasis between this and the Puritan teaching has already been noticed! I thought it would be profitable to outline a sermon of Baxter's called "Right Rejoicing." His text, be it noted, was Luke 10:20: "Not withstanding in this rejoice not, that the spirits are subject unto you; but rather rejoice because your names are written in heaven."

Baxter opens by showing that the disciples had "abundant matter for rational, warrantable joy. . . . For the subjection of the devil was a gift of Christ, foretold by the prophets, it was victory over the strongest enemy, over the most subtle enemy, the most malicious enemy. It was an honour to be instruments and to be partakers in the success of the Gospel." Where, then, was their fault?

> 1. They looked too much at the matter of dominion over the subjected and ejected devils, and relished most delightfully in the external part. But the great end of these miracles they too much overlooked; they left out of their rejoicings the appearances of God, the advantages of faith, the promotion of the spiritual Kingdom of Christ, and the greater mercies of the Gospel as to themselves and others.

2. They took too great a share of the honour to themselves, being more affected to see what great things they
were made the instruments to accomplish, than what
honor did thereby accrue to God and benefit to man.

Thus, our Lord was here curing what Baxter terms their "dis-
eased joys," "lest Satan should take advantage of their carnality."
Hence we learn what joy is allowed and commanded to those who
serve. It is joy in the greater mercies of God which should call
forth our greatest joy. Our interest in heaven is a greater mercy
than any service here on earth. Our joy must be in reference to
His honor—for this greatest honor arises from His greatest mercies and thus He called on the disciples to look upon the greatest
of His gifts. Moreover, as Baxter puts it, "As to the degree of their
rejoicing, he would not have them give the greater share to the
lesser mercies but to rejoice so much more in their heavenly interest." "He alloweth them no joy in this or any temporal or created thing whatever, but as it proceedeth from God, and tendeth
to him as our ultimate end. We must not rejoice in our victories
over Satan, or any other enemy for itself, and as our end, but as
it is a means to the glory of God and men's salvation."

The error of our well-intentioned teachers was not that it is
wrong to rejoice with the angels over one sinner that repenteth
but that our greatest joy should be in Him who made it possible—
the Father who sent the Son, the Son who saves, the Spirit who
works, and the Kingdom which is being extended to the glory of
God the Father, Son, and Holy Ghost. And even the joy of service
should be drowned in the greater joy of the eternal inheritance
that is ours in and through Christ.

Joy and Heaven

All Puritan teachers exhort their congregations to contemplate heaven and its unspeakable joys in the strongest terms possible. I will conclude with a few extracts from Baxter on this. First,
the latter part of *Right Rejoicing*:

1. What should be rejoiced in, if not the Lord of life Himself who is the everlasting joy and glory of the Saints? . . . Other things may be the means and conveyance, but God is the matter of our joy. . . . What is heaven but the fruition of God?

2. It is congruous that we now rejoice in that which we must everlastingly rejoice in. Heaven is the state of everlasting joy, and therefore the foresight of it by faith is the only way to rational, solid comfort here.

If heaven be the matter of your joy, you may go on in your rejoicing and everyday may be your festival. For God is the same yesterday, today, and for ever. You *only* have the Day that hath no night and the feast that hath no end, or intermission, unless it is caused by your errors and misapprehensions. If once you have a God, a Christ, a heaven to rejoice in, you may rationally indulge in constant joy and may rationally rejoice in poverty, reproach, contempt and calumny, in imprisonment, banishment, sickness, or in death as well as in a prosperous state: and you transgress the Laws of Reason if you do not.

3. Rejoice if your names are written in heaven: for this is a divine, a pure, a profitable, and a warrantable joy. . . . Here is joy that you need not be ashamed of: of which you can scarcely take too much: of which you need not to repent. The more you are thus joyful, the more acceptable to God. . . .

O that our souls and our assemblies did more abound with this holy joy! And O that Christians understood the excellency and the usefulness of it, and would set themselves more constantly to the promoting and the maintaining of it in themselves! Whoever of you is most joyful in the Lord, I dare persuade you to be more joyful yet: and so far should you be from checking yourselves from this Holy Joy, that the rest of your duties should intend it, and you should make it your work by the help of all God's ordinances and mercies to increase it.

And lastly, from *The Saints' Everlasting Rest:*

The Christian knows by experience now, that his most immediate joys are his sweetest joys: those that have least of man, and are most directly from the Spirit. That's one reason, as I conceive, why Christians who are much in secret prayer and in meditation and contemplation (rather than they who are more in hearing, reading and conference) are men of greatest life and joy: because they are nearer to the well-head, and have all the more immediately from God Himself. There is joy in these remote receivings; but the fulness is in his presence.

Compare the joys which thou shalt have above with the foretastes of it, which the Spirit hath given thee here. Judge of the lion by the paw, and of the ocean of joy by that drop which thou hast tasted. Alas, all this light that so amazeth and rejoiceth me, is but a candle lighted from heaven, to lead me thither through this world of darkness! If the light of a star in the night be such, or the little glimmering at the break of day; what then is the light of the sun at noonday. If some godly men that we read of, have been overwhelmed with joy till they have cried out, Hold, Lord, stay Thy hand. I can bear no more! Like weak eyes that cannot endure a great light, O what will then be my joys in Heaven, when as the object of my joy shall be the most glorious God, so my soul shall be made capable of seeing and enjoying him. And tho' the light be ten thousand times greater than the Sun's yet my eyes shall be able for ever to behold it.

I close with the answer to the first question in the Westminster Larger Catechism—"Man's chief and highest end is to glorify God and fully to enjoy him for ever."

8

MISSIONS IN THE
REFORMED TRADITION

B. R. Easter

We do not need to look far for reasons to justify a missionary paper at this conference. The first could be the recent World Council of Churches meeting in New Delhi, stressing service and witness and inaugurating the Commission on World Mission and Evangelism. The second would be that this is Bible Year, and the Bible's message is missionary—the Gospel for the world. A third reason might be the bicentenary of the birth of William Carey, the great Calvinist and missionary pioneer. A fourth—to consider the current charge that Calvinism chokes and jeopardizes missionary concern and zeal. But there is a deeper reason still, that embraces all these—our obligation to know and understand the missionary thought and achievement of our Reformed predecessors. Then we can make our distinctive contribution to the contemporary missionary situation. With this in mind, may we (1) survey the Reformed contribution to missions; (2) draw some conclusions; and (3) suggest our contribution to world evangelism today.

The Sixteenth Century

Here we must consider John Calvin in relation to the churches' missionary task and face a question which is of real perplexity; first, because he did not write a missionary treatise; also, because there are many opinions regarding his missionary attitude. Many assert his lack of missionary concern, among them Warneck, Graham, Hunter, and McLeod Campbell. Others emphasize it, as for instance, Schlatter, Zwemer, Holsten, and van den Berg.

We must remember the times in which Calvin lived. Roman Catholic powers had sea control and access to non-Christians; Protestants had neither. The Reformed churches were fighting for life and existence and their theologians were almost entirely engaged in strengthening and extending their faith in Europe. As Zwemer writes: "John Calvin lived in the sixteenth not the nineteenth century. We cannot expect of him a world view and a world vision like that of Carey!" We cannot judge Calvin by our standards. We can only ask whether he had a vision of the Kingdom's advance in the world and the churches' duty to proclaim Christ to it. Here we examine briefly his theology and practice.

1. *Theology.* Calvin relaid the foundation of missions by re-discovering the Gospel. He sought to remove error and expound the Gospel as the Bible presents it. The *Institutes* profess to do just this. Calvin stressed the sovereignty of God's Word over the church.[1] Scripture must rule and dictate her message and activity. He also stressed the sovereignty of God's grace in salvation. The heart of the *Institutes* (books 2 and 3) is an exposition of man's need of justification and God's provision of it in Christ. Calvin's watchword *sola gratia,* speaks of God's free mercy, and this is the Church's proclamation: it gives her a full Gospel and purified evangelistic motives. Then, he further taught God's sovereignty over all life. The Christian must glorify God in every area

of existence. He must live entirely to God's glory. This means life-long obedience.[2]

Calvin made a penetrating analysis of man's relation with his Creator. He drew the lines of an approach to non-Christian religions that still influences thought today. Man has a natural instinct for God.[3] He is created in His image and cannot avoid meeting God's revelation in himself, nature, and history.[4] By reason of man's rebellion against God and His revelation, man now lives in a labyrinth of darkness and foolish imaginings.[5] Man's continuous reaction to that revelation is heathendom.[6] He will not acknowledge his Creator, but turns to other gods and philosophies in affront to the true God. God, however, still cannot be avoided and in common grace he restrains men in sin, enables some outwardly in good living, and gives some hunger for Himself.[7]

What is Calvin's thought on the spread of the Kingdom? He expects the Kingdom to advance. The apostles began the work and it still continues.[8] To Bullinger he writes, "The Kingdom of Christ should be extended not only inwardly but in every part of the world, for this is the will of God." Again: "God has created the entire world to be a theatre of His glory by the spread of the Gospel." This advance is a continual conflict of Christ with Satan. The coming of the Kingdom is God's work. "The Kingdom . . . is neither to be advanced or maintained by the industry of men, but by God alone." We depend on God's opening the door.[9] This should not, however, lead to passivity, but to action in dependence upon God. The Church's task is to pray[10] and to preach the Gospel to all men, as opportunity is given. Calvin teaches a universal offer of Christ to all as our duty. "This is our duty, everywhere to make known among the nations the goodness of our God."[11] "There is a universal call by which God . . . invites all men alike."[12] The performance of this duty expresses Christian compassion.[13]

One thing is not clear in his teaching—the relevance of the Great Commission to the post-apostolic Church. He maintains the uniqueness of the apostles' office, and specifically limits it to the Twelve, in view of Roman claims. But he does not clearly distinguish between the unique apostolic office and the universal commission to the whole Church.[14] We notice that in Calvin's thought belief in election is no impediment to world-wide evangelism. It neither minimizes, nor limits, the universal offer. This notion Calvin repudiates: "Because we do not know who belongs to the number of the predestined, or does not belong, our desire ought to be that all may be saved; and hence every person we meet we will desire to be with us a partaker of peace."[15]

2. *Practice.* We have one example of Calvin's active missionary concern. In 1555 he was asked to send clergy with a Huguenot colony to Brazil. He promptly sent fourteen divines to minister to the colonists and to preach to the natives. Also, Calvin corresponded with these first Protestant missionaries. This shows him as being anxious to reach the heathen when given the opportunity.

All the aspects of Calvin's thought which we have noted are important for the missionary enterprise. He was truly missionary minded in that he saw man's plight, God's grace in Christ, and the Church's duty to preach to all men; also, because his whole life circled around concern of these beliefs overseas, his concern for the spread of biblical faith in Europe shows a missionary spirit. That his followers practiced missions when opportunity came proves this. The cause of Calvin's apparent inaction is to be found in external circumstances, not in his thought. This is the considered view of Dr. van den Berg after thorough study of the evidence.[16] In his theology lay deep missionary impetus which in changed circumstances blossomed into action. Today, Calvin guides us to the Word to subject our missionary message, motives, and methods to its direction.

Later on there was more activity. In 1577 a Czech nobleman, Vaclav Budovec, became ambassador at Constantinople, after study at Reformed colleges, including Geneva. There he engaged in evangelism among Moslems. Islam's influence staggered him. He wrote *Anti al Koran* to defend Christianity against Islam, and he did win a Moslem to Christ.

As Spanish sea power waned, the English began to explore and colonize. To discover and open the world was a religious as well as a political and economic venture. To extend the nation was to spread the faith. During the 1576 voyage Martin Frobisher's chaplain, Wolfall, "desired to save souls and reform infidels to Christianity." With expansion came desire for a Protestant world empire accompanied by missionary endeavor. Christians felt that it was God's time for the non-Christian world, and that their duty as colonists was "to bring those who know not God to a reverence of the Divine Name" (Robert Hakluyt in 1587). The first Virginia settlement in 1584 had this purpose: "The propagation of the Christian religion to such people as live in darkness." Harriot, a scientist, expounded the Bible to the Indians there.

In 1590 a Dutch theologian and Anglican clergyman, Adrian Saravia, wrote defending Anglican orders and episcopacy in *Diversis Gradibus Ministrorum Evangeli*. He was "of no mean repute and great learning," and a friend of Richard Hooker. He appeals to the Great Commission to defend his view of ministry and missions. The Church's authority to carry the Gospel to the world rests on this Commission. The obligation to make disciples is her duty everywhere and in all ages. Saravia's assertion of the permanent validity of the Great Commission was an important step forward. His thesis, "that the command to preach the Gospel to all peoples is obligatory upon the Church since the apostles were taken up into heaven, and that for this purpose the apostolic office is needful," was not well received because of its controversial overtones. But Reformed Christians accepted Saravia's view of the Great Commission in the next century.

The Seventeenth Century

Overseas opportunities, renewed study, and personal devotion, led to further enterprise.

1. In Holland, as the Republic grew, the East Indies, Formosa and Ceylon became colonies. Beside this came a reviving of spiritual life and missionary interest. The leaders of the "Second Reformation" pioneered this new movement. The Synod of Dordt (1618) showed evident missionary concern: "This promise (of

the Gospel) together with the command to repent and believe ought to be declared and published to all nations, to all persons promiscuously and without distinction. . . ."[17]

A clarion call came from Heurnius in *De Legatione Evangelica ad Indos* (1618). This "cry from the heart" sparked off latent interest. The Great Commission is unreservedly appealed to with emphasis on gratitude, sacrificial obedience, and compassion as motives for fulfilling it. Teellinck in *Ecce Homo* (1622) challenged the East India Company to action. Hornbeck of Leyden University taught all ordinands "missions" and sought to awaken interest. Grotius wrote *Of the truth of the Christian Religion* as a missionary handbook. It was reprinted and translated thirty times.

Voetius, a learned Professor at Utrecht, took on "the task of laying the foundations of a theological discussion of the principles and methods of the missionary enterprise"[18] in his *Politica Ecclesiastica* (vol. 3) and *Disputationes Selectae*. This was a first Protestant attempt at what is nowadays called missiology. The missionary aim, according to Voetius, is to plant the Church and convert the heathen, an enterprise of which "the ultimate and supreme final cause is the glory and manifestation of divine grace." Voetius also discussed and assessed the world religions in the light of Scripture. J. H. Bavinck writes, "he honestly sought the principles of missions within the Scriptures."[19]

From the appeal came action. Antony Walaeus founded a missionary seminary in 1622, teaching theology, other religions, and languages. In Java, from 1619 onwards, schools and churches were founded, leaders trained, and the New Testament translated into Malay and Arabic. In Formosa a deep work was done by Candidus (1626) followed by Robert Junius (1631). Junius learnt the language, baptized 5,900 converts, and wrote Bible helps in Formosan. In Ceylon, work was shallower, but Baldaeus did evangelical work there. Later missionaries also reached Amboyna, South India, and even Brazil.

2. We find also in Britain growing missionary feeling, particularly among the Puritans. Richard Sibbes in *Light from Heaven* (1633) on 2 Timothy 3:16, urges taking the Gospel to all since

"no one is now shut out." He sees "hope for those Western peoples" and foresees that the message "may in God's time proceed yet further West." The Westminster Divines recommended prayer "for the propagation of the Gospel . . . to all nations."[20] Interest was concentrated on the American colonies. Many had a missionary purpose. Massachusetts colony, 1628, aimed to "invite the natives . . . to the knowledge of the only God and Saviour of mankind." Its seal was an Indian crying, "Come over and help us." In 1641 the Mayhew family began missionary work on Martha's Vineyard which continued for 150 years!—"a persistent family missionary effort which has few, if any, equals."[21]

Puritan interest focused mainly on John Eliot. Born in 1604, after leaving Cambridge he helped at Thomas Hooker's school, was converted, and followed Hooker to Massachusetts in 1631. An accomplished scholar, he produced the *New Bay Psalter* (1640). In 1646, having learned the language, he began work among Indians near his Roxbury pastorate. He was well received, and many were converted and became "praying Indians." This fine life's work gained him the title of the Indian Evangelist. We notice: (1) He understood and befriended Indians. He learned their language and culture, and accepted their hospitality and kindnesses. His attitude was the pattern for later missionary approach. (2) He tended Christians as a true pastor. He translated the Bible by 1663: a vast job for one man. Puritan classics, catechisms and primers, and evangelistic literature such as Baxter's *Call to the Unconverted*, were made available. Eliot gave what we should call elementary education, and schools were organized. Communities were formed where Indian Christians lived to God's glory in obedience, service, and witness. He encouraged farming, home industry, and self-government. His "indigenous principles" produced results. By 1690 there were 24 Indian preachers, 20 men studying at Harvard, 14 congregations, and 25,000 Christians. (3) His example made a profound impression. He mirrored the ideal of the "Reformed" missionary, engaging in evangelism, preaching to all within reach with awful urgency. It was his example that challenged Brainerd, Fuller, and Carey. He was a man of invincible resolve to glorify God, regardless of cost, with determination and fearlessness. In his "pittie," he loved, understood, and gave himself to, the Indians. His part in God's work was acknowledged with humility: "It is the Lord who hath done what is done: it is becoming to . . . lift up Jesus Christ and ourselves to lie low." He summarized his work thus: "Prayer and pains through faith in Jesus can do anything."

Eliot influenced many Puritans by correspondence, but to a greater extent by published reports of the work, which awakened much interest and stirred others to action. In 1644 English and Scottish supporters petitioned Parliament for decisive missionary help. Parliament then formed "The Society for the Propagation of the Gospel in New England" (1648) which, "was without counterpart in the earlier spread of Christianity or any other religion. Through it the Christian impulse was giving birth to a new type of organization."[22] Nation-wide collections brought subsidies for American missionaries. Cromwell projected a Council for the worldwide extension of Christianity, having four departments and a missionary seminary at Chelsea College. Baxter wrote to Eliot, supported him by prayer, stimulated concern, and revived this first S.P.G. after the Restoration (1663).

The Eighteenth Century

In the early eighteenth century there came a decline in devotion and missionary zeal. Nevertheless, some possessed world vision. Within Anglicanism, Thomas Bray's industry resulted in the formation of the present S.P.G. (1701) and S.P.C.K (1698). Philip Doddridge was outspoken in demanding a missionary society and definite action. Isaac Watts kept alive the hope that "Jesus shall reign" through his hymns and organized missionary collections. In 1709 a praying ministerial group founded the Scottish S.P.C.K. to evangelize the Highlanders; later they supported American work. At Paisley, Robert Millar, "the Latourette of 2¼ centuries ago," wrote *The History of the Propagation of Christianity*—a pioneer history of missions and a call for missionary activity.

Then came the Revival movements, almost simultaneous and largely independent of each other—the "Methodist" movement with Wesley and Whitefield; the "evangelical" movement within Anglicanism, and the New England "Awakening" under Tennent and Edwards. These stimulated missionary enterprise and produced immediate results.[23] Edwards himself was a missionary at Stockbridge (1751). The most moving result of the revival in the missionary sphere, however, was the short, tragic career of the man who would have been Edwards's son-in-law had he lived—David Brainerd. Supported by Scottish S.P.C.K., he inspired Doddridge, Carey, Martyn, Livingstone, and many others. Converted in 1738, and trained at Yale (1739–42), he began evangelizing Indians in 1743, aged 25. He lived a lonely, hard life, often depressed and ill, and died of tuberculosis in 1747. Four things impressed later generations: (1) his devotion to Christ's Kingdom; (2) his concern in prayer; (3) his preaching, covering the "whole counsel of God," emphasizing Calvary. Revival came "when he discoursed on the condescension and love of a dying Redeemer . . . it was astonishing how they were melted by the love of the Redeemer."[24] (4) The results. He saw ninety baptized, a Christian community formed, and a school built. He saw the Spirit at work in deep conviction, bringing changed and ordered lives. God honored his brief effort with deep, permanent results.

Nearly fifty years later twelve Baptists met in Kettering to launch a missionary Society. Their decision flowed directly from the Revival movements. Among them were Sutcliffe, Ryland, Fuller, and Carey. What lay behind this step of faith? In the background was Jonathan Edwards. It was he, not Wesley, who most influenced them. Edwards weaned Fuller from "hyper-calvinism" to the classical position, according to which the unreserved character of the Gospel offer was maintained alongside unconditional election. Edwards's *Humble Attempt* (1748), an appeal to worldwide prayer, was sent to Sutcliffe, whose own *Call to Prayer* led to prayer associations being formed in 1784. This prayer movement was decisive for the new society. Brainerd's Journal, published by Edwards, also made a great impression on them.

In the foreground was Carey. He pressed for action, wrote his *Enquiry* (1792), preached the famous Nottingham sermon, and cried "cannot something be DONE!" Edwards's biblical theology, Brainerd's example, concerted prayer, and Carey's drive lay behind the inauguration of the Particular Baptist Missionary Society in October 1792. In this bicentenary year we recall that William Carey was (1) a Reformed Christian. He joined the Particular, or Calvinistic, Baptists. Dr. Smith calls him "a Calvinist of the broad missionary type of St. Paul."[25] From Fuller's *The Gospel Worthy of all Acceptation* (1781) he learned Edwardian Calvinism. His Calvinism was biblical and balanced: "We are firmly persuaded that Paul might plant, and Apollos water, in vain . . . did not God give the increase. We are sure that only those who are ordained unto eternal life will believe . . . nevertheless, we cannot but observe with admiration that Paul, the great champion for the glorious doctrines of free and sovereign grace, was the most conspicuous for his personal zeal in the work of persuading men to be reconciled to God."[26]

(2) Carey was a missionary theologian. No emotional zealot, he thought through his missionary principles with care and thoroughness in light of Holy Scripture. His *Enquiry* is noble, masterly, lucid, and factual, comparable with later and larger missionary treatises. This booklet proves "that the shoemaker minister . . . had already professorial thoughts in his mind."[27] The *Form of Agreement* also gives his basic ideas. His main principles were

> (a) The Word of God is the basis and instrument of the missionary task. The Enquiry, section 1, proves the Great Commission's permanence, removes objections, and founds our missionary "duty" upon the Scriptures. He lived by the Bible, and it was his foundation and tool. His use of the Word was varied, but in everything he was determined by it. "We must use every means within our power to excite . . . attention and reverence . . . to it (God's Word) as the fountain of eternal truth and the message of Salvation" (Agreement 9).

(b) He viewed the world as the sphere of the missionary task. Section 3 of the Enquiry is a masterly and accurate survey with "sweep of purpose combined with wealth of detail." He gained world vision from the Bible, from Captain Cook's *Voyages,* and wide reading.

(c) The Church was the agent of the missionary task. He called the whole Church and every Christian in it, to action. A Society was to him a "second best." He challenged the Church from its past and presented a threefold motive for action—the value of immortal souls, love for them, and obedience to Christ's commands.

(3) Carey was a great missionary. The vastness of his achievement is overwhelming. His methods are up to date and fresh. Preaching is central—all other work surrounds and flows from it. "We must make the greatest subject of our preaching Christ crucified. The doctrine of Christ's expiatory death . . . must ever remain the great means of conversion."[28] Indigenous principles were used. On arrival in India the missionaries formed themselves into a Church which converts could join. They stressed the need for national evangelists and pastors and adequate training.[29] Translation work was phenomenal—six Bibles, twenty-four Testaments, in all thirty-five languages! Training of nationals was given priority—Serampore College trained clergy and gave a comprehensive Christian education to all. Carey tried to understand Indian culture. He studied Bengali and Sanskrit, printed Indian holy books, and sought to enter the Indian's thought-life.

(4) What of his character? Two things strike us: (a) His dogged determination as a man of action. To quote his own words, "I can plod, I can persevere in any definite pursuit. To this I owed everything." (b) His deep humility as a man of God. "What do we live for but to promote the cause of our dear Redeemer in the world. If that be carried on we need not wish any more."[30]

The next step was the beginning of the London Missionary Society in 1795. Many factors converged in its formation: Carey's letters were read by the Calvinist Independent David Bogue, the

Warwickshire Prayer Association considered action, and the *Letters* of the Anglican chaplain, Melville Horne, had quickened Haweis and other Anglicans. The Society had no definite leaders, embracing all of "Evangelical sentiments" and world concern, Independents, Anglicans, and Presbyterians. It was thus an early attempt at evangelical cooperation. Their general standpoint is said to have been "Calvinistical."[31] Missionaries were sent to the South Seas, Africa, and Jamaica.

An early recruit, Vanderkemp, began the Netherlands Missionary Society (1797), which was mainly supported by Reformed Churches.

Among Anglicans, Grant of the East India Company appointed evangelical missionary chaplains and asked for missionary effort in India (1792). Evangelical clergy of the Eclectic Society discussed "missions" on several occasions. The members in 1799—among them Charles Simeon, Thomas Scott, Richard Cecil, Newton, and Venn—asked: "What can be done?" Venn outlined plans: Follow God's leading, depend on God's Spirit, select spiritual men, begin in a small way, launch a decidedly Anglican Society. The Church Missionary Society was founded a month later, in April 1799, with Scott as first secretary. After early difficulties and despised beginnings it became the world's largest society. It found its roots in Reformation theology.[32] These attempts led to the great efflorescence of missionary endeavor in the nineteenth century.

The Nineteenth Century

Latourette has called 1800 to 1914 the "great century" involving ever wider missionary expansion and zeal. By 1900 there were 20,000 missionaries, 558 agencies, and 80,000 national workers throughout the world. The Reformed churches played an important part in this, and some of the finest missionaries were of Reformed stock: Judson, Livingstone, Moffatt, Morison and Martyn, Paton and Williams. A missionary, an institution, and a theologian will illustrate the vast Reformed contribution.

1. *The Missionary*. Alexander Duff, first missionary of the Church of Scotland, ranks among the greatest of missionaries. Dr. Pierson links him with Carey and Livingstone. Educated under Chalmers, reared in the Westminster theology, he went to India in 1830. His church accepted the challenge of the "evangelicals," deciding in 1824 to engage in "missions."

His life aim was "to be a missionary to the heathen; abroad, labouring directly among them; at home, pleading their cause among the Churches of Christendom." (1) In India (1830–63) he was a missionary educator, making an epoch-making contribution, stressing higher education as a means of evangelism, Christian instruction, and spread of the Gospel. This education was biblically based; Christianity was the foundation and atmosphere of the curriculum. He also edited Christian newspapers and helped in the founding of Calcutta Hospital and University. (2) At home he was a missionary advocate, using his great preaching gifts for the cause. His preaching was "rapturous passionate eloquence"—his lecture tours were stirring trumpet calls to action, seeking to reach the whole Christian public. For twenty-three years he pressed for a Professor of Missions to train ministers with missionary zeal. In 1867 Duff became the first full Professor of Missions in the world. He established congregational associations, and wrote many articles to arouse interest. Pierson writes, "No man since St. Paul has done more to feed the fires of enthusiasm for world evangelism."

2. *The Institution*. In 1812 Princeton Theological Seminary, U.S.A. was born as "a Gibraltar of orthodoxy and a school of eminent scholarship," teaching Calvinism without modification and functioning as "a nursery for missions to the heathen." It always fostered missionary and evangelistic zeal. The earliest Professors, Samuel Miller, Archibald Alexander, and Charles Hodge, encouraged this. They suggested in 1830 a Professor of "Pastoral Theology and Missionary Instruction" who "would promote among all . . . missionary zeal and active effort for the advancement of the Redeemer's Kingdom." Their reasons: to nurture missionary spirit, giving new ministers missionary zeal and through them the Church, and to call out recruits. Charles

Breckenridge, appointed in 1836, gave the first definite missionary course in the world. Alexander used his personal influence
and the great, devout Charles Hodge "did more for the heathen
than this world knows" through conversation, sermons, and edit-
ing and writing in the *Princeton Review*. No wonder that some of
Princeton's most brilliant men became missionaries: within its
first hundred years 410 went overseas, one out of every thirteen
students.

3. *The Theologian.* Abraham Kuyper, eminent Dutch churchman and statesman, ranked with Bavinck and Warfield as the
greatest Reformed thinker at the end of this century. He devoted
his brilliant intellect and talents to reviving and reconstructing
Reformed faith and life against the background of European ra-
tionalism and liberal theology. His writing and activity still wield
influence. He edited a newspaper, entered politics, and became
Prime Minister. He played a prophetic part in Church reform
and also founded the Free University. His writings are profound
contributions to Reformed thought. A prolific writer, he gave real
attention to missions, which he ardently advocated, outlining aspects of a Reformed missionary theology as follows:

(1) He defined the study of missions as "Prosthetics," the
study of God's adding to His church, considering it a distinct
branch of the theological curriculum. (2) He insisted that Christians must understand accurately, and face directly, the other religions of the world. Their origin is found in man's perverse reaction to God's revelation. Our approach to them must be
personal and humble. (3) He regarded "common grace" as God's
merciful activity upon mankind, restraining sin's curse and blessing and directing life's progress. (4) The Gospel, said Kuyper, asserts Christ's kingship over all life. There is no sphere of life
about which He cannot say, "It is Mine." (5) In 1890 Kuyper
called for a more God-centered viewpoint: "The missionary sent
by Christ must follow the trail blazed by the Lord; if God in His
election does not precede, the word of the missionary can bear
no blessing." His ideas were accepted by Middleburg Synod in
1896.

These examples indicate that last-century Reformed orthodoxy, so far from being bereft of missionary concern, actively stimulated it.

The Twentieth Century

Over the last sixty years have come dramatic changes. The great Missionary Conference at Edinburgh, 1910, set the pattern for modern missionary thought and activity. Three subjects discussed reflected the dominant lines of approach.

1. *The Younger Churches.* The increasing importance of national churches began to be realized. Many encouraged independence and self-expression in new churches. John L. Nevius, a Presbyterian, practiced "indigenous church principles" in China, emphasizing that the local church must be self-supporting, self-governing, and self-propagating from its inception. He reacted against paid mission workers advocating spontaneous witness. In Korea the "Nevius Method" produced amazing results: one hundred communicants in 1890 became 800,000 in 1958.[33]

2. *Missionary Cooperation.* Concern about this produced the International Missionary Council for world consultation and action. Reformed statesmen were active here, notably Dr. Samuel Zwemer, who made a considerable contribution until his death in 1952. A great Moslem missionary, he founded and edited *The Moslem World.* He became Professor of Missions at Princeton, and wrote over thirty books on missionary themes. "His zeal and devotion . . . inspired and decided thousands . . . to devote themselves . . . to the service of God."[34]

3. *Approach to Other Religions.* Theological liberalism weakened the uniqueness of the Gospel—missions came to be seen as "a common search for truth." Already in 1923, with many others, J. Gresham Machen recognized this threat; his *Christianity and Liberalism* was a masterly statement of the case against the new trend. At the 1928 Missionary Conference liberalism dominated, and this was followed by W. Hocking's *Rethinking Missions* (1932). Machen analyzed this shrewdly: "It presents missions . . . (as) that of seeking truth together rather than . . . presenting the Truth."[35] The cli-

mate has changed somewhat since Kraemer's *The Christian Message in a Non-Christian World* (1938), and the renewed biblical study of the past generation has had its effect—but the debate continues.

Today, Reformed missionaries are scattered throughout the world, and Reformed thinkers are attending to missionary topics. Dr. John Bavinck, of Amsterdam, has done much here, especially in his *Introduction to the Science of Missions* (1960).

Conclusions

We may say in general the Reformed have not been backward in either thought or action in the missionary enterprise; rather, the opposite. In particular

1. We see a definite pattern in our review. The Reformed missionary movement began as a trickle, became a stream, and eventually, a flood. In each century there was more activity than in the preceding. "As each century passed Protestants were progressively more energetic in spreading the Christian Faith."[36] There was ebb and flow, first comparative inactivity and then, increasing zeal. New activity was born of deep religious revival. Here we detect the Hand of God.

2. God used a variety of ways to stimulate action. He used the examples of Eliot and Brainerd, Carey's writings, Horne's Letters, and Buchanan's Sermons. He used students—Judson, and Mills; businessmen—the Clapham Sect; clergy—The Eclectic Society. He used prayer for revival and awakening—Edwards and Sutcliffe. All were goads to decisive activity, showing that God never allows Christians to avoid His commands.

3. Each new advance sprang from a revival, not a weakening of Reformed doctrine. For instance—in seventeenth century Holland, "those in whom the piety of Dordt had become flesh and blood were the most enthusiastic advocates of . . . missionary obligation."[37] In eighteenth century England, "leadership was prevailingly Calvinist, and expansion of the Evangelical movement, which apart from Wesleyan Methodism, was informed with Calvinist piety."[38] This is so in every instance.

4. This leads us to assert, lastly, that the Reformed faith possessed within itself the dynamic and power for missionary outreach. Dr. Payne states, "Classical Calvinism had within itself the essential evangelistic impulse; when the rock was smitten, water gushed forth."[39] And Dr. Forsyth writes: "Missions have more to hope for from a narrow creed which remains great, than a wide humanism that runs thin . . . the width of the Gospel really springs from its depth."[40]

What in Calvinism has demanded missionary activity? First, its willingness to listen and submit to God's voice in the missionary Scriptures. Second, its view of Christ and the vital need of faith in Him for salvation. The unique Christ is the dynamic for missions. He must be proclaimed to be believed. Missionary action is also demanded by Calvinism's adherence to the universal offer. Nothing in Calvinism minimizes or hinders this—election does not frustrate or overshadow here. Missionary duty rests on God's will of command, not His secret purpose. The doctrine of definite atonement is also a missionary dynamic, indicating an achieved salvation, a sufficient Savior to proclaim, and a worldwide multitude purchased by Him (Rev. 5:9). The universal offer rests on this. Missionary action is prompted, too, by the doctrine of election, pointing to God's free compassion, accentuating His activity, giving confidence and assurance; showing that the salvation of His chosen ones is God's world purpose (Mark 13:27). Finally, Calvinism is compelled to missionary zeal by its concern for God's glorification in the gathering of a worldwide Church. Clearly, Reformed missionary activity was stimulated, not choked by its theology, when this was united to a vigorous piety.

The Reformed Contribution Today

When I speak of the Reformed contribution, I do not advocate unwillingness to learn from the past or from others—but my point is that the Reformed tradition has a distinctive message in this field. Let me suggest here some lines of thought which need emphasis:

First, we need to make it clear that missionary work is not a merely human enterprise but is, primarily, the activity of the living, sovereign God. In and through our works, God works; He is the real missionary. Dr. Bavinck concludes after reviewing the biblical material: "The work of Missions is God's work." As salvation is of God, so are missions. 1 Corinthians 3:5–6: "We are simply God's agents . . . I planted . . . Apollos watered but God made it grow. Thus it is not the gardeners . . . who count, but God" (N.E.B.). The work of missions also has a trinitarian character; it is the work of the Father, Son, and Holy Spirit. In salvation—planned by the Father, achieved by the Son, applied by the Spirit—missions have a vital place. This all has wide implication: (1) It makes missions a continuing task, to be finished only when God's own work concludes at Christ's return. (2) It shows missions as one task. The One God, by the one Gospel calls one Church throughout the world. There is thus no tension between the claims of the Church at home and overseas: both must be met, for both are one. (3) It makes the fulfillment of the missionary task certain. God will certainly accomplish His purpose of calling out His Church through missions. This gives confidence and hope amid darkness, difficulty, and opposition. (4) It gives perspective to missionary thought, making our standpoint God-centered. The knowledge that the Triune God controls and directs the work is our rock in today's changing world.

If missions are God's work, then our guide in it is God's Word. The Word must control our message, our motives, and our methods. We must allow God's Word to decide our problems and direct our conduct, whatever our situation. This makes Reformed Christians radicals—testing past history and present experience in missions by Holy Scripture.

Next, we stress the importance of proclamation. Preaching is the central function of the missionary task in Scripture. It involves, of course, more than the spoken word—it includes the missionary and his personal attitudes also. We lay emphasis on the comprehensive message rather than the comprehensive approach. Here the comprehensive Calvinist view of Christ's offices of Prophet, Priest, and King, is important. To the liberal we emphasize Christ's Saviorhood as essential. To the pietist, we insist that Christ is LORD as well as Lamb—the One Who not only saves the soul, but also rules the life, transforming the whole man and his environment. He wills to renew and rule man's language, customs, and culture (see Matt. 28:19; 2 Cor. 5:17).

The question of Christianity and other religions is still urgent. Here Reformed Christians stand on *Scripture* in its assessment of and approach to non-Christian faiths. Accordingly, they see, first, the reality of God's general revelation in creation, history, and human life. This is still clear and unmistakable—from it man ought to know God. Second, they see that other religions are rejection of the revealing God: a deliberate denial, exchange, and turning from Him to darkness and chaos. General revelation now brings guilt and wrath (Rom. 1:18–19). Third, Reformed Christians recognize God's present activity among those religions in common grace. Then, they stress the absoluteness and uniqueness of the biblical revelation in Christ bringing men the reconciliation to God, and the new light and power, that they need. We emphasize also the importance of a loving, personal approach to those of other faiths: appreciating the others' position, feeling united with them in sin and need of grace, loving them as our neighbors depending on God's Word to convict and lead to faith.

We must *declare*, too, that missions are directed utterly and finally to God's glory. God's purpose is to save a Church to His own glory, and the glory of His grace. The aim of missions is God's self-glorification. His aim is ours too—concern for God's glory must be our own ultimate motive. We glorify Him in obeying His command, in loving the lost, in sharing His concern to see His Church planted throughout the world.

What of our practical contribution? One thing is certain; if the contemporary revival of Reformed ideals among us is to be true to its own history and its own heart, one result will be missionary advance. This will mean Reformed Christians playing full, active, and vital parts in the missionary prayer, study, and service of their own congregation or group, and throwing themselves into every worthy missionary effort. It means ministers who have missionary vision themselves, stirring and challenging their people to wider world vision. It means that the movement will produce dedicated thinkers and missionaries of Reformed principles concerned supremely for man's salvation and God's glory. One way to meet the current charges of Calvinist missionary indifference is to "outlive" them, by showing practically that Calvinism still possesses the dynamic that reaches out to the world. Let the true missionary attitude which becomes us be explained to us by John Venn (1806): "Deeply affected by the sinful and ruined state of mankind, especially the heathen, he (the Christian) devotes his life, with all its faculties, to promote their salvation. With the world under his feet, with heaven in his eye, with the Gospel in his hand, and Christ in his heart, he pleads as an ambassador for God, knowing nothing but Jesus Christ, enjoying nothing but the conversion of sinners, hoping for nothing but the promotion of the Kingdom of Christ, and glorying in nothing but the cross of Christ. . . ."

SOLI DEO GLORIA

9

PREACHING — PURITAN
AND REFORMED

J. A. Caiger

It is common among us to think and to speak of C. H. Spurgeon as a Puritan born out of due time. I think this overstates the matter. Spurgeon was not entirely a Puritan. Dare I say that in certain respects he lacked the precise discipline of the Puritans, and, on the other hand, there was about him an expansiveness, a wide-embracing humanitarianism, which was distinctively Spurgeonic rather than Puritan. He was great enough to create his own forms and patterns of influence, and in any case it is easy enough to see that each were reacting in powerful ways upon the times in which they lived and worked—the Puritans upon the seventeenth century and Spurgeon upon the nineteenth. The Puritans were still fighting the battle of the Reformation. Spurgeon preached in an age of humanitarian reform.

But for all the differences which may be discernible Spurgeon had a great heart for the Puritans. His theological roots were thrust deep into the truths which they held dear, and which they expounded so powerfully, and he was always most ready to acknowledge his great debt to their rich and prolific writings. I want now to follow his eminent example, and, after this brief introduction, to lay before you the ground-plan of this paper, in order that you may have some idea as to what we hope to do and where we hope to go.

First, I want to take a general view of the Westminster Directory for Public Worship in order to give you some idea of the place which the Puritans gave to preaching in their services. Then we shall look in more detail at the section in this Directory which is concerned with the preaching of the Word in order to see what they intended by this exercise. And third and last I hope to give you some examples of the preaching of Reformers, Puritans, and Evangelicals, so that we may be able to see what they had in common, and wherein lay their essential points of difference.

The Place of Preaching in Reformed Worship

As a matter of history the title page of the Directory makes interesting reading. It runs as follows: "The Directory for the Public Worship of God; agreed upon by the Assembly of Divines at Westminster, with the Assistance of Commissioners from the Church of Scotland, as a part of the Covenanted Uniformity in Religion betwixt the Churches of Christ in the Kingdoms of Scotland, England, and Ireland. Established and put in execution by Act of the General Assembly February 3, 1645; and approved and established by Act of Parliament February 6, 1645."

The Directory opens with a preface which in characteristically dignified language expresses serious dissatisfaction with the liturgy of the Church of England, and sets out the reasons which lay behind the production of this new form of worship. "We have, after earnest and frequent calling upon the name of God, and after much consultation, not with flesh and blood, but with his holy word, resolved to lay aside the former liturgy, with the many rites and ceremonies formerly used in the worship of God; and have agreed upon this following Directory for all the parts of public worship, at ordinary and extraordinary times."

We are not concerned here with the relative merits of the Anglican and Presbyterian forms of worship, but with the place given to preaching in this Presbyterian order. Worship begins with the assembling of the congregation, and the Directory has a section dealing with the grave and reverent behavior of the people, and their entire concentration upon the greatness and majesty of the Lord. There is to be no whispering, no gazing or sleeping, and no reverence paid to any person present. The people are wholly to attend upon the worship of God. To this end a brief prayer is to be uttered by the minister seeking for them God's pardon, assistance, acceptance, and His blessing upon the portion of His Word to be read.

Then follows the reading of the Scriptures—ordinarily one chapter of each Testament at every meeting, and all the canonical books (and only the canonical books) being read over in order "that the people may be better acquainted with the whole body of the Scriptures." Expository comment is permissible in conjunction with the reading (Spurgeon used regularly to give this), but with this significant qualification: "regard is always to be had unto the time, that neither preaching, nor other ordinances be straitened, or rendered tedious." Even exposition must not be allowed to prejudice preaching!

After this a psalm is sung, and then the minister leads his people in the great public prayer before the sermon. This is offered with a view to the worshippers being rightly affected with their sins, "mourning in sense thereof before the Lord," and hungering and thirsting after the grace of God in Jesus Christ. This is the purpose of the prayer, and there follows in four and a half pages of close print in small type the material points which should find mention in it.

First, mention is made of our great sinfulness, by reason of original sin, the seed of all other sins; by reason of actual sins— our own and those of rulers and of the whole nation; by reason of sinful dispositions of the soul, and of particular sins in the congregation; and by reason of our sense of guilt and of our deserving of God's fiercest wrath and heaviest judgments.

This is followed by a supplication of God for His grace "in the free and full remission of all our sins, and that only for the bitter sufferings and precious merits of that our only Saviour Jesus Christ"; for the work of the Holy Spirit in shedding abroad the love of God in our hearts, in sealing to us the full assurance of pardon and reconciliation, in comforting, healing, and convicting men according to their state and need, and in mortifying, quickening, and sanctifying His people in order to make them strong, obedient, and holy.

The horizon then widens as prayer is offered for the spread of the Gospel and Kingdom of Christ to all nations. The detailed mention of so many centers and circles of life and influence is bewildering to our less disciplined minds. Jews and Gentiles, persecuted Christian brethren, the Reformed churches, their missionary outposts, the King's majesty, the Queen's conversion, the religious education of the Prince, the High Court of Parliament, nobility, judges, magistrates, gentry "and all the commonalty," the ministry, universities and other institutions of learning, the local congregation in its varied relationships and trials, including mention of the local government, the weather, and any natural or civil calamities which might be oppressing the locality—all these are given full and specific intercession.

The prayer moves on to embrace petitions for "God's grace and effectual assistance to the sanctification of His holy sabbath, in all the duties thereof, public and private," for the outpouring of the Spirit of grace that the people may taste "the first-fruits of the glory that is to be revealed" and "may long for a more full and perfect communion" with Christ, and, finally, "that God would in a special manner furnish His servant (now called to dispense the bread of life unto His household) with wisdom, fidelity, zeal, and utterance, that he may divide the word of God aright, to every one his portion, in evidence and demonstration of the Spirit and power; and that the Lord would circumcise the ears and hearts of the hearers, to hear, love, and receive with meekness the ingrafted word, which is able to save their souls . . . that so Christ may be so formed in them, and live in them, that all their thoughts may be brought into captivity to the obedience of Christ, and their hearts established in every good word and work for ever."

All this, then, is by way of preparation of the congregation for the preaching of the Word which immediately follows, and which we shall examine more closely in a few moments.

The sermon finished, the minister again leads the congregation in prayer, giving thanks for the blessings of the Gospel in its many glorious aspects "as, namely, election, vocation, adoption, justification, sanctification, and hope of glory," praying for the continuance of the Gospel and its ordinances, "turning the chief and most useful heads of the sermon into some few petitions; and praying that it may abide in the heart, and bring forth fruit." He further prays for preparation for death and judgment, "a watching for the coming of our Lord Jesus Christ," and God's acceptance of the spiritual sacrifice offered, having entreated His forgiveness "of the iniquities of our holy things."

"The prayer which Christ taught his disciples" is recommended for use at this point, after which, a psalm is sung, the chief care of which must be to sing with understanding, and with grace in the heart, making melody unto the Lord. The minister then dismisses the congregation "with solemn blessing."

Thus the sermon is viewed as being the central act in the public worship of God. It is not an addendum to a period of corporate prayer and praise. Nor is it viewed as a preparation for some culminating act of corporate intercession or communion. The foundation is laid in the opening prayer and in the public reading of the Holy Scriptures. Then set within the framework of the singing of the psalms come the two prayers, the first of which prepares the people for the preaching of the Word and leads up to it; the second follows the preaching and seeks the blessing of God upon its matter and its message. The preaching of the Word was therefore, to the Puritans, central to the whole structure of praise and prayer in the public worship of God.

The Preaching of the Word in Reformed Worship

The introductory paragraph to this section is infused to an impressive degree with words and phrases from the New Testament. "Preaching of the word, being the power of God unto salvation, and one of the greatest and most excellent works belonging to the ministry of the gospel, should be so performed, that the workman need not be ashamed, but may save himself, and those that hear him."

Here is laid the foundation of the biblical doctrine of preaching, and it is laid, as the foundations of all biblical doctrine must be laid, with stones quarried from the Scripture itself. The Puritan approach to preaching was squarely based on the emphatic declarations of the Word of God. What is the power of God unto salvation to every one that believeth? It is the gospel of Christ (Rom. 1:16). How is the power of God in the gospel communicated to those that believe? By the foolishness of preaching (1 Cor. 1:21). What therefore is the responsibility of the minister of the gospel? It is to study to show himself approved unto God, "a workman that needeth not to be ashamed, rightly dividing the word of truth" (2 Tim. 2:15). And if the preacher diligently takes heed to himself and to the doctrine of the gospel, what effects will follow? He will save both himself and those that hear him (1 Tim. 4:16).

And the preaching is so to be performed that these effects do follow. Is there an echo here, intentional or otherwise, of Acts 14:1? "Paul and Barnabas went both together into the synagogue of the Jews, and so spake, that a great multitude both of the Jews and also of the Greeks believed."

Are we ashamed of our preaching? Probably we do well to be: but we should not need to be. Is our preaching saving those that hear us? We wish it so: it should be so.

If the preaching of the gospel is the instrument of the Spirit in the saving of men, certain things must be presupposed in the preacher. There is material for study here both with respect to ministerial training and to subsequent ministerial discipline. The minister of Christ, we are told, must be gifted in some good measure for so weighty a service by his skill in the original languages, and in such arts and sciences as are handmaid unto divinity. The reference here evidently is to those basic skills which make possible the study and exposition of the Scriptures. Clearly the intention behind this qualifying phrase is to ensure that such preliminary studies as are desirable and necessary should be cultivated in order to increase the youthful minister's ability to understand and to believe the Gospel.

It is further presupposed that he will be gifted with knowledge in the whole body of theology. Notice this characteristically Puritan view of the counsel of God as a body of divinity, with all its parts properly fashioned, proportioned, and related. The minister of the Gospel must be able to see it whole. But "most of all" (this is the phrase used in the Directory) he must be distinguished by his knowledge in the holy Scriptures, "having his senses and heart exercised in them above the common sort of believers." In this sense the minister is to be no ordinary Christian. He is to be "primus inter pares," first among equals, but yet in a real sense first, by reason both of his Divine calling, and of his excelling in those spiritual exercises to which every Christian is called.

It is here that the idea of ministerial training passes over into that of perpetual and increasing discipline. The minister must be gifted "by the illumination of God's Spirit, and other gifts of edification, which (together with reading and studying of the Word) he ought still to seek by prayer, and an humble heart, resolving to admit and receive any truth not yet attained, whenever God shall make it known unto him." You will observe the clear recognition that truth is revealed from heaven when God chooses to reveal it, and it is attained, when He does so, by reading and studying of the Word—but not only by these, but also by the continual discipline of prayer, of humility of heart, and of willingness to submit the intellect to whatever God may make known.

And all these gifts the preacher is "to make use of, and improve, in his private preparations, before he deliver in public what he hath provided."

The section then moves into a detailed statement concerning

the methods to be used in preaching. The subject of a sermon is to be a text of Scripture—either "holding forth some principle or head of religion, or suitable to some special occasion emergent." It is noteworthy that preaching for some special occasion still calls for an exposition of Scripture. And, for the encouragement of those of us who find delight and edification in extended series of sermons, we are told, "he may go on in some chapter, psalm or book of the holy scripture, as he shall see fit." It is he who determines what he will preach—not his congregation, and since the Directory does not say how long he is to go on with his chapter, psalm, or book, presumably he is free to go on as long as he likes!

The introduction is to be brief and perspicuous, "drawn from the text itself, or context, or some parallel place, or general sentence of scripture." If the text is long, as will be the case with a history or a parable, a brief summary should be given. If it is short, a paraphrase may help. But in either case the aim must be to show the scope of the text and to point at the chief heads and grounds of doctrine which are to be raised from it. Was it this that influenced Spurgeon in his method of introducing his sermons?

"In analysing and dividing his text, he is to regard more the order of matter than of words." His concern must be theological rather than philological, with the food itself, rather than with the manner in which it is served. And he must not "burden the memory of the hearers in the beginning with too many members of division, nor trouble their minds with obscure terms of art." Presumably this means that he must not weary his congregation with technicalities. The sermon must have its skeleton, but it is the living body which is to be presented to the people. A skeleton may be an edifying sight for students of anatomy, but it has little to offer the world as a whole.

The preacher's primary concern must be to *raise doctrines* from the text. In this he must exercise a three-fold care. First, he must ensure that the matter he expounds be the truth of God. Second, it must be a truth "contained in or grounded on that text, that the hearers may discern how God teacheth it from thence." Third, he must "chiefly insist upon those doctrines which are principally intended, and make most for the edification of the hearers." His concern then is to be with truth—but not only with truth. He is not merely to display it, and perhaps to dazzle his hearers with the brilliance of the display. He is to communicate it. He must do everything he can to help them to see whence it is derived, and to grasp it and to receive it for themselves.

For this reason "the doctrine is to be expressed in plain terms." Parallel passages may be adduced to confirm the doctrine, but these also must be plain and pertinent, and not too many. They must be added to support the doctrine—not to suffocate it. Arguments and reasons must be solid and convincing. Illustrations must be full of light, "and such as may convey the truth into the hearer's heart with spiritual delight." Notice again the emphasis on conveying, or communicating, the truth. The illustration must never be a thing in itself, or an end in itself.

Doubts and differences arising from Scripture, reason, or prejudice should be dealt with, if indeed they are matters of serious concern. "Otherwise it is not fit to detain the hearers with propounding or answering vain or wicked cavils, which as they are endless, so the propounding and answering of them doth more hinder than promote edification." Here the same essential principle is set as a limit to controversy—the aim at all times must be the edification of the people.

The exposition and vindication of the doctrine, essential and demanding as it is, is only preliminary to an application of the truth to the hearts of the hearers. This may prove to be a work of great difficulty to the preacher, and it will be very unpleasant to natural and corrupt hearts in his auditory, but it must be done. "He is to endeavour to perform it in such a manner, that his auditors may feel the Word of God to be quick and powerful, and a discerner of the thoughts and intents of the heart; and that, if any unbeliever or ignorant person be present, he may have the secrets of his heart made manifest, and give glory to God."

Great care must be taken in dealing with erroneous teachings. Undue extravagance in this matter may only serve to create in the minds of the people an interest in the very ideas the preacher wishes them to avoid. "In confutation of false doctrines, he is neither to raise an old heresy from the grave, nor to mention a blasphemous opinion unnecessarily: but, if the people be in danger of an error, he is to confute it soundly, and endeavour to satisfy their judgments and consciences against all objections." There must be no trifling with threatening error. It must be clearly exposed, and systematically destroyed.

The approach to the duties of the Christian life must be a practical one. It is not enough to deduce ethical principles. The preacher must declare specific obligations ("duties" is the word properly used), and he must "teach also the means that help to the performance of them." The pastor is there to care for, and to help, the sheep.

A paragraph follows which stresses the special wisdom required in "dehortation, reprehension and public admonition," where the preacher has to deal faithfully with some sin in his congregation. He must disclose its nature, emphasize its seriousness, describe the misery which attends it, and indicate the remedies which may be applied to it.

The Puritans had a great feeling for troubled hearts. Not only was comfort to be found and applied to such, but also care was to be taken "to answer such objections as a troubled heart and afflicted spirit may suggest to the contrary." And where possible able and experienced ministers were to help their congregations in the work of self-examination by giving what are called "notes of trial," that is, tests based on the teaching of Scripture, by means of which the people could try themselves, and judge their spiritual state and Christian progress.

The preacher is under no obligation to expound every doctrine implied in his text, and similarly he must make a wise choice of those "uses" or applications which "by his residence and conversing with his flock, he findeth most needful and seasonable; and, amongst these, such as may most draw their souls to Christ, the fountain of light, holiness, and comfort."

Finally, seven points are enumerated dealing with the spirit and manner of the ministry. These are best quoted as they stand since every phrase is important, and to summarize them would be to lose their effect:

The servant of Christ, whatever his method may be, is to perform his whole ministry:

1. Painfully, not doing the work of the Lord negligently.

2. Plainly, that the meanest may understand; delivering the truth not in the enticing words of man's wisdom, but in demonstration of the Spirit and of power, lest the cross of Christ should be made of none effect; abstaining also from an unprofitable use of unknown tongues, strange phrases, and cadences of sounds and words; sparingly citing sentences of ecclesiastical or other human writers, ancient or modern, be they never so elegant.

3. Faithfully, looking at the honour of Christ, the conversation, edification, and salvation of the people, not at his own gain or glory; keeping nothing back which may promote those holy ends, giving to every one his own portion, and bearing indifferent respect unto all, without neglecting the meanest, or sparing the greatest, in their sins.

4. Wisely, framing all his doctrines, exhortations, and especially his reproofs, in such a manner as may be most likely to prevail; showing all due respect to each man's person and place, and not mixing his own passion or bitterness.

5. Gravely, as becometh the Word of God; shunning all such gesture, voice and expressions, as may occasion the corruptions of men to despise him and his ministry.

6. With loving affection, that the people may see all coming from his godly zeal, and hearty desire to do them good.

7. As taught of God, and persuaded in his own heart, that all that he teacheth is the truth of Christ; and walking be-

fore his flock, as an example to them in it; earnestly, both in private and publick, recommending his labours to the blessing of God, and watchfully looking to himself, and the flock whereof the Lord hath made him overseer.

So shall the doctrine of truth be preserved uncorrupt, many souls converted and built up, and himself receive manifold comforts of his labours even in this life, and afterward the crown of glory laid up for him in the world to come.

All this the Directory prescribes with respect to the preaching of the Word of God.

English Preaching in the Reformed Tradition

The preaching with which we are concerned is that of sixteenth, seventeenth, and eighteenth centuries—that of the Reformers, the Puritans, and the Evangelicals. It was marked by certain characteristics which are common to them all. There are particular differences in style and approach which may be best appreciated from the examples we hope to quote, but these general characteristics are to be noticed in them all, and it is probably from these that we should chiefly learn.

If we may work from the periphery of the matter into the center, so that the points appear in inverse order to their importance, I suggest that one of the most powerful impressions registered upon the mind is that this preaching was *intellectual* in character. By this I do not mean that it was academic in a merely theoretical sense. It was the work of minds that were utterly submitted to the mighty influences and the rich nourishment of revealed truth—but there we have said it, it was the work of minds. This preaching was the product of arduous mental exercise, and it was designed to provoke an exercise of mind in those to whom it was addressed. These men were concerned with truth. Their view of the Gospel was that it is the truth "as it is in Jesus," and it is therefore as truth that it must be declared. Truth demands understanding in the preacher, and is addressed to the understanding of the hearer.

The style, as we have indicated already, varied. The preaching of the Reformers and the Puritans is reminiscent of the altars which the Israelites were permitted to make for their sacrifices. They were to be made either of earth, or of unhewn stone. They were rough; they were rugged; but they robbed God of none of his glory, and He came and blessed them there. The Evangelicals of the eighteenth century had more polish in their preaching. But if the preaching of men like Jonathan Edwards was polished, as indeed it was to a remarkable degree, it was polished granite— not plastic!

But whether we are impressed at one point by the earthiness of the Reformers, or at another by the greater precision and polish of the Evangelicals, we cannot fail to be impressed by the powerful intellectual quality of their preaching.

In the second place their preaching was essentially *biblical.* They all believed what Luther expressed in No. 62 of the Theses which he posted so boldly on the Cathedral door in Wittenburg: "The true and precious treasure of the Church is the Holy Gospel of the glory and grace of God." They were not interested in preaching anything else. If we may make Luther the spokesman again: "A man's word is a little sound that flies into the air and soon vanishes; but the Word of God is greater than heaven and earth, yea, greater than death and hell, for it forms part of the power of God, and endures everlastingly." This they believed, and therefore they looked for inspiration and authority, for matter and example, only to the Bible.

Third, their preaching was *theological.* This we might expect, but it is right that it should be stressed. There are preachers who claim a great respect for the Bible, and who base their preaching upon it—yet their ministry is anything but theological. The approach to the Bible may be psychological, or philosophical, or merely sentimental, in which case what is preached will bear no recognizable relation to the message of the men whose ministry we are considering. Their view of Scripture compelled them into preaching which was expository. It was inevitable that this should happen, once their minds were submitted to the Bible as the Word of God. God had spoken. He had caused His Word to be placed in their hands. Now they had but one duty—it was to expound to the people *that* Word, and *only* that Word, in terms which people could understand and receive.

This leads us to our fourth point, which is that their preaching was pre-eminently *pastoral.* I submit that this is true of all those we have mentioned. They were not all "pastors" in the more limited sense of being settled ministers of churches—although, of course, many of them were. But all of them preached to their hearers, each as "a dying man to dying men," and they revealed in their whole manner, as well as in the content of their message, their profound concern for the souls of those who listened to them. They had no interest in building for themselves reputations as scholars, as social reformers—or even as preachers. They burned with zeal for the salvation of souls, and they gave themselves to a ministry which promised healing for the brokenhearted, and which could set at liberty those who were bruised. Let me quote Whitefield here in 1737 at the age of 22:

> The tide of popularity (in London) now began to run very high. In a short time, I could no longer walk on foot as usual, but was constrained to go in a coach, from place to place, to avoid the hosannas of the multitude. They grew quite extravagant in their applauses; and, had it not been for my compassionate High Priest, popularity would have destroyed me. I used to plead with Him, to take me by the hand and lead me unhurt through this fiery furnace. He heard my request, and gave me to see the vanity of all commendations but His own.

That surely is the spirit of New Testament preaching, which seeks not the aggrandizement of the preacher, but the glory of God in the salvation of those for whom Christ died.

Fifth, and last under this head, let me say that their preaching was beyond all else *spiritual.* By this I mean that in their preaching they consciously depended upon the Holy Spirit. They did not trust for effect to their oratorical power, their wit, or their charm. With Paul they denied themselves the luxury of exploiting the magnetism of their personalities, in order that their hearers might be impressed, not by the natural gifts of the preacher, but by the spiritual gifts and graces of God. Their speech and their preaching was not with enticing words of man's wisdom, but in demonstration of the Spirit and of power, that the faith of their hearers should not stand in the wisdom of men, but in the power of God.

Let me give you two quotations on this point from the sermons of Dr. Richard Sibbes, Master of Catherine Hall, Cambridge, and Preacher of Gray's Inn, London.

> And to this end beg of God His Spirit, which is above all impediments. The more Spirit, the more strength and courage against impediments. The more we attend upon holy means, the more spiritual and heavenly light and life is set up in the soul. The more spiritual we are, the more we shall tread under foot all those things that stand between us and heaven. Let us therefore labour more and more for the Spirit, and then we shall offer an holy violence unto good things. . . . Therefore, go on boldly and resolutely in good things, always remembering to beg the Spirit of God, that may arm our spirits with invincible courage.[1]

> (Reproof) must be done with a sweet temper, keeping our distance, and reserving the due respect unto those in whom we shew our dislike. As we see Nathan, when he came to tell David of his fault, how he doth it, what art he useth! It must be so done as that it may appear to be done out of pure zeal, that it is no wild-fire nor no heat of nature; but that it cometh merely from the Spirit, and in much love, with mildness and pity, in which case it carrieth a wondrous authority.[2]

And here is the opening paragraph from a sermon by C. H. Spurgeon on Romans 9:30–33:

For several Sabbath mornings I have sought the comfort and edification of God's people, although I trust I have not, even in such discourses, overlooked the unconverted. How can we forget them, while they are in such peril? At the same time, the main drift of the service has been for the people of God, and it will not be wise to continue long in that line. We must not forget the lost sheep: it were better that we left the ninety and nine than that we neglected the rambler. We must, therefore, this morning seek to go after that which is gone astray until we find it. Oh, that God the Holy Spirit would make every word to be full of His power! He can fill each sentence with a celestial dynamite, an irresistible energy, which will blast the rocks of self-righteousness, and make a way for the gospel of the grace of God through the impenetrable barriers of sin. For that end I am anxious that, while I speak on God's behalf, the prayers of the faithful may bring down God's power, and make the feeble voice of man to be the vehicle for the omnipotence of God.

This brings us finally to some random examples from the preachers themselves, that we may gain some impression of the way in which these principles were exemplified and expressed in their preaching. To draw so small a selection from a field so rich and so wide seems almost to be impious, but the discipline of choice must perforce be exercised, in the hope that the passages chosen may be adequately representative of some aspects of this great preaching tradition.

Let us begin with Luther—vulgar, no doubt, but then Germany was vulgar in his day. The Italian scholars may have prided themselves on their elegant and refined Latinity, but north of the Alps learning was happy to parade itself in much homely and earth-stained garb. Vulgar then, and volcanic, pouring out great masses of material with enormous force and at great heat; but he spoke to the heads and to the hearts of the common people, and they heard him gladly. Here are two unusual extracts, both char-

acteristic of the humanity, the pastoral warmth, and the doctrinal
power of his ministry.

The first is from a sermon on the Nativity.

> Think, there was no one there to bath the Baby. No warm
> water, nor even cold. No fire, no light. The mother was
> herself midwife and the maid. The cold manger was the
> bed and the bathtub. Who showed the poor girl what to
> do? She had never had a baby before. I am amazed that
> the little one did not freeze. Do not make Mary a stone.
> For the higher people are in the favour of God, the more
> tender are they.
>
> Let us, then, meditate upon the Nativity just as we see it
> happening in our own babies. Behold Christ lying in the lap
> of His young mother. What can be sweeter than the Babe,
> what more lovely than the mother! What fairer than her
> youth! What more gracious than her virginity! Look at the
> Child, knowing nothing. Yet all that is belongs to Him, that
> your conscience should not fear but take comfort in Him.
> Doubt nothing. To me there is no greater consolation given
> to mankind than this, that Christ became man, a child, a
> babe, playing in the lap and at the breasts of His most gra-
> cious mother. Who is there whom this sight would not com-
> fort? Now is overcome the power of sin, death, hell, con-
> science, and guilt, if you come to this gurgling Babe and
> believe that he is come, not to judge you, but to save.

The second is concerned with the fruits of saving faith.

> O it is a living, busy, active, mighty thing, this faith! It is
> impossible for it not to do good perpetually. It never asks
> whether good works are to be done, but before the ques-
> tion can be put it has done them, and is always doing
> them. . . . Hence without constraint the man is joyously
> willing to do good to everyone, to serve everyone, to suf-
> fer all things, for the love and praise of God Who has
> shown him such grace. So that it is impossible to separate

work from faith, yes, just as impossible as to separate heat
and light from fire.

These are not the words of an arid theoretician, but of a man
whose earthly humanity was blazing with the light and fire of a
truly spiritual divinity, who discerned the profoundest doctrine in
the most homely records of the Gospel, and who had the power
to clothe this doctrine with words which ordinary men and
women received hungrily for the warmth and shelter and security
which they brought.

Now a few extracts from the Puritans themselves. Thomas
Brooks was the saintly rector of St. Margaret's, Fish-Street Hill.
His *Heaven on Earth* is a treatise, rather than a book of sermons,
but the style and content are more characteristic of preaching
than of ordinary writing. I quote him that we may see and feel
something of the pastoral heart of the man, and his shepherd-
feeling for those to whom he ministered.

> I would fain have as free, as large, and as sweet a heart to-
> wards saints, as Christ hath. For a wolf to worry a lamb is
> usual, but for a lamb to worry a lamb is unnatural; for
> Christ's lilies to be among thorns, is ordinary, but for
> these lilies to become thorns, to tear and fetch blood of
> one another, is monstrous and strange. Ah, Christians!
> can Turks and Pagans agree? Can Herod and Pilate
> agree? can Moab and Ammon agree? can bears and lions,
> can wolves and tigers agree? yea, which is more, can a le-
> gion of devils agree in one body? and shall not the saints,
> whom heaven must hold at last, agree? . . . All saints are
> fellow-members, fellow-soldiers, fellow-travellers, fellow-
> heirs, fellow-sufferers, and fellow-citizens; and therefore I
> cannot, dare not, but love them all, and prize them all.

Now a typical word on the exercise of faith.

> Faith is an appropriating grace; it looks upon God, and
> saith with David, "This God is my God for ever and ever,

and He shall be my Guide unto the death." It looks upon Christ, and saith with the spouse, "I am my Beloved's, and His desire is toward me." It looks upon an immortal crown, and saith with Paul, "Henceforth is laid up for me a crown of glory." It looks upon the righteousness of Christ, and saith, "This righteousness is mine to cover me." It looks upon the mercy of Christ, and saith, "This mercy is mine to pardon me." It looks upon the power of Christ, and saith, "This power is mine to support me." It looks upon the wisdom of Christ, and saith, "This wisdom is mine to direct me." It looks upon the blood of Christ, and says, "This blood is mine to save me."

And here is an exhortation to deeper Christian experience in an essentially Puritan vein:

Now is it not as easy a thing as it is pleasant, for a man that hath several sweet springs in his garden, to sit down, draw water, and drink? O believing souls! there are springs, there are wells of living water, not only near you, but in you; why, then, do you, with Hagar, sit down sorrowing and weeping, when you should be a-tasting or a-drinking not only of the springs above you, but also of the springs within you? A man that hath fruit in his garden may both delight his eye and refresh his spirit with tasting of it. Certainly we may both eye and taste the fruits of the Spirit in us, they being the first-fruits of eternal life. I think none but mad souls will say that grace is the forbidden fruit that God would have us neither see nor taste. We ought not so to mind a Christ in heaven, as not to find "Christ in us the hope of glory." Christ would not have His spouse so to mind her own blackness, as to forget that she is all fair and glorious within.

William Gurnall, of Lavennham in Suffolk, was another Puritan with a great pastoral compassion. Two brief extracts from his *The Christian in Complete Armour* must suffice. First, an encouragement to the Christian beset by satanic temptation.

Take God into thy counsel. Heaven overlooks hell. God at any time can tell thee what plots are hatching there against thee. Consider Satan as he is God's creature; so God cannot but know him. He that makes the watch, knows every pin in it. He formed this crooked serpent, though not the crookedness of this serpent; and though Satan's way in tempting is as wonderful as the way of a serpent on a rock, yet God traceth him, yea, knows all his thoughts together. Hell itself is naked before Him; and this destroyer hath no covering. Again, consider him as God's prisoner, who hath him fast in chains, and so the Lord, Who is his keeper, must needs know whither His prisoner goes, who cannot stir without His leave.

Second, a word on the Christian's vision of the power of God.

The Christian's comfort increaseth or wanes, as the aspect of his faith is to the power of God. Let the soul question that, or his interest in it, and his joy gushes out, even as blood out of a broken vein. It is true, a soul may scramble to heaven with much ado, by a faith of recumbency, relying on God as able to save, without this persuasion of its interest in God; but such a soul goes with a scant sidewind, or like a ship whose masts are laid by the board, exposed to wind and weather, if others better appointed did not tow it along with them. Many fears like waves ever and anon so cover such a soul, that it is more under water than above; whereas one that sees itself enfolded in the arms of almighty power, O how such a soul goes mounting afore the wind, with her sails filled with joy and peace!

Before we leave Gurnall here is a word of his wisdom concerning the work of the ministry: "It is not the least of a minister's care and skill in dividing the word, so to press the Christian's duty, as not to oppress his spirit with the weight of it, by laying it on the creature's shoulders, and not on the Lord's strength." By this I take him to mean that the duties of the Christian life rest upon, as they are rooted in, the power of Christ, and the minister must point to them there.

It would be remiss of us to fail to mention the allegorical method of interpretation so beloved of the Puritans. Here is Sibbes preaching on Canticles 4:16: "Awake, O north wind; and come, thou south; blow upon my garden, that the spices thereof may flow out." He is dealing with the question as to why the Spirit of God, in the use of means, is compared to wind. Here are his points:

1. *The wind bloweth where it listeth,* as it is in John 3:8. So the Spirit of God blows freely, and openeth the heart of some, and poureth grace plentifully in them.

2. *The wind, especially the north wind, hath a cleansing force.* So the Spirit of God purgeth our hearts from dead works to serve the living God, making us partakers of the divine nature.

3. *The wind disperseth and scattereth clouds, and makes a serenity in the air.* So doth the Spirit disperse such clouds as corruption and Satan raise up in the soul, that we may clearly see the face of God in Jesus Christ.

4. *The wind hath a cooling and tempering quality, and tempers the distemper of nature.* As in some hot countries there be yearly anniversary winds, which blow at certain times in summer, tempering the heat; so the Spirit of God allayeth the unnatural heats of the soul in fiery temptations, and bringeth it into a good temper.

5. *The wind being subtle, searcheth into every corner and cranny.* So the Spirit likewise is of a searching nature, and discerneth betwixt the joints and the marrow, betwixt the flesh and the Spirit, searching those hidden corruptions, that nature could never have found out.

6. *The wind hath a cherishing and a fructifying force.* So the Spirit is a quickening and cherishing Spirit, and maketh the heart, which is as a barren wilderness, to be fruitful.

7. *The wind hath a power of conveying sweet smells in the air, to carry them from one to another.* So the Spirit in the word conveyeth the seeds of grace and comfort from one to another. It draws out what sweetness is in the spirits of men, and makes them fragrant and delightful to others.

8. *The wind, again, bears down all before it, beats down houses, and trees, like the cedars in Lebanon, turns them up by the roots, and lays all flat.* So the Spirit is mighty in operation. There is no standing before it. It brings down mountains, and every high thing that exalts itself, and lays them level: nay, the Roman and those other mighty empires could not stand before it.

For these respects and the like, the "blowing of the Spirit" is compared to wind. For which end Christ here commands the wind to "blow upon His garden."

The danger of this method is that it may tend to sentimentality, but the Puritans were safeguarded by their concern to interpret everything in terms of doctrine. Spurgeon could use this method with great effect, but no man is safe in employing it unless his mind is steeped in scriptural truth, and his character poised in balance upon the whole counsel of God.

Lastly, we must turn to the eighteenth century Evangelicals, in order to hear preaching at its greatest. We shall notice certain differences as we do so. The sermon form changed considerably in the hundred years between 1650 and 1750. The sermons of the Evangelicals were not nearly so much extended in their analytical detail as those of the Puritans, but were, as I think, more powerfully concentrated within a much simpler outline. But there is a difference discernible which is of far greater importance than this matter of the form in which the message was presented.

The preaching of the Evangelicals impresses me as being generally more powerful in its evangelistic thrust. It appears to have a much more direct approach to the soul of the hearer. There is a sharper point and a keener edge about it all, and a greater urgency. Bishop Ryle makes this point in his description of the preaching of George Whitefield:

> Whitefield was a singularly bold and direct preacher. He never used that indefinite expression "we," which seems so peculiar to English pulpit oratory, and which only leaves a hearer's mind in a state of misty confusion. He met men face to face, like one who had a message from God to them, "I have come here to speak to you about your soul." The result was that many of his hearers used often to think that his sermons were specially meant for themselves. He was not content, as many, with sticking on a meagre tail-piece of application at the end of a long discourse. On the contrary, a constant vein of application ran through all his sermons. "This is for you, and this is for you." His hearers were never let alone.

If we enquire into the reason for this difference between the Puritans and the Evangelicals, we may find it in the preoccupation of the Puritans with covenant theology, and in their view of the Church and the ministry. It may be true in some cases, though certainly not in all, that their view of the covenant of grace tended to militate against a forthright and dogmatic approach to the individual: and these words from *The Form of Presbyterial Church-Government* approved by the General Assembly in 1645, shed an interesting light on their view of the ministry:

> The officers which Christ hath appointed for the edification of His Church, and the perfecting of the saints, are, some extraordinary, as apostles, evangelists, and prophets, which are ceased. Others ordinary and perpetual as pastors, teachers, and other Church governors, and deacons.

The failure to recognize the evangelist as belonging to the present order of the ministry of the Church is certainly significant, and this was not true of the preachers of the Revival in the century which followed.

Here then is the mighty Jonathan Edwards, preaching in the midst of revival:

> Are there not many here who have lived long in the world, and are not to this day born again? and so are aliens from the commonwealth of Israel, and have done nothing ever since they have lived, but treasure up wrath against the day of wrath? Oh, Sirs, your case, in an especial manner, is extremely dangerous. Your guilt and hardness of heart is extremely great. Do not you see how generally persons of your years are passed over and left, in the present remarkable and wonderful dispensations of God's mercy? You had need to consider yourselves, and awake thoroughly out of sleep. You cannot bear the fierceness and wrath of the infinite God. And you, young men and young women, will you neglect this precious season which you now enjoy, when so many others of your age are renouncing all youthful vanities, and flocking to Christ? You especially have now an extraordinary opportunity; but if you neglect it, it will soon be with you as with those persons who spent all the precious days of youth in sin, and are now come to such a dreadful pass in blindness and hardness.
>
> Therefore, let every one that is out of Christ, now awake and fly from the wrath to come. The wrath of Almighty God is now undoubtedly hanging over a great part of this congregation. Let every one fly out of Sodom: "Haste and escape for your lives, look not behind you, escape to the mountain, lest you be consumed."

And now to conclude our paper let Whitefield speak:

> Awake, then, you that are sleeping in a false peace, awake, ye carnal professors, ye hypocrites that go to church, re-

ceive the sacrament, read your Bibles, and never felt the power of God upon your hearts; you that are formal professors, you that are baptized heathens: awake, awake, and do not rest on a false bottom. Blame me not for addressing myself to you; indeed, it is out of love to your souls. I see you are lingering in your Sodom, and wanting to stay there; but I come to you as the angel did to Lot, to take you by the hand. Come away, my dear brethren—fly, fly, fly, for your lives to Jesus Christ, fly to a bleeding God, fly to a throne of grace; and beg of God to break your hearts, beg of God to convince you of your actual sins, beg of God to convince you of your original sin, beg of God to convince you of your self-righteousness—beg of God to give you faith, and to enable you to close with Jesus Christ. O you that are secure, I must be a son of thunder to you, and O that God may awaken you, though it be with thunder; it is out of love, indeed, that I speak to you.

My design is to bring poor sinners to Jesus Christ. O that God may bring some of you to Himself! May the Lord Jesus now dismiss you with His blessing, and may the dear Redeemer convince you that you are unawakened, and turn the wicked from the evil of their way! And may the love of God, that passeth all understanding, fill your hearts. Grant this, O Father, for Christ's sake; to Whom, with Thee and the blessed Spirit, be all honour and glory, now and for evermore. Amen.

10

THE PURITAN CONCEPT
OF DIVINE INTERCESSION

Eifion E. Evans

Through the tender mercy and loving kindness of God our Savior, His elect, in times of fearful declension and deadly lassitude, have not been left without a divine cordial of the most stimulating kind, prepared in the divine purpose, according to the terms of His gracious covenant, and providing the sweetest comfort, encouragement, and consolation. For those of His oppressed and despairing ones in Egypt He prepared a deliverer of divine appointment and a deliverance beyond human imagination. The mere sighs, cries, and groans of His people drawn from them by reason of the excessive yoke of insufferable bondage, coming up unto God, brought His covenant into remembrance and His power into operation. When opposition, persecution, or accusation is arraigned against them, though with considerable show of force, malice, and hatred, all will come to nought through the cancelling and overcoming quality of God's provision. Thus, though Satan himself should stand at the

right hand of Joshua the high priest, vigorously resisting and defi-
antly accusing God's anointed servant, and though his garments are
filthy and defiled, yet is Satan the loser and Joshua the better by it,
for God, who has chosen Jerusalem has undertaken the rebuke of
His enemy and the protection of His people. Whence comes this
timely intervention, and what office has God inaugurated in the
eternal counsel to manage such vital affairs? The answer must be—
through the gracious, compassionate, and effective intercession of
His own beloved Son, Jesus Christ!

For such times as ours, then, few considerations are more
necessary, few truths more invigorating, than those of the intercession of Christ and of His Spirit.

Among Christians, there seems to be a prevalent and widespread ignorance concerning these valuable doctrines. The sad
consequences of this lack of knowledge are to be felt in many aspects of the Christian's spiritual experience, but particularly is
this true in the realm of prayer. For herein lie those motives
which move us to fervency, boldness, and confidence, and they,
in their turn are tokens of blessing and an earnest of success in
prayer. A serious investigation of the subject should therefore
prove to be most timely and beneficial. Nor are we alone in recognizing its importance. Oliver Heywood's estimate, in Puritan
days, was not extravagant.

> The subject is exceedingly necessary; our persons and our
> prayers would be lost, had we no intercessor. . . . This is a
> high privilege, a doctrine worth studying, for next to
> Christ's satisfaction upon the cross, a Christian's safety
> lies in Christ's intercession.[1]

What Heywood says of Christ's intercession, John Bunyan
says, in effect, of Christ's advocacy.

> I fear the excellency of that doth still too much lie hid;
> though I am verily of the opinion that the people of God
> in this age have as much need of the knowledge thereof,
> if not more need, than had their brethren that are gone

before them. These words, "if not more need," perhaps
may seem to some to be somewhat out of joint; but let the
godly wise consider the decays that are among us as to the
power of godliness, and what abundance of foul miscarriages the generality of professors now stand guilty of, as
also how diligent their great enemy is to accuse them at
the bar of God . . . and I think they will conclude, that, in
so saying, I indeed have said some truth.[2]

The greatness of the subject's importance is paralleled only by the
wideness of its scope, for who can plumb the depths or measure the
heights of Christ's love in His intercession for sinners? Are the ex-
panses of sin to which we have sunk vast? So are the pleadings of
Christ for us comprehensive. Are there countless, grave, overwhelming hindrances which prevent our access to God and communion with Him? Then take note of the majesty of the Person, the
sufficiency of the sacrifice, and the prevalency of the intercession of
our great High Priest to remove these obstacles and guarantee not
only entrance, but welcome, to the presence of the Most High!

From an honest enquiry into the nature of God and the state
of man the evidence is conclusive that there is need for a Mediator. God's majesty and holiness is separated infinitely from man's
creatureliness and sinfulness. It was to undertake the bridging of
this gulf that the Son of God was delegated in the eternal purpose, to the office of High Priest with the authority, gravity, and
finality of the divine oath. It was to accomplish the same that He
appeared once on earth to bear our sins, and that He ascended
into heaven to appear before God, to exhibit His perfect sacrifice, and to intimate His gracious will. Not only so, but, in His capacity of Advocate, He opposes and annuls the monstrous rage
and fierce accusation of Satan against those whom the Father has
given Him. Furthermore, so that their link with heaven may be
preserved intact and guaranteed effective, He has sent His Spirit
to determine and direct their heavenly traffic, and to manage
those affairs on earth which He works in heaven. Thus have believers a dual comfort: for Christ appears on their behalf above,
and the Spirit dwells, on Christ's behalf, within.

There are, then, three main things to consider in our examination of the Puritan understanding and statement of intercession. First, Christ's intercession in heaven; second, Christ's advocacy against Satan; and third, the Spirit's intercession in the believer. The Puritans determined their doctrines from scriptural rather than from philosophical or rational considerations. They surveyed them in the light of Reformed principles, and expressed them, with the aid of logic and method, in a clearly defined and typical manner. From the Scripture text they distilled the doctrine, adduced reasons in support thereof, and finally applied the teaching by way of exhortation. The texts principally expounded, to a lesser degree (comparatively) in commentaries, and to a greater degree in sermons or treatises, in respect of the concept of intercession were: Isaiah 53:12; Zechariah 3:2; Romans 8:26, 34; Hebrews 7:25 and 9:24; and 1 John 2:1–2.

Christ's Intercession in Heaven

Christ's intercession in heaven is a direct correlate of His atonement on earth, and the Puritans thought of it in this way. His present activity in heaven is declared to be an essential counterpart of His substitutionary sacrifice on the cross, and is correlative to it, just as "father" is to "son," or "creation" to "providence." Intercession is complementary to atonement and founded upon it, as Oliver Heywood states in his *Treatise on Christ's Intercession.*

> Thus doth our blessed Jesus step up to be arbitrator, mediator, and referee betwixt God and sinners. This is the case; God and man are at variance in consequence of Adam's apostacy. . . . How must these be made friends? Infinite love and wisdom have found out an expedient that is sufficient to effect it, even the second person of the Trinity, assuming the nature of man, and interposing two ways:—(1) By suffering the penalty that man had de-

served, and satisfying justice by his meritorious oblation of himself . . . and thus he hath reconciled God and man by his death on the cross. . . . (2) The intercession of Christ now in heaven; he is our advocate, because he is the propitiation for our sins, 1 John 2:1, 2. Thus Christ is now in heaven to pursue the same design he had upon the cross, so that Christ's intercession sets out the perpetual efficacy of his sacrifice, and the continual application of it to believers. . . .[3]

The concept of correlation is also in accord with Old Testament typology, and here Thomas Goodwin shall speak for his Puritan brethren.

In the old Levitical priesthood, the high priest's office had two parts, both which concurred to make them high priests. *First*, Oblation, or offering the sacrifice. *Secondly*, Presentation of it in the holy of holies, with prayer and intercession unto God, to accept it for the sins of the people. The one was done *without*, the other *within* the holy of holies. . . . Now then, in answer to this type, there are two distinct parts of Christ's priesthood. *First*, The "offering himself a sacrifice" up to death, as Heb. 9:26, which answers to the killing of the sacrifice without the holy of holies; for answerably he was crucified without the city, Heb. 13:12. *Secondly*, He carried this his blood into the holy of holies, namely, the heavens, Heb. 9:12, where he appears, ver. 24, and there also prays in the force of that blood. And the type of those prayers was that cloud of incense made by the high priest. . . . Which incense is his own prayers in heaven, which he continually puts up when the saints pray on earth, and so perfumes all their prayers, and procures all blessings for them.

Indeed, the same author goes as far as to maintain that this second part of the sacerdotal office is the crowning part—and he has scriptural proof for it.

This part of his priesthood is of the two more eminent, yea, the top, the height of his priesthood. And this is held forth to us in the types of both these two orders of priesthood that were before him, both that of Aaron and Melchisedek: *First,* this was typified out in that Levitical priesthood of Aaron and his fellows: the highest service of that office was the going into the holy of holies, and making an atonement there; yea, this was the height of the high priest's honour, that he did this alone, and did constitute the difference between him . . . and other priests. . . . *Secondly* . . . by Melchisedek's priesthood. . . . Now Melchisedek was his type, not so much in respect of his oblation . . . but in respect of that work which he ever performs in heaven: therefore that same clause *for ever* still comes in, in the quotation and mention of Melchisedek's priesthood in that Epistle. . . . And, *thirdly,* to confirm this, you shall find this to be made the top notion of this Epistle to the Hebrews, and the scope of it chiefly, to discourse of Christ's eternal priesthood in heaven, and to shew how therein Melchisedek was a type of him . . . more expressly in chap. 8:1 . . . "we have such an high priest as is set down at the right hand of the throne of the Majesty in the heavens."[4]

The contrast between the shadow and the substance is very vivid, for by reason of death the high priests of old were not able to continue. Our High Priest, having offered Himself up for our sins, and having been raised and exalted by the power of God, ever lives to make intercession for us, not in an earthly tabernacle, but in heaven itself. This is the wonder of the divine economy.

Wherein, then, does his intercession lie? For whom is this blessed privilege secured, and for what does the Son appear before His Father? John Owen speaks of the "safest conception and apprehension that we can have of the intercession of Christ" as being, his continual appearance for us in the presence of God, by virtue of his office as the "high priest over the house of God," representing the efficacy of his oblation, accompanied with tender care, love, and desires for the welfare, supply, deliverance, and salvation of the Church. Three things, therefore, concur hereunto: (1) *The presentation of his person* before the throne on our behalf, Heb. 9:24. This renders it sacerdotal. His appearance in person for us is required thereunto. (2) *The representation of his death, oblation, and sacrifice for us*; which gives power, life, and efficacy unto his intercession. . . . But (3) Both these do not render it prayer or intercession; for intercession is prayer, 1 Tim. 2:1, Rom. 8:26. Wherefore there is in it, moreover, a putting up, a requesting, and offering unto God, of his desires and will for the Church, attended with care, love, and compassion, Zech. 1:12.[5]

Thus, even as it was necessary that a righteous substitute should suffer our penalty on the cross, so also it is necessary that a worthy representative should appear in heaven to claim our deliverance. As on earth we could not endure the infinite penalty incurred by our sin, so in heaven we dare not appear before a holy God. So that on earth, Christ alone, by virtue of the divinity and righteousness of His Person, can pay our penalty, while in heaven Christ alone, by virtue of the sufficiency and efficacy of His oblation, dare plead our cause. Thomas Horton, in his comments on Romans 8:34, makes this clear:

As for ourselves, we have so much sin and guiltiness upon us, and defilement in us, as that we know not how with any face to make appearance in the presence of God; now therefore does Christ himself, who is our Surety, appear in our stead. He that has paid the Debt for us, is not ashamed to shew his Head; but does *boldly and confidently* present Himself in our behalf: Here I am as the Surety, and Advocate, and Mediator for all mine Elect; what-ever thou hast against any of *them,* charge it upon me. As he

was ready at first to *undertake* the Work. . . . So he is as
ready now to own it, and to stand by it, being undertaken
by Him.

Horton further enlarges upon those three elements in Christ's
intercession noted by Owen:

> This Intercession of Christ . . . does not consist in a for-
> mal *prostrating* of the *Body* of Christ, but especially in these
> following particulars. First, In his *appearing* and *presenting*
> of Himself for us to his Father in both his Natures. . . .
> Look as in the Courts of men, there is usually answer
> made by the Attorney, who appears in the behalf of the
> Person cited, and speaks for him; even so does the Lord
> Jesus Christ sitting at the right hand of God *appear* in the
> behalf of all his Members, to satisfie the justice of God
> concerning those Complaints and Accusations which are
> brought against them. This was shaddowed out to us in
> the Dispensations of the *Levitical Law*, Exod. 39:7, where
> it was the custom and manner of the *High Priest* to go into
> the *Holy of Holies* with the *Names* of the Children of *Israel*
> written in precious stones, for a *Memorial of them*, that he
> might remember them to God in *his prayers*. And thus now
> in like manner, Christ Jesus being entred into the *Holiest
> of all*, which is Heaven itself, does there present to his Fa-
> ther the Names of all his *elect Children*, and makes re-
> membrance of them, that he may obtain reconciliation
> for them, and free them from condemnation. . . . Sec-
> ondly, As Christ does *appear* in Heaven for us, so He does
> likewise further urge, and exhibit, and present to God the
> Father the *vigor and merit*, and efficacy of that Sacrifice
> which he once *made on Earth* for us. Christ deals with God
> now in a way of justice and *equal demand*; that whereas he
> has paid the price, and made full satisfaction to Him, that
> now therefore He may obtain that of Him which he bar-
> gain'd and agreed with Him *for*, which is the Salvation of
> the Souls of his people. . . . Thirdly, He does also actually

apply this his Death and Merit, and Satisfaction to *Believers themselves*. . . . As Christ stands upon his *own price*, the justifying and maintaining of *that as full and sufficient*, so he does likewise *make over* this his price and payment to the *benefit of the faithful*. He perpetually *wills and desires* that this Satisfaction should be imputed to *all* whom his Father hath given unto him.[6]

It will be evident by now that Christ's intercession is a privilege extended only to the elect, as is consistent with John 17:9, "I pray for them; I pray not for the world, but for them which thou hast given me." It is also clear that Christ's intercession is for all the elect; that is to say, it embraces His elect before their coming into a state of grace as well as subsequent to it. Christ's intercession is thereby related to the restoration and reconciliation of sinners, so that what the Spirit on earth does in the hearts of the unconverted, Christ in heaven pleads for before the Father, namely, the application of His redemption, John 17:20, "Neither pray I for these alone, but for them also which shall believe on me."

Christ's intercession for the elect is not necessary merely to their justification. The body of sin is still with them, they are not yet free from weakness. Their best aspirations, motives, desires, services are all clouded with imperfections. Nonetheless, those to whom communion with God had been before most distasteful now count that to be most delightful; those who before shunned God's face now long for it. How else can their thirst after God be assuaged, how else their persons be acceptable, and their petitions answered, other than through the mediation of their blessed Redeemer? To the Puritans this truth was a veritable fountain of good things, bringing renewal and refreshment to the weary, boldness and confidence to the hesitant, assurance and gladness to the despondent. Those matters therefore which relate to the complete, final, and utter salvation of the saints are also the concerns of Christ's intercession. The bestowal of the Holy Spirit, union and fellowship with the Father, sanctification, prayer, perseverance in the way of grace, and final participation in glory, all these, and more besides, belong to the activity of Christ in heaven for the saints. As Bunyan says, "justi-

fication will stand with imperfection. . . . Justification . . . only cov-
ereth our sin from the sight of God; it maketh us not perfect with
inherent perfection. . . . And this is . . . one reason, why they that
are justified have need of an intercessor—to wit, to save us from the
evil of sin that remains in our flesh after we are justified by grace
through Christ, and set free from the law as to condemnation."[7]
Heywood recommends as "the best way to ascertain what our Lord
prays for now, in the highest heavens, on the behalf of believers,"
the observation of "Christ's prayer for his Church when he was on
earth," and proceeds to enumerate the several signal blessings desired by Christ according to John 17. Bunyan reduces them to four
heads, "(1) . . . that the elect may be brought all home to him, that
is, to God. (2) . . . that their sins committed after conversion may be
forgiven them. (3) . . . that their graces which they received at conversion may be maintained and supplied. (4) . . . that their persons
may be preserved unto his heavenly kingdom."[8]

One matter of Christ's intercession deserves our particular attention, namely, the offering up of our prayers to the Father.
Here are the relevant comments from Anthony Burgess's exposition of John 17:9, together with his applications:

> *This Mediatory praier of Christ is the ground of all the acceptance
> of our praiers;* Our Praiers if not found in him are provoca-
> tions rather than appeasements. . . . He is the Altar upon
> which all the oblations are sanctified, and from hence it is
> that the Incense of their Praiers are performed, so that God
> finds a sweet savour in them. . . . And this may unspeakably
> support under sad Temptations, when thou canst not pray,
> thy heart is bound up, Thy affections are faint and cold.
> Thou criest out, Oh the sinnes and infirmities of thy Praiers,
> yet Christ's Praier is full and fervent for thee, There is no
> Imperfection, no fault to be found with him; Oh, it's a good
> refuge to run unto, when thou art almost overwhelmed be-
> cause of thy dull, formal and distracted Praiers![9]

This work of Christ was according to one of three ways in
which His intercession was "typed out" in the Old Testament. The

living fire which was continually on the altar typified Christ's prayers on earth, in His State of humiliation. The daily sacrifice was destined "to make continual application of the great, solemn, annual expiation, unto the consciences of the people." The incense that was burned in the sanctuary every day by the priests represented prayer. Christ's prayer for us in heaven, however, is the expression of His will and desires for us, and this was typified by the incense wherewith the high priest entered once a year into the most holy place on the day of atonement. "So did our high priest," says John Owen, "he filled heaven with the coals of that eternal Fire wherewith he offered himself unto God." He elaborates the point further,

> We may apprehend its relation unto the types in this order: His prayer, John 17, was the preparation of the sweet spices whereof the incense was made and compounded, Exod. 30:34. His sufferings that ensued thereon were as the breaking and bruising of those spices; wherein all his graces had their most fervent exercise, as spices yield their strongest savour under their bruising. At his entrance into the holy place this incense was fired with coals from the altar; that is, the efficacy of his oblation, wherein he had offered himself unto God through the eternal Spirit, rendered his prayer as incense covering the ark and mercy-seat—that is, procuring the fruits of the atonement made before God.[10]

How necessary it is that we should remind ourselves continually of these glorious truths! How fitting for downcast souls are the gracious words of Hebrews 4:14–16. "Seeing then that we have a great high priest, that is passed into the heavens, Jesus the Son of God, let us hold fast our profession. For we have not an high priest which cannot be touched with the feeling of our infirmities; but was in all points tempted like as we are, yet without sin. Let us therefore come boldly unto the throne of grace, that we may obtain mercy, and find grace to help in time of need."

No less comforting than the matter of His intercession are His qualifications for the office. Our intercessor is the Son of God, our advocate is Jesus Christ the righteous. The Puritans multiplied their adjectives in their attempts to describe the eminent fitness of Christ to represent us in heaven before the Father. Here, for example, are some of the words Heywood uses to commend Christ's worthiness in this respect: able, judicious, skillful, just, condescending, easy of access, free, willing, nigh at hand, compassionate, gracious, faithful—and there are many more. Their very profusion should serve to convince us of the tremendous benefit of meditation upon this neglected subject. Let Bunyan draw the first part of our subject to a conclusion with a stirring exhortation.

> Believers should not rest at the cross for comfort; justification they should look for there; but, being justified by his blood, they should ascend up after him to the throne. At the cross you will see him in his sorrows and humiliations, in his tears and blood; but follow him to where he is now, and then you shall see him in his robes, in his priestly robes, and with his golden girdle about his paps. Then you shall see him wearing the breastplate of judgment, and with all your names written upon his heart. Then you shall perceive that the whole family in heaven and earth is named by him, and how he prevaileth with the Father of mercies, for you. Stand still awhile and listen; yea, enter with boldness into the holiest, and see your Jesus as he now appears in the presence of God for you; what work he makes against the devil and sin, and death, and hell, for you. Heb 10:9. Ah! it is brave following of Jesus Christ to the holiest, the veil is rent, you may see with open face as in a glass, the glory of the Lord.[11]

Christ's Advocacy against Satan

It is Bunyan who also deals principally with the second section of our study, in a treatise entitled *The Work of Jesus Christ as an*

Advocate. George Offor, who edited Bunyan's works a century ago, makes the following relevant remarks in his "advertisement" to this treatise:

> This is one of the most interesting of Bunyan's treatises, to edit which required the Bible at my right hand, and a law dictionary on my left. We are indebted for this treatise to Bunyan's having heard a sermon which excited his attention to a common, dangerous, and a fatal heresy. . . . In this sermon, the preacher said to his hearers, "see that your cause be good, else Christ will not undertake it." Bunyan . . . exposes the fallacy and uses his scriptural knowledge to confute it, by showing that Christ pleads for the wicked, the lost; for those who feel themselves so involved in a bad cause, that no advocate but Christ can bring them through.[12]

It is Nathaniel Hardy, however, in his exposition of 1 John 2:1, who provides us with the most succinct statement of the concept of advocacy.

> Whensoever this title (*paracle/tos*) is given to the Holy Ghost, it is either in respect of the world, and then it noteth his pleading for God with men by way of conviction, John 16:7–8, or in respect of believers, and then it noteth his encouraging them in all their distresses, chap. 14:19 and enabling them by strong groans to plead with God for themselves, Rom. 8:28: but when it is given to Christ, it importeth his taking our cause upon himself, and undertaking to intercede with God on our behalf. . . . This will the better appear if we consider that advocate is . . . a judicial word, so that look, as in all such proceedings, there is the guilty, the accuser, the court, the judge, and the advocate, so it is here: heaven is the court, man is the guilty, Satan the accuser, God is judge, and Christ the advocate; and look as the advocate appeareth in the court before the judge, to plead for the guilty against the ac-

cuser, so doth Christ before God in heaven, to answer
whatsoever the devil can object against us.[13]

That is to say, an advocate presupposes an adversary, antagonist,
or accuser, so that this office of Christ is a specialized one. Furthermore, Christ's office as advocate can be distinguished from
his office as intercessor, and Bunyan does so in this way:

> (1) They differ in name. . . . (2) In the nature of office. A
> priest is to slay a sacrifice; an advocate is to plead a cause.
> . . . (3) As to their extent. The priesthood of Christ ex-
> tendeth itself to the whole of God's elect, whether called
> or in their sins; but Christ, as Advocate, pleadeth only for
> the children. (4) As to the persons with whom they have
> to do. We read not anywhere that Christ as Priest, has to
> do with the devil as an antagonist, but, as an Advocate, he
> hath. (5) As to the matters about which they are em-
> ployed. . . . (6) So that Christ, as Priest, goes before, and
> Christ, as an Advocate, comes after; Christ, as Priest, con-
> tinually intercedes; Christ, as Advocate, in case of great
> transgressions, pleads: Christ as Priest, has need to act al-
> ways, but Christ, as Advocate, sometimes only.[14]

This particular office of Christ therefore has reference to the sins
of the believer after conversion, for which sins Satan indicts us in
the court of heaven. In our absence our cause is taken up by our
blessed Advocate, who takes our part before the Father, and
pleading against Satan on the grounds of His atoning work for us,
brings about our acquittal, thereby restoring to us communion
with the Father and joy in the Holy Ghost.

While the offices of intercessor and advocate are distinguished, they are nevertheless related. For in Christ's advocacy
His work is not to deny our crimes but to argue His substitution
for us; it is not to deny God's justice, but to claim it on our behalf.
He neither ignores our guilt nor neglects God's law, but through
the supreme efficacy of His unique satisfaction for sin, and
through the prevalence as well as the excellence of His advocacy,

His clients are released, their opponent thwarted, and His Father's justice and mercy honored and glorified. The harmony between Christ's being a sacrifice, a priest, and an advocate, is explained by Bunyan in this way: "As a sacrifice, our sins were laid upon him, Isaiah 53. As a priest, he beareth them, Exodus 28:38. And as an Advocate, he acknowledges them to be his own, Psalm 69:5. Now, having acknowledged them to be his own, the quarrel is no more betwixt us and Satan, for the Lord Jesus has espoused our quarrel, and made it his. All, then, that we in this matter have to do, is to stand at the bar by faith among the angels, and see how the business goes. . . ."[15]

Finally, for the comfort of those who need such an advocate Hugh Binning reminds us of His superb qualifications.

> (*With the Father,*) speaks out the Relation he and we stand in to the Judge . . . therefore, there is great Hopes that our Advocate *Jesus Christ* shall prevail in his Suites for us, because he, with whom he deals, *the Father,* he loves him, and loves us, and will not stand upon strict Terms of Justice, but rather attemper all with Mercy and Love . . . *he is the Christ of God,* anointed for this very Purpose, and so hath a fair and lawful calling to this Office. . . . If a Man had never so great Ability to plead in the Law, yet, except he be a licentiate and graduate, he may not take upon him to plead a Cause. But *our Lord Jesus* hath both Skill and Authority . . . the Council of Heaven did licentiate him, and graduate him for the whole Office of *Mediatorship:* In which there is the greatest Stay and Support for a sinking Soul, to know that all this Frame and Fabrick of the Gospel was contrived by God the Father . . . he is called *Jesus the Saviour,* he is such an *Advocate,* that he saves all he pleads for . . . that never succumbed in his Undertaking for any Soul, be their Sins never so heinous, their Accusation never so just and true, their Accuser never so powerful, yet they who put their Cause in his Hand, who flee in hither for Refuge, being Wearied of the Bondage of Sin and Satan, he hath such a Prevalancy with *the Father,*

that their Cause cannot miscarry . . . *Jesus the Righteous*. If he were not righteous in himself, he had need of an Advocate for himself, and might not plead for Sinners.[16]

Just as Binning argues for Christ's qualification to this office, so Bunyan is earnest in urging us to make application of this to our own needs.

Is Christ Jesus the Lord mine Advocate with the Father? Then awake, my faith, and shake thyself like a giant; stir up thyself, and be not faint; Christ is the Advocate of his people, and pleadeth the cause of the poor and needy. . . . As we should make use of Christ's advocateship for the strengthening of our faith, so we should also make use thereof to the encouraging us to prayer. As our faith is, so is our prayer; to wit, cold, weak, and doubtful, if our faith be so. . . . And according as a man apprehends Christ in his undertakings and offices, so he will wrestle with and supplicate God . . . we should use of this doctrine . . . to keep us humble; for the more offices Christ executeth for us with the Father, the greater sign that we are bad; and the more we see our badness, the more humble we should be . . . we should improve this doctrine . . . to encourage perseverance . . . to the driving of difficulties down before us, to the getting of the ground upon the enemy.[17]

See what strong consolation and lively hope is held out to us in the advocacy of Christ! How the consideration of it should reestablish our comfort and quicken our affections!

The Spirit's Intercession in the Believer

Thus we come to a brief examination of the third and last section of our subject, the intercession of the Spirit in the believer. That this is a necessary employment of the Spirit none will deny who have any acquaintance with the corruption of their hearts and the strength of the enemy. These hindrances militate against the spiritual exercises of the believer, and there is a resultant disinclination to prayer which is lethal to spiritual health and progress. Here, however, the Holy Spirit renders His assistance and by His work of intercession within disposes, teaches, and enables the believer to pray "according to the will of God." "Here note how the whole Trinity hath a worke in this holy exercise of prayer," says William Gouge. "The holy Ghost frameth our requests. The Son offereth them up unto his Father. The Father accepteth them thus framed, and offered up."[18] Thus the Spirit's intercession secures assistance, and Christ's intercession secures acceptance, to our prayers. Henry Lukin, in a treatise on *The Interest of the Spirit in Prayer*, draws on a scriptural example to illustrate the distinction between Christ's intercession and that of the Spirit.

> As Advocates do not only plead for their Clients, but many times dictate to them what they should say; So both Christ and the Spirit are as Advocates to us. And as *Nathan* did first suggest to *Bethsheba* what she should say (1 Kings 1:12, etc.), and then came in himself to confirm her Word, to second them, further to urge them: So the Spirit doth first assist us in drawing up our Petitions, for which Cause we are said to pray in or by the Spirit. . . . And when we have presented our Petitions, when Christ doth by his Intercession further confirm them, and plead with the Father on our Behalf.[19]

The manner of the Spirit's assistance in prayer is, according to John Owen, twofold; by working in us inclination and ability. Though He is called the "Spirit of Supplications," he does not Himself pray for two reasons; first, because He is divine and prayer implies inferiority of nature; second, because such interposition on our behalf is attributed by the Scripture to the priestly office of Christ and His intercession. Therefore, concludes Owen, the Holy Spirit is a Spirit of Supplications only in the two ways noted.

To the end therefore that we might pray effectively, the Holy Spirit acquaints us with the depravation of our nature, the grace and mercy which are prepared in the promises of God, our failure in view of the precepts or commands of God, and the proper motives and matters of our prayers. Owen continues,

> He doth not only enable them to pray, but worketh affections in them suitable unto what they pray about . . . the Spirit is said to "intercede for us with groanings"; which can be nothing but his working in us and acting by us that frame of heart and those fervent, labouring desires, which are so expressed, and these with such depth of intention and labouring of mind as cannot be uttered. . . . Secondly, Having truly affected the whole soul, enlightened the mind in the perception of the truth, beauty, and excellency of spiritual things, engaged the will in the choice of them and prevalent love unto them, excited the affections to delight in them and unto desires after them, there is in the actual discharge of this duty of prayer, wrought in the soul by the power and efficacy of his grace, such an inward labouring of heart and spirit, such a holy, supernatural desire and endeavour after union with the things prayed for in the enjoyment of them, as no words can utter or expressly declare.[20]

To stir up our affections in this salient duty the Holy Spirit works within us a delight in God, especially from a sense of his relation unto us as our Father. A "prospect of God as on a throne of grace," an enlarged liberty, and a confidence of acceptance are also the products of this work of the Spirit within. Finally, says Owen, "It is the work of the Holy Spirit in prayer to keep the souls of believers intent upon Jesus Christ, as the only way and means of acceptance with God."[21] In this way, the Spirit's work in prayer is consistent with His expressed concern, namely, to glorify the Son, our Lord Jesus Christ.

Having attempted a survey of the Puritan concept of intercession, it behooves us to ponder over these things and apply them to our own condition. Have we an interest in Christ's intercession? Have we engaged Him to be our advocate? Have we felt the movings of His Spirit in prayer? As we reflect on these great concerns of our souls, Christ should become more precious, and the Holy Spirit more necessary, to us. For surely we have seen in the office of Christ as our intercessor and advocate, and of the Holy Spirit as the inspirer of prayer; in the divine wisdom and according to sovereign purpose, that God is vitally concerned with His people and ever active on their behalf. The saints have assured for them their personal restoration and safety, their spiritual welfare and prosperity, their perseverance in grace, and their participation in eternal bliss. To God alone be the glory!

11

SUMMING UP

D. Martyn Lloyd-Jones

You have heard in the announcement that it is not my intention to deliver an address at this session but simply to say a few words before we turn to God in prayer. A number of friends expressed a desire that we should have a session of prayer, and as mine was the only session for which no subject had been announced and as in any case it is the last session, it was the obvious choice for this purpose. It is right and fitting that we should do this—although we are not quite clear about adopting this as a regular part of each Conference. There are those who feel that as we are all praying men and women who belong to churches which pray, and as it is very difficult to get together to a Conference such as this for two days, the primary object of this gathering should be to discuss these great matters together so that we may pray more efficiently when we go home. I am quite sure that that is right.

It must not be assumed therefore that this will always be the character of the last meeting. But we must be fluid in these matters, and not become set. If therefore we have the feeling, as I certainly have had on this occasion, that we should give this session to prayer in this way, well then you will understand the reason for it. But perhaps it is a good thing that we should on this one occasion at any rate remind ourselves that there should be an "end" to all we do here.

In order to direct attention to that I would like to consider with you briefly the words of our Lord, "If ye know these things, happy are ye if ye do them" (John 13:17). In many ways the greatest danger confronting us, all of us, is the danger of being content with a knowledge of these things, an intellectual knowledge and apprehension. Such knowledge is most valuable, but if it stops at that it can be quite useless and, indeed, positively harmful because it may drug us into a condition in which we feel that nothing further is necessary.

Now there was nothing that was more characteristic of the Puritan method of preaching than the way in which they always came to the "application." They were always very insistent upon that. I have sometimes wondered whether the trouble with many of us is our tendency to forget the application. There are many reasons for this. The chief one, I believe, is the danger of reaction, and of an over-violent reaction, against something else. It is a very subtle thing, but quite unconsciously we allow other people, and other positions, and other ideas, and other movements to determine ours. That, surely, must always be wrong. We should always be in control, we should always be positive, we should not merely be a "reaction" against something. This is a principle, you will agree, which can be worked out along many lines. I feel that we are always in danger of allowing an opponent, or somebody who is obviously wrong, to determine the grounds of argument and the matter to be argued about. Now up to a point that is inevitable, but that is merely the negative part of our work, and it is essential that we should be positive. It is a bad state when we are just "reactions" against various things, because that means that having reacted against them we stop, and so our witness is nullified and becomes quite ineffective. Now if it is true to say of us, as has been suggested once or twice in this conference, that we

are a people who seem to be lacking in an active urgent concern
for souls and in activity and action, it is a very serious matter. I am
not admitting the charge for a moment, but if there is some suspicion of truth here, well then this conference should have made
us examine ourselves very seriously. In fact, I feel that that is the
way in which one can sum up this conference this year. It seems
to have been a repeated challenge along that particular line. Are
we always a little liable to be content with just knowing? And having known, to stop at that and to do nothing? The first challenge
came to us with respect to missionary activity. We must examine
ourselves very seriously about that. We of all people should have
a concern for the glory of God, and therefore for the salvation of
men's souls. Have we got that as we should have it? Does our understanding of these doctrines lead us to a great compassion for
the lost? Have we real zeal for the glory of God? Not in theory,
not in statement only, but in actual practice?

Then take the second session where we were dealing with the
vital matter of communion with God. To what extent is our communion with God real? We are all clear about what is bad, what is
false, and what is wrong, but what of this matter positively? What
is the condition of our praying, our "prayer life" if you like? How
much time do we spend in prayer? What kind of prayer is it? What
do we really know about praying "in the Spirit," which is surely
the essence of real communion with God? "If ye know these
things, happy are ye if ye do them." If we merely feel upbraided
and searched and condemned, and stop at that, we shall just become miserable and we shall probably analyze ourselves and the
situation still more and then become introspective and morbid
and spend our time in utter discouragement, just thinking about
ourselves and our own failure. That, of course, is utterly hopeless
and useless. Surely, the effect it should have upon us is to make
us realize what is possible and to be concerned about arriving at
that. If we really have grasped what is possible for us in this whole
matter of communion, well then we must go on, and we must not
give ourselves peace or rest until this has become a living reality
to us in our experience. And so with all the other themes that
have been put before us. Prayer came up again in the session de-

210 ~ D. Martyn Lloyd-Jones

voted to the subject of intercession and the Spirit's work in us. We did not deal with that sufficiently in the discussion. These matters are so large that it is very difficult to find time to take up these points as we ought.

Then in the last session we faced the duty of rejoicing in the Lord, and of always rejoicing in the Lord. Now of all people, surely, we should be rejoicing most of all in the Lord, because the more you know about Him, as we were shown so clearly, the more you delight in Him and the more you rejoice in Him. There is something wrong somewhere, otherwise these charges, these suspicions about our position, should never arise at all. The introduction this afternoon reminded us of that—that people normally think of the Puritan as a miserable person. It is wrong of course, but why have they got that impression? It would be folly and untrue to say that there is no foundation for it at all. There is a misunderstanding of Puritanism that does lead to misery. There are some people who are so afraid of false joy that they are only really happy when they are more or less unhappy. There is no doubt about this. I once listened to a man preaching a sermon on "the rainbow in the cloud"; but the whole of the sermon was devoted to warnings against false joy, so instead of going out of the service filled with thoughts about the rainbow, we were sent out with thoughts about the cloud! It was just that the good man was obsessed by this fear of the false.

Now the Puritans—we are reminded of this constantly—were always warning against the false, but they did not stop at that. And we must not stop at that. Otherwise we just become reactions, we are merely and only against the false. But that is of no value, it does not lead anywhere. Surely we ought, if we understand these things at all, to have such knowledge of God, and such access to God through the Lord Jesus Christ by the One Spirit, that we should be increasingly men and women who come out of His Presence in such a way that people will know that we have been in His Presence.

What is needed today above everything in the Church is the type of knowledge of God which is seen in such a man as Robert Murray McCheyne. When that saintly man entered his pulpit on

Sunday morning people began to weep at the mere sight of him, before he had uttered a sound. Like Moses, having spent time on the mountain with God, it was evident to the people when he came down that he had done so. There was a radiance about him. Do we know anything about that? Is it going to be obvious to our families and our friends and fellow church members as the result of these two days we have spent here that we really have been with God? That is the object of all this. Otherwise it becomes a kind of scholasticism, it becomes a coterie. God forbid that we should ever degenerate into that! The end and object of all this, and all we have done, is to bring us to a knowledge of God. And if it does not do that we shall just have been turning around in circles, giving a good deal of satisfaction to the flesh, and we shall go away proud of our knowledge and our understanding, but it will be no help to anybody at all. No, there is always an end to these things. Take the New Testament Epistles, take the great Pauline Epistles with their great doctrines—yet every single one of them was written with a pastoral intent. We tend to forget that! They all have a pastoral intent and object. All our knowledge must be applied. It is sinful not to do so. "If ye know these things, happy are ye if ye do them."

There is just one other word I want to say. I am not sure but that the danger confronting some of us, our greatest danger at the moment, may just be this—and there have been indications of it in this Conference this time—the danger of our estimating and judging aspects of doctrine in terms of our own experience and thereby "limiting the Holy One of Israel." There is a great deal of that at the present time. Take for instance what was said in passing by several about people's reactions to the *Journals* of George Whitefield. You noticed the tendency to say about them, "Ah, excess of youth," etc! How many of us are in danger of having that charge brought against us? Thank God, I say, for a man who is subject or exposed to that charge! Or let us put it like this. To how many churches today do you think it would be necessary to write the First Epistle to the Corinthians? How many of our churches are so thrilling with spiritual life that you have to tell them about control and of being aware of excesses? I do not know of one. That is because there is no life.

When you have life and vitality there is always a danger of excess. I would not venture to suggest that Whitefield had no failings, but I cannot understand the type of person who can read those *Journals* of Whitefield and simply feel that this was just a young man who was carried away by animal excitement. We were actually given a quotation, which proved that he was not. We thanked God for the way in which he had been kept by the Spirit from losing his head, or losing himself in any respect, in spite of the phenomenal success that attended his ministry. No man was more humble, no man was more aware of the dangers.

But what I am afraid is happening is this, that we read of a man like Whitefield lying on his bed badly in need of physical rest in the midst of strenuous preaching but finding sleep quite impossible because God was pouring His love upon him, and having read that we simply say, "Ah, this is ecstasy, this is excess, this is enthusiasm." Why do we say that? I am afraid there is but one reason for it. It is that we know nothing whatsoever about such experience. And because we do not know it, we criticize it in Whitefield. In other words, we are reducing what is offered us, and promised us, in the New Testament to the level of our own experience. Because there are so few Christian people today who know this "real" joy of the Lord, these "real" manifestations of the Son of God, these overwhelming experiences of the Spirit being poured out—because that is such a rare experience today, our tendency is to criticize, to query, and to doubt its spiritual character. We are defining doctrine in terms of our experience and of our understanding.

We must come back to the New Testament itself and see how then the people of God knew what it is to pray in the Spirit. Look at them in the Book of the Acts of the Apostles, and look at the teaching given in the Epistles. What do we know about the Spirit coming down? What do we know about being in prayer meetings where you forget time altogether? Now that happened in the early Church, and it has happened in the subsequent history of the Christian Church. What right have we to express our criticisms and to say, "Ah, this is just youthful effervescence, something which a man outgrows"?

The fact was that those men never outgrew that. Whitefield and others were aware of the fact and ready to admit that they used certain unguarded expressions in their preaching and in their writing, but the whole glory of that period is—I am referring particularly to the eighteenth century—the way in which the amazing spiritual experiences persisted. And we know something of the way in which these people died. Exalted spiritual experience was not something that applied to their youth only; some of them had their greatest experiences during their last days on earth. Thank God you cannot explain these things psychologically or in terms of age or of anything else.

Let us be careful lest we become guilty of "quenching the Spirit." We can easily become guilty of this. In our fear of certain things we can become so careful and so wary and so cautious and so afraid, that nothing at all will ever happen to us, and nothing will ever happen to our churches. And so the position will continue as one of utter discouragement and may even go from bad to yet worse.

I feel that we have to be careful about these things and that we must come back again to the New Testament and see what is possible and open to God's children, to Christian people, while here on earth. Is this kind of "pneumatic" element as prominent among us as it should be? That seems to me to be the great question. Doctrine after all is a foundation, and no more. It is not an end, it is only a beginning. It is the means. We must never stop at it. It is always designed to bring us, by faith, into that knowledge, that intimacy, that deep experience of the Living God, for which we really meet with Him, know that He is present, and are conscious of the energies of the Spirit in us and among us.

Do let us, therefore, examine ourselves very seriously about these things. It is very wonderful and enjoyable to have fellowship of kindred minds. How delightful to discuss and to talk about these things. What is more enjoyable than this? But it can lead to nothing—nothing at all—if we are not ever mindful of the fact that it is merely the means provided by God to bring us to a knowledge of Himself.

With that word let us turn to God together. Let us worship

Him, let us praise Him, let us thank Him. But above all let us plead with Him to have mercy upon us and to visit us. Let us take the phrase of Isaiah, and "lay hold upon God." How many are there that stir themselves up to lay hold upon God? That is the call to us, it seems to me, at a time like this. Here is the Truth. Yes, but why is it so ineffective? It needs this power to come upon it, the Spirit and the Word, the Spirit upon the Word, the Spirit using the Word, the Spirit through the Word. Let us pray to God to give us this "demonstration of the Spirit and of power," this power and unction that can take a word that often sounds so dead, a mere letter, and turn it into a living flame that will do its saving and transforming work in the minds and the hearts of men and women. Let us pray.

O Lord our God, we come into Thy holy Presence and we come, O Lord, to worship Thee, we come to praise Thy Name. Great God of wonders, all Thy ways are Godlike, matchless, and divine. We thank Thee for the opportunity we have had together to remind ourselves of this. O help us, we pray Thee, at this hour to realize that Thou art the Living God, and that Thou are looking down upon us in this room.

O Lord, we come in the Name of Thy dear Son. We recognize we have nothing else to plead, we have nothing which we can present before Thee. We were all by nature the children of wrath, even as others, and we have sinned against Thee deliberately and spurned the Voice Divine so often, followed our own wills, been proud of ourselves, of what we are, not even recognizing that what we are was the result of Thy gracious gifts to us. O God, we see how poor and sinful and vile we all had become as the result of man's original disobedience and sin and fall, and our own misdeeds and transgressions. So we come and we plead only the Name and the Blood of Thy dear Son, and we do thank Thee that in Him we know that we have this access. Lord, make us all sure of it, forgive us if we ever come into Thy Presence in His Name, yet uncertainly. Grant us all the full assurance of faith that we may know our acceptance, that we may rejoice in Thy Presence and praise Thy Name.

We thank Thee together for the energies of Thy blessed Spirit. We thank Thee that He does work within us both to will and to do of Thy good pleasure. We know that we would not be here even this afternoon were it not for this. We thank Thee that He brings us back to Thee, that suddenly

He visits us and causes us to read Thy Word and to turn unto Thee in prayer.

O Lord, we have never seen and known so clearly that, were not this salvation Thine from beginning to end, we would still be undone. We know it is Thy work and that Thou art continuing it within us, and we humbly thank Thee for His disturbing us, for His convictions, for His drawings, for all His movements within us. O God, we thank Thee for this and our prayer is that we may know this in a greater, a mightier manner. O Lord, enable us to pray in the Spirit. O come, we pray Thee therefore, upon us in this very gathering and enable us so to pray.

Lord, Thou knowest our desire is that Thy great Name may be magnified, that men and women may be humbled before Thee; yea, that the very nations be humbled before Thee. O God, authenticate Thy Word, grant power by Thy Spirit unto those who preach it in sincerity and truth. Revive Thy work, O Lord, in the midst of these evil days. Hear us in our prayer, and lead us on now by Thy Spirit that we may pray truly unto Thee.

We ask it in Christ Jesus' Name. Amen.

Part 3

Faith and a Good Conscience

❧

1962

12

THE CASUISTRY
OF WILLIAM PERKINS

I. Breward

Outside the Roman Church, the word casuistry has rather unpleasant associations. We tend to link it automatically with words
such as priestcraft, with the confessional and a moral judgment
which is capable of twisting any obligation to its own ends. The
word has never been the same since Pascal published his devas-
tating exposure of Jesuit casuistry.[1] Even if we were to look at
modern Roman treatments, many of us would be repelled by the
contents and methods used, feeling that we had strayed into an
alien world.

Yet we have all indulged in casuistry at some time or other, for
it is simply the science of bringing general moral principles to
bear on particular cases. Most people would subscribe in the abstract to the principle of speed limits in built up areas, but few
would feel that they were bound by the speed limit law in an
emergency. Clearly, there could be good and bad reasons for

breaking this law, and the fact that some people justify their actions by bad reasoning would not make us want to prevent people exercising their moral judgment altogether, in order to avoid the possibility of abuse.

Casuistry can be good or bad, and the fact that there are some blundering practitioners should not lead us to reject it without careful consideration. It may be that it can be formulated in such a way as to avoid the dangers of legalism or laxity. To be sure, modern Protestant writers on the subject of ethics tend to reject any form of casuistry, holding that it rests on a fundamental misunderstanding of the Christian ethic, which, according to them, is not based on an abstract law, but is founded on living encounter with Christ in the situations in which we find ourselves. Love, they say, transcends any law.

Working on these assumptions, it is not surprising that the Protestant casuistry of the seventeenth century gets a bad press from them. The verdict of W. F. Forrester on Baxter's *Christian Directory* is perhaps typical: "Any such system of legalistic attitudes or codification of duties is quite repugnant to our Protestant faith and way of life."[2] But I wonder if it is quite as simple as that! Certainly, we must not underestimate the perennial danger of legalism in ethical thinking, but have we not gone to the other extreme and called wooliness Christian freedom, simply because we are reluctant to sort out the principles by which we live, thinking clearly and biblically about the way in which we should apply them?

For this reason, I think that a fresh look at the beginnings of Protestant casuistry might be useful. We might not feel that we can go all the way with the exhaustive treatments which the subject received; we might even want to disagree with some of the principles which seventeenth-century casuists used. But it is hard to resist admiration for the pastoral ideal on which Protestant casuistry was based, or for its attempt to build up an all-inclusive theoretical and practical theology, in which there was no attempt to bypass any of the thorny problems which arise when one tries to apply the Christian ethic to the multifarious situations of daily life.

To begin with, we must remember that, for Protestants, the word "casuistry" had a far wider connotation in the seventeenth century than it has nowadays in Roman literature. It included many subjects which would make a modern casuist blink, subjects which nowadays would be allotted to systematic and practical theology, psychology, and apologetics, as well as dealing with issues which we would consider belonged to the province of ethics or moral theology. There was no trace of the divorce between moral and ascetical theology which was beginning to appear in the Roman casuistry of the sixteenth and seventeenth centuries, leading eventually to the undoubted excesses which were condemned by the Roman hierarchy. As I hope to show, the development of Protestant casuistry was by no means the theological fall from grace which Karl Barth conceives it to have been. "By the end of the 16th century," Barth writes, "matters had gone so far that the Puritan William Perkins was willing and able to write a book *De Casibus Conscientiae* in which he gave a systematic account of the correct individual decisions enjoined upon the Christian."[3] This seems to Barth very regrettable, and he quotes Calvin in his support, but what Calvin was attacking and what Perkins wrote about were two very different things.

Reformation Background

Certainly, both Luther and Calvin denounced medieval moral theology in no uncertain terms, putting in place of the mechanical and legalistic codification of offences found in medieval collections of "cases" (offences which could usually be commuted for cash!) a system of pastoral care which expressed in practical terms their theology of justification, the principle of the priesthood of all believers, and their concern to give freedom from the oppressive ordinances of men which had been such a burden to scrupulous consciences. Medieval casuistry had been written to help priests assess guilt when hearing confessions; but the Reformers abolished the medieval confessional. In their hands, confession was no longer a compulsory search for the yearly tally of mortal sins, but became simply the last recourse for those whose consciences were not set at rest by the regular preaching of the word and the administration of the sacraments. As Luther put it, confession was "a cure without equal for distressed consciences." And in fact all the Reformers stressed the power given by God to the minister to declare God's forgiveness of the sins which had been causing the distress. In this respect the voice of the minister was as the voice of God himself. Perkins stood firmly in this tradition, stressing the value of voluntary confession, not only from the point of view of the minister, who needed to know what was at the root of the troubled conscience, but also for its value to the distressed.[4]

The Reformers may have repudiated casuistry in the traditional sense, but they all gave guidance on matters of Christian duty, often in considerable detail. One has only to glance at the correspondence of Luther and Calvin to see the extent to which they continued to resolve cases of conscience, though they did not formalize their treatment as Perkins was to do at the end of the century in his *Cases of Conscience*.

Without exception, the Reformers realized the importance of instructing the conscience. Ideally, conscience was an infallible guide, the voice of God in man. In practice, it was corrupted like the rest of man's faculties and even when regenerated still needed to be guided by the law (i.e., the Decalogue) and the great affirmations of the Christian faith. Catechisms were frequently based on the Apostles' Creed, the Decalogue, and the Lord's Prayer, and these played an increasingly important role in the popularization of Reformed theology and ethics.

By the end of the sixteenth century, it was becoming obvious that the inherited ideas of the past, the resistance of vested interests, the revival of Romanism, and the cooling of Protestant zeal, were all combining to make the maintaining of the Reformation's highest ideals increasingly difficult. Christian freedom is all very well, but it presupposes a certain level of spiritual maturity. Fear of antinomianism was widespread, and there was much laxity among Protestant layfolk. It should not altogether surprise us if other complementary emphases, more pedagogic and disciplinary, came to the forefront of Reformed ethical thinking at the end of the sixteenth century. Nurturing believers capable of responsible action is in any case a staggering task, as every minister knows. It is in this kind of context that we should try and see why Perkins wrote his *Cases of Conscience.*

Not that Perkins was in every respect breaking new ground. Isolating him from the ethical thinking and pastoral practice of Luther, Melanchthon, Calvin, and Peter Martyr makes his work appear far more novel than it actually was. And there were important precedents in the Church of England too. I need not dwell on the pastoral deficiencies of many of the sixteenth-century Anglican clergy and the attempts of the Puritans to remedy a very difficult situation by means of "prophesyings," and later through the classical movement. By no means all the clergy labelled "Puritan" were interested in introducing a Presbyterian form of Church government, and even those that were still found time to discuss cases of conscience, as the minutes of the Dedham classis show. Perkins himself was a moderate Puritan, more interested in building up the Church than in worrying about the finer points of Church government. He stood in the tradition of men like Foxe, Wilcox, Dering, and Greenham, who were all noted for their skill in resolving cases of conscience. People came for miles to consult clergy of Greenham's stamp about problems of conscience, and books of letters written by godly ministers to troubled souls were starting to appear, for instance *Large Letters* by Thomas Wilcox, published in 1589.

Books on moral problems were also starting to appear, in which the Christian attitude to dancing, gambling, and so on was discussed, sometimes in rather lurid detail. People were very conscience of the problem of right conduct. There was a large secular literature of a moralizing kind, and ethical principles culled from the classics were drilled into every schoolboy in the process of acquiring some kind of facility in the classics. It is not surprising that people should have been willing and, indeed, anxious to read handbooks on how to live the Christian life. Francis Bacon no doubt spoke for many when, in 1589, he complained about the way preachers failed to apply their directions for Christian living to cases of conscience, "that a man may be warranted in his particular actions, whether they be lawful or not."[5]

Having now said something about the kind of society in which Perkins lived, and the activities of his predecessors, I hope that I have made it clear that this element of ethical thinking is found from the very beginning of the Reformation, and that far from being an innovator, Perkins is building on the foundations of the original Reformers.

Perkins's Purpose

I wish now to have a look at the aim, methods, and contents of Perkins's casuistry.

His casuistry must not be seen apart from the rest of his theology, but as an integral part of it. One of his earliest works, *A Treatise Tending unto a Declaration Whether a Man Be in the Estate of Damnation or the Estate of Grace* (1589), sought to show the reader the ways in which the signs of grace could be recognized, settling the conscience and enabling the Christian to bear the sorrows and pains of this world with a courageous spirit. He knew that if one is afflicted with a wounded spirit "the grief is so great, the burden so intolerable, that it will not by any outward means be eased or assuaged."[6] The same preoccupation with conscience appears in all Perkins's works. The cure of afflicted consciences was, he held, part of the work of Christ's prophetic office, which He has now committed to ministers of the gospel.[7] One is not surprised to find that Perkins spent his Sundays resolving problems of conscience. In all this there was nothing new, as I have already shown. What was new was Perkins's collection of these cases in a systematically arranged treatise, which was published after his death by Thomas Pickering as *Cases of Conscience* in 1606.

Perkins had two kinds of readers in mind. First, he was concerned to publish something which would be of value to his fellow ministers in their dealings with troubled consciences. This was the first Protestant attempt of its kind, and evidently met a long-felt need, for it went through at least fifteen editions in English, Latin, and German and inspired many other similar treatises by both Lutheran and Reformed theologians in the seventeenth century.

Perkins modestly disclaimed any pretensions to complete-
ness. Likening the subject to a vast sea, it is, he said, impossible to
present an exhaustive treatment. "I will only (as it were) walk by
the banks of it, and propound the heads of doctrine that thereby
I may at least occasion others, to consider and handle the same
more at large."[8] In composing this kind of production for ministers, Perkins was doing something which was common practice in
the Roman Church, though it must be remembered that he presupposes a different kind of pastoral relation: he was not writing
a manual for confessors!

That he wrote in the vernacular and not in Latin shows us
that he did not only have his ministerial brethren in mind, but
was also writing for laymen who wished to keep their consciences
sound and know how to act in their callings. In this sense, his
work was a kind of popular health manual for the soul. Sixteenth-
century ministers frequently saw themselves as doctors of the soul
and used medical analogies to describe their work. Troubles of
conscience were held to have certain very definite causes and certain equally definite cures. Then, as now, it was the complicated
cases that aroused the greatest interest. A successful physician of
the soul like Perkins could expect a large reading public (just as
some famous modern doctors do) when he explained the ways in
which he worked.

In offering guidance for his fellow Christians, Perkins believed that it was not enough to preach the great principles of the
gospel and leave the small issues of conduct to take care of themselves. As his pupil Ames remarked, "through the neglect of this
husbandry, a famine of godliness hath followed in many places,
and out of that famine a grievous spiritual plague."[9] There seems
no reason to doubt that Perkins was attempting to fill a gap in
spiritual direction about which Romanists had waxed scornful.
One T. Hill, in *A Quatron of Reasons*, published in 1600, con-
trasted the way in which Catholics had the advantages of being
guided by priests expert in cases of conscience, whereas a Protestant did not meddle with these matters of conscience, "but
freighteth his ship only with faith, and never beateth his brain
about sins, for that he thinketh none to be imputed to such Pre-

destinated, as they all ween themselves to be, which causeth the people their followers to be utterly ignorant of the nature, differences, and quality of sins, and consequently nothing fearful, or stayed by conscience to commit the same."[10] Hill exaggerates, but when a generation later we find Ames commenting on the lack of Protestant case-divinity prior to Perkins, it becomes obvious that Perkins's contemporaries felt that he was performing a real service to the Church of God when he wrote on this aspect of theology.

The final thing which Perkins set out to do was to set out a theory of pastoral care which would make it unnecessary for theological students to read Roman manuals of casuistry, which contained many serious errors. They gave too much power to the priest, they taught the validity of implicit faith, denied the need for assurance, insisted on yearly confession to the priest of all mortal sins on pain of damnation if the command was neglected, distinguished sins into mortal and venial, and, worst of all, taught that men could satisfy for the temporal punishment due to their sins. It was only the Word of God that could bind and direct conscience correctly. What was probable and conjectural, what was based on the conceits and opinions of men could only lead to despair and damnation.

Conscience and the Word of God

Perkins's theory of conscience was intimately related to his casuistry, and he appears to have written the first systematic treatise on conscience in English—*A discourse of conscience*, printed in 1596. I shall not say more about this than the minimum necessary to explain the methods which Perkins used for comforting and informing troubled consciences.

Conscience works by means of a syllogism. Perkins illustrated from the mind of a murderer. His theoretical understanding knows the natural law that every murderer is cursed. His practical understanding tells him: you are a murderer. With the major and minor premises of the syllogism thus supplied, the conclusion should follow in his conscience automatically—therefore I am cursed. Unfortunately, the Fall has corrupted the working and judgment of conscience so that neither the premises nor the conclusion may be given to the mind. Though the conscience was placed in our reason as the voice of God, determining of things done, telling us, as it were, what God thought of our actions, it was an exceedingly sensitive organ. Perkins likened it to the eye of the soul which became blinded if wounded often enough by acts of insubordination against its judgments. It was to be found in every man in varying degrees of sensitivity, even in the veriest atheist. All the writers of the period speak in terms of awe of the horrors of conscience which were a foretaste of the judgment of God. Perkins taught that they caused swooning, feverish heat, and rising of the entrails to the mouth,[11] terrors which could only be assuaged by the blood of Christ[12] assuring a man that his sins no longer stood between him and God.

This brings me to the relation of conscience and the Word of God. Since conscience was from God, only He could bind it and guide it to its true end. This He did through His Word. By contrast, human laws, oaths, and duties only bound insofar as they agreed with the Word of God. The Word was a gift to sinful men to guide them in a sinful world. Men should only do what God commanded and do nothing where there was no warrant in the Word. Perkins believed that there was no action that could eventuate, for which there was not sufficient guidance set down in Scripture: "All actions that please God, must be done in faith; therefore all actions that please God, must have some ground and direction in the word of God, without which word of God there can be no faith."[13] Certainly this attitude could lead to a new kind of legalism and scrupulosity, every bit as bad as the kind the Reformers had sought to escape from, if interpreted in a very literalistic kind of way which saw the Scripture as a lawbook. Hooker was quite right to attack some of the manifestations of this spirit among the Puritans,[14] but Perkins was too balanced to fall into some of the excesses of his contemporaries.

If the Bible played such an important part in the direction of conscience, it was clearly very important to set down some principles of interpretation. The distinction between law and gospel was fundamental. Ministers must preach the law to wake erring consciences to their true situation. Again and again Perkins emphasized the dangers of a superficial pastor failing to bring the sinner to see himself as he was before God. Only when the sinner was truly humbled should the gospel be applied. Otherwise the wounded conscience could not be healed, but would still retain some of the germs of sin and shortly fester again. Nor had Perkins any time for the pastoral care which was based on the theory that all men would be saved. Salvation could only be found within the covenant founded by Christ and this salvation could only be received by repentance and faith. Without faithful preaching of the law men would not be able truly to repent. Perkins himself was noted for the way in which his sermons mixed law and gospel, so that sinners were humbled and the humble healed.

When Perkins used the word "law" he meant the moral law which was summed up in the Decalogue, not the ceremonial law or the civil law of the Jews. This moral law was a republication of the law of nature and thus served not only to remind the sinner of his responsibilities, but also to guide the believer in his ethical decisions. Law bound both positively and negatively, but it was the gospel which was completely binding on the believer, for in this God had shown us perfect righteousness, demanding faith that excluded doubt. Consequently, Perkins did not need to spend any great attention on the problems of erring or doubting consciences. Men either had a good or a bad conscience. There could be no doubt about the Word binding. The task of conscience was simply to discern obligations as set forth in the Word.

Perkins discussed what the believer should do when there was a seeming clash between the precepts of the Word, or when there was no clear biblical injunction. In the former case Perkins suggested that commandments of the first table (the first four) took precedence over commands from the second table. Thus when the state commanded something contrary to the worship of God, we were to obey God rather than men. Alternatively, the summary of Christ helped us to decide the priority of obligations. If our neighbor's house caught fire while we were on the way to church, it would not be a sin to fight the fire rather than worship God, because service of our neighbor was equally a way of serving God.

Where there was no clear definition in the Word, Perkins advised taking the safer course rather than run the risk of falling into sin. Roman casuists tend to regard this counsel as dangerous, leading to rigorism, but the solution to this problem which was adopted by contemporary Roman casuists like Medina led to the laxity of the following century which Pascal so rightly castigated. Within the context of Perkins's theology, the dangers latent in rigorism (i.e., the risk of Pharisaic unreality and self-righteousness) were nonexistent. Perkins held that the best we could do was incapable of pleasing God. Our status with God depended on the work of Christ, not on our ethical achievements.

A more important question to ask is whether Perkins's attitude to Scripture ran the risk of degenerating into legalism, as many modern writers would feel. Certainly there are risks in Perkins's tendency to see Scripture as a kind of moral lawbook, but I would point out that in the context of his whole theology this is not the whole story. To begin with, the Holy Spirit enables us to do what God commands in the Word. Perkins saw the Bible as a charter of liberty, giving a good conscience, rather than as a code of restricting practices. Then, second, an examination of some of his cases shows that he does not give cast-iron solutions to every scruple. He attempts to set forth the scriptural principles on which right actions should be based, leaving a great deal of leeway to the individual conscience in making decisions.

Take for instance his discussion of the case whether it was right to flee in time of persecution. He insists that every case must be decided according to circumstances. Tertullian was wrong to say that flight was never justified. Perkins cited Matthew 10:25 ("When they persecute you in one city, flee into another") and the examples of Jacob, Moses, and Paul, to justify his position. He then looked at the contention that since persecution was sent by God it should be borne. Using the analogy of illness in which it was valid to use every possible means of cure, Perkins held that it was valid to flee in certain circumstances: when there was no hope of doing good, when one was expelled by the authorities, when one withdrew only for a time, when after due consideration one decided that one did not possess the strength to stand, when God offers a lawful way out, or when the persecution is personal and flight will bring peace to the church. Clearly in all these there was plenty of room for the exercise of personal judgment, a factor which Perkins himself recognized to be of vital importance when he insisted that the pastor in such a situation must be sure he is acting from moderation of mind.[15] If, on the other hand, we are taken by the authorities, escape is illegal, as also when God cuts off the means of escape, or when we are bound by our calling. In no circumstances must we do evil that good may come.[16] This example shows that Perkins's casuistry was more in the nature of a moral compass than a detailed plan of action binding in all circumstances.

If Perkins used Scripture to resolve cases, in contrast to the human authorities used by Roman casuists, he also rejected their distinction between mortal and venial sin. He felt, like all the other Reformers, that it was pastorally pernicious to deny the seriousness of some kinds of sin. Yet clearly it was equally senseless to put murder on the same level as some minor fault. He gave a careful discussion of the various types of sin, according to their origin and circumstances, going into greater detail than other Reformed scholars, like Peter Martyr and Ursinus, who had also attempted to draw some kind of distinction between the various kinds of sin. His position can best be summed up in the principle that "though every sin of itself be mortal, yet all are not equally mortal."[17] He went much further than Romanists were prepared to go, in that he defined sin as whatever wanted conformity to the law of God, "whether it be with the consent of will or no."[18] An erring conscience was no excuse. Sin was sin and must be recognized as such.

Even when a person had grasped the structure of conscience, the varying kinds of sin, and the way in which problems ought to be resolved, there was still a great danger of wrong diagnosis. It was essential to be able to distinguish between a genuinely afflicted conscience and what was curable by medicine. In this connection Perkins discussed the ways in which the disease of melancholy could be distinguished from an afflicted conscience. Even in the sixteenth century it was desirable for ministers to be able to recognize the boundaries between medicine and what was distinctively spiritual, just as today being able to recognize curable mental disorders is an important part of the minister's task, so that he does not apply the wrong medicine. Perkins also discussed the various types of affliction which the Christian could be expected to meet and suggested the methods appropriate to the cure of each.

In all cases the application of the law receives emphasis. Worldly sorrow for sin was not enough. Men must be sorry because they have sinned against God and repent for distinct sins. Without this feeling of humility, Perkins believed that the healing promises of the gospel could have no effect. He lists certain conditions which should be observed if the application of the promises of the gospel is to bring relief: the comfort must still contain some admixture of the law; if the grief of sinners is great, they must on no account be left alone in case they fell into despair; they must learn to submit themselves to the judgments of the wise; they must not be told of the fearful accidents which had befallen those in like case, lest they be cast into despair; and the minister must bear patiently with all their perversities and not expect speedy results, because sin is often very deeply rooted.[19]

Perkins's Ethical Teaching

Having briefly examined the aims and methods by which Perkins sought to comfort afflicted consciences, I want to conclude with a quick look at some of the treasures in the contents of his treatise on casuistry. It was characterized by brevity, order, and simplicity, falling neatly into three sections—man as man, man in relation to God, and man in relation to other men. Many of the cases were discussed in other earlier works, and it seems hardly accurate to accuse Perkins of declension from Reformed truth, simply because he had ordered his material! It is the contents of Perkins's *Cases of conscience* which illustrate most clearly the basic differences between Protestant and Roman casuistry. Perkins ignores the complicated legal issues about the sacraments and their validity which occupy so much space in Romanist treatments, discussing instead matters which at first sight would seem to have little relation to ethics at all. He saw very clearly that ethics and theology are inseparable and would have no time for those moderns who cry for a "simple gospel" and would gladly relegate theology to the rubbish heap, believing that the Christian ethic can get on well enough without it.

Thus in his section on man as man, Perkins discusses three things—what a man must do to be saved, how men are assured of their salvation, and how we can be restored to God's favor when we have fallen. Judging by his constant reference to the problem of assurance, Perkins regarded it as the greatest "case" of all. Some scholars have seen in Perkins's interest in feelings a fall into subjectivism which led ultimately to the excesses of pietism, but when this emphasis is seen in the context of his whole theology, it is clear that the decisive emphasis is on the sovereignty of God. To those who do not know what assurance and joy relationship to Christ conveys to the believer, the doctrine of assurance will always seem rather peculiar. For myself, I believe Perkins was right to spend so much energy on discussing the various sides of this "case." If a man is assured of God's favor to him in Christ, he is able to live victoriously in whatever state he finds himself. Perkins's theology was eminently practical (he defined theology as "the science of living blessedly for ever"), and his whole teaching on the living of the Christian life is based on the good conscience which comes from being assured of God's favor in Christ.

In his second section, Perkins again discussed matters theological rather than ethical in the narrow sense, bringing out very clearly the way in which ethics is founded in God and our relation to Him in Christ. Under man's relation to God he discussed the existence of God, the divinity of Christ, the authority of the Scriptures, and the nature of worship. Clearly Perkins was interested in producing an educated people, not just a group in clerical leading strings dependent for their thinking upon the ministry. It is a sad commentary on the dreary moralizing that so often passes for preaching these days that it is rare indeed for it to be related meaningfully to the fundamentals of the faith as Perkins sought to do here. Most people today regard the question of God's existence as a rather abstract issue. For Perkins it stood at the heart of theology and ethics. He disclaimed any intention to answer sophistical quibbles.

> Rather my purpose is, in showing that there is a God, to remove, or at least help an inward corruption of the soul, that is great and dangerous, whereby the heart and conscience by nature denieth God and his providence. "If the removal of the heart means the death of the body" that opinion that taketh away the Godhead, doth in effect rend and pluck out the very heart of the soul.[20]

His final section on the relation of men to men is concerned with the nature of the virtues. Perkins's treatment owes something to Aristotelian ethics, but is basically biblical. Unfortunately this section is not complete. Perkins seems to have died near the end of his series of sermons. However, enough remains to give a fairly complete idea of the kind of approach that he adopted. He discussed six virtues—prudence, which was found in the mind, and those which were found in the will, clemency, temperance, liberality, justice, and fortitude.[21] He defined virtue as "a gift of the spirit of God, and a part of regeneration whereby a man is made fit to live well."[22] The virtue of a Christian was quite different from the virtue of a heathen. This latter was due to God's restraining grace, and not to the regenerating Holy Spirit. Perkins rejected the ideal of the mean as a guide to virtue, as well as some of the Aristotelian virtues. Magnanimity, for example, was to him a vice, tempting men to leave their calling and to eschew humility.

His discussion of prudence shows how deeply his ethics had been influenced by the insights of the Reformers into the bibli-

234 ∞ I. BREWARD

cal message. Two cases were discussed in this section—how a man should practice prudence, or wisdom, and whether a man may lawfully and with good conscience use "policy" in the affairs of this life.[23]

Prudence, said Perkins, begins in the fear of God, as one lives in the presence of God, obeying Him, discerning truth from falsehood, and resolutely following the best in all things. He summed up the practice of prudence in nine rules. First of all, a man must above all things in the world provide for his own salvation and the forgiveness of his sins. Second, we must be watchful against our spiritual enemies, for Satan is strong and subtle in his suggestions. Third, every man must measure himself by his own strength, and do nothing beyond his ability, a principle which is far from rigorism. Linked with this is the need for confining our activities to those for which God has called us, and choosing only the actions which are good and true. Perkins's seventh rule was that things of profit and pleasure must give place to things that belong to virtue and honesty. Following prudence also meant that we should not trust the fair pretences of men without careful trial. His two final rules are perhaps the most interesting. He suggested that we should adapt ourselves to the times in which we live insofar as this agrees with the Word and keeping a good conscience. This is a perennial problem for the Christian and we need constantly to be examining what we present as the faith in case we are either moving too slowly or too fast. Perkins was very realistic and was content to have something of his ideal rather than nothing.

> If we cannot do the good things that we desire, in that exquisite manner that we would, we must content ourselves with the mean; and in things which are good, and to be done, it is the safest course to satisfy ourselves in doing the less, lest in venturing to do the more, which cannot be, we grow to the extremity, and so fail or offend in our action.[24]

Perkins saw the problem of usury in this light, maintaining that it was better that it should be restrained if it could not be eradicated altogether. Is this the kind of attitude we should be content with in matters which we regard as serious social problems? The balance between realism and idealism in the Christian life is very necessary, even if few manage to achieve it.

Perkins's teaching on temperance shows that the best Puritan practical divinity was far from the gloomy asceticism with which it is usually associated in the popular mind. Certainly Perkins is full of warnings about the dangers of indulgence and becoming enslaved to the things of this world by concentrating on the gift rather than on the Giver. But we must not ignore the equally frequent passages in which he insists that the gifts of God must be used with joy because of the liberty purchased for us by Christ, though this joy must always be in the Lord and presupposes a regard for the glory of God and the good of our neighbors. Perkins even speaks of using meats not simply for the satisfying of our hunger and the quenching of our thirst, "but also freely and liberally, for Christian delight and pleasure."[25] We should receive the creatures as tokens of our reconciliation to God, and being content with what He had given us, we can treat our table as "a lively sermon to us, of God's special providence over our bodies" and "as every creature serves our use, even so we should consecrate ourselves to God, and serve Him with both our souls and bodies."[26]

The fine flower of Perkins's casuistry appears in his little treatise on equity, called *Epieikia,* published in 1604. He saw this virtue as the very marrow of the commonwealth, applying at all levels of society, teaching men when to moderate the extremity of the law and when to enforce it. To follow equity in our dealings with other people meant bearing the infirmities of others and interpreting their actions in the best possible light, for "the more a Christian is rooted in true love, the more infirmities he will pass by."[27] This attitude is not an easy-going tolerance which accepts anything because it has no standards, but is grounded in the attitude of God to sinful men. If God was to deal with us as we deserved, exacting our full debt to him, we would be prostrated by the horrors of conscience and cast into the fires of hell. But in fact God treats us with mercy: "Shall the Lord deal thus moderately with thee, for thy many, and so great sins, and wilt thou deal so hardly with thy brother, in his few small offences against thee?"[28] It is our mercy to others that shows what God's mercy is like to other men.

In brief compass I have attempted to survey Perkins's casuistry. When we read his work, several centuries after he wrote it, there might be questions we would like to raise about the methods and contents of his casuistry. But we can scarcely disagree with his aim of so instructing his hearers and readers that they were able to live responsible lives, expressing the deepest insights of the Reformed faith in conduct characterized by joy, service, and love. Perkins's balanced judgments, deep pastoral insight, and sensitivity to the needs of his day, produced not only books that are still worth the reading, but many imitators, both Puritan and Anglican, in the seventeenth century. In the words of Ames, "left he behind many affected with that study; who by their godly sermons (through God's assistance) made it to run, encrease, and be glorified throughout England."[29]

13

THE PURITAN CONSCIENCE

J. I. Packer

Giving evidence in the recent lawsuit about D. H. Lawrence's novel, *Lady Chatterley's Lover,* Richard Hoggart startled the court by calling Lawrence a Puritan. Asked what he meant (a natural question), he replied that to him a Puritan was a man supremely concerned about conscience. This definition as it stands is either sophistical or stupid, for you could hardly have two more different things than the concern about conscience which Hoggart finds in Lawrence and that which marked the Puritans of history. Nevertheless, Hoggart's formula is a pointer to an important truth. The concern which was really supreme in the minds and hearts of the people called Puritans was a concern about *God*—a concern to know Him truly, and serve Him rightly, and so to glorify Him and to enjoy Him. But, just because this was so, they were in fact very deeply concerned about conscience, for they held that conscience was the mental organ in men through which God brought His Word to bear on them. Nothing, therefore, in their estimation, was more important for any man than that his conscience should be enlightened, instructed, purged, and kept clean. To them, there could be no real spiritual understanding, or any genuine godliness, except as men exposed and enslaved their consciences to God's Word.

In saying this, the Puritans were doing no more than maintain an emphasis which went back to the first days of the Reformation. One thinks, for example, of Luther's momentous words at Worms—"My conscience is captive to the Word of God. I cannot and will not recant anything, for to go against conscience is neither right nor safe. God help me. Amen." One thinks, too, of the famous sentence about the doctrine of justification in chapter 20 of the Augsburg Confession of 1530—"This whole doctrine must be related to that conflict of a terrified conscience (*illud certamen per terrfactae conscientiae*), and without that conflict it cannot be understood." Statements like this make plain the centrality of conscience in the Reformers' understanding of what it meant to be a Christian.

Conscience, to them, signified a man's knowledge of himself as standing in God's presence (*coram Deo*, in Luther's phrase), subject to God's Word, and exposed to the judgment of God's law, and yet—if a believer—justified and accepted nonetheless through divine grace. Conscience was the court (*forum*) in which God's justifying sentence was spoken. Conscience was the soil in which alone true faith, hope, peace, and joy, could grow. Conscience was a facet of the much-defaced image of God in which man was made; and vital Christianity (the "Christian religion" of which Calvin wrote the *Institutes*) was rooted directly in the apprehensions and exercises of conscience under the searching address of God's quick and powerful Word, and the enlightenment of His Holy Spirit. So the Reformers held; and the Puritans too.

But where do we find such an emphasis today? The frightening fact is that at the present time this note is scarcely ever struck. In Western society as a whole, conscience is in decay: apostasy has set in and hence, as always, moral standards are falling. Among intellectuals, conscience is on occasion perverted: one thinks again of D. H. Lawrence and of his camp-followers, and also of Isaiah's curse—"Woe unto them that call evil good, and good evil!" (Isa. 5:20).

In the Christian Church, consciences should be sharp and
alert; but are they? It is to be feared that we whom Christ calls to
be the salt of the earth have lost much of our proper savor. Are
evangelicals noted these days for goodness and integrity? Are we
distinguished in society for sensitiveness to moral issues, and
compassion towards those in need? Do our preachers, earnest
and eloquent as they may be, win for themselves the name that
God gave to Noah—"a preacher of *righteousness*" (2 Peter 2:3)?

Once the so-called "nonconformist conscience" meant something in national life; but does it mean anything now? Once,
Christians were taught to commune with their consciences daily,
in the regular discipline of self-examination under the Word of
God; but how much of this remains today? Do we not constantly
give evidence of our neglect of this secret discipline by unprincipled and irresponsible public conduct? We profess our anxiety
to keep clear of legalistic bondage, but are we not in much
greater danger of antinomian license?

We rightly repudiate the common view that doctrine does not
matter so long as one is upright in life; but if we let our reaction
drive us into the opposite extreme of supposing that one's life
does not matter so long as one is "sound" ("a good Calvinist," we
say), then the beam in our own eye will be worse than the mote
in our brother's. A study of the Puritan conscience, therefore,
may well be bracing and salutary for us at the present time.

The Puritan Idea of Conscience

All Puritan theologians from Perkins are agreed in conceiving of conscience as a rational faculty, a power of moral self-
knowledge and judgment, dealing with questions of right and
wrong, duty and desert, and dealing with them authoritatively,
as God's voice. Often the Puritans appealed to the form of the
word (con-science, from the Latin *con-scientia*) as pointing to
the fact that the knowledge which conscience possesses is
shared knowledge, joint knowledge, knowledge (*scientia*) held
in common with (*con-*) another—namely God. The judgments

of conscience thus express the deepest and finest self-knowledge that a man ever has—i.e., knowledge of himself as God knows him.

William Ames starts his textbook on conscience and casuistry by reproducing Aquinas's definition of conscience as "a mans judgement of himselfe, according to the judgement of God of him,"[1] and variants of this definition often appear in Puritan writings. Ames appeals to Isaiah 5:3 and 1 Corinthians 11:31 as affording its biblical basis. The Edinburgh professor, David Dickson, gives a fuller analysis along the same lines, as follows: "Conscience, as it doth respect ourselves, is . . . the understanding power of our souls examining how matters do stand betwixt God and us, comparing his will revealed, with our state, condition and carriage, in thoughts, words or deeds, done or omitted, and passing judgment thereupon as the case requires."[2]

Conscience, says Thomas Goodwin, is "one part of practical reason,"[3] and the Puritan theologians, still following Aquinas—for they never hesitated to borrow from medieval writers when they judged their teaching to be scriptural—all depict the reasonings of conscience as taking the form of a *practical syllogism*: that is, an inference from two premises, major and minor, concerning either our duty (what we should or should not do) or our state before God (obedient or disobedient, approved or under censure, justified or condemned). Dickson gives the following example of a syllogism about duty:

> *What God hath appointed to be the only rule of faith and maners, I must take heed to follow it as the rule.*
>
> But, *the holy Scripture, God hath appointed to be the only rule of faith and maners.*
>
> Therefore, *I must take heed to follow the Scripture as the only rule.*[4]

Another illustration would be this: God forbids me to steal (major premise); to take this money would be stealing (minor premise); therefore I must not take this money (conclusion).

In a practical syllogism about one's state, the major premise is a revealed truth, functioning as a rule for self-judgment, and the minor is an observed fact about oneself. Ames illustrates with two syllogisms, in the first of which conscience condemns, in the second of which it gives comfort. The first is: "*He that lives in sinne, shall dye: I live in sinne; Therefore, I shall dye.*" The second is "*Whosoever believes in Christ, shall not dye but live. I believe in Christ; Therefore, I shall not dye but live.*"[5]

Though in experience the reasonings of conscience, like most of our thinking processes, are so compressed that we are consciously aware only of the conclusion, anyone who reflects on the way his conscience functions will soon see that this doctrine of the practical syllogism is in fact a correct analysis.

It is a universal experience that conscience is largely autonomous in its operation; though sometimes we can suppress or stifle it, it normally speaks independently of our will, and sometimes, indeed, contrary to our will. And when it speaks, it is in a strange way distinct from us; it stands over us, addressing us with an absoluteness of authority which we did not give it and which we cannot take from it. To personify conscience and treat it as God's watchman and spokesman in the soul is not, therefore, a mere flight of fancy; it is a necessity of human experience.

So then, when the Puritans call conscience "God's deputy and vice-regent within us,"[6] "God's spy in our bosoms,"[7] "God's serjeant, which he employs to arrest the sinner,"[8] we must not dismiss these ideas as just quaint fancies; they represent a serious attempt to do justice to the biblical conception of conscience, which every man's experience reflects—namely, the conception of conscience as a witness, declaring facts (Rom. 2:15; 9:1; 2 Cor. 1:12); a mentor, prohibiting evil (Acts 24:16; Rom. 8:5); and a judge, assessing desert (Rom. 2:15; cf. 1 John 3:20–21). Such passages amply warrant the Puritan conception of conscience as the faculty which God put in man to be a sounding board for His Word in its application to our lives, or (changing the metaphor) a mirror to catch the light of moral and spiritual truth that shines forth from God and to reflect it in concentrated focus upon our

deeds, desires, goals, and choices. The Puritans are simply following the Bible when they depict conscience in this fashion, as
God's monitor in the soul.

To amplify the last thought, we will now cite three typical and
detailed Puritan presentations of conscience and its activity.
Here, first, is Richard Sibbes's picture of conscience as *God's court*
within us, where the last judgment is anticipated (a very common
Puritan thought).

> To clear this further concerning the nature of conscience
> [Sibbes is expounding 2 Cor. 1:12], know that God hath
> set up in a man a court, and there is in man all that are in
> a court.
>
> 1. There is a *register* to take notice of what we have done.
> . . . The conscience keeps diaries. It sets down everything.
> It is not forgotten, though we think it is . . . there is a reg-
> ister that writes it down. Conscience is the register.
>
> 2. And then there are *witnesses.* "The testimony of con-
> science." Conscience doth witness, this have I done, this I
> have not done.
>
> 3. There is *an accuser with the witnesses.* The conscience, it
> accuseth, or excuseth.
>
> 4. And then there is the *judge.* Conscience is the judge.
> There it doth judge, this is well done, this is ill done.
>
> 5. Then there is an *executioner,* and conscience is that
> too. Upon accusation and judgment, there is punish-
> ment. The first punishment is within a man alway before
> he come to hell. The punishment of conscience, it is a
> prejudice (*i.e.* a pre-judgment) of future judgment.
> There is a flash of hell presently (*i.e.* in the present) af-
> ter an ill act. . . . If the understanding apprehend dolor-
> ous things, then the heart smites, as David's "heart

smote him," 1 Sam. 24:5. . . . The heart smites with grief
for the present, and fear for the time to come.

God hath set and planted in man this court of conscience,
and it is God's hall, as it were, where he keeps his first
judgment . . . his assizes. And conscience doth all the
parts. It registereth, it witnesseth, it accuseth, it judgeth,
it executes, it doth all."[9]

Here, second, from John Bunyan's *Holy War*, is an account of
the career of "Mr. Recorder" of the town of Mansoul, first under
sin and then under grace.

Mr. Recorder . . . (was) . . . a man well read in the laws of his
king, and also a man of courage and faithfulness, to speak
truth at every occasion; and he had a tongue as bravely
hung as he had a head filled with judgment. . . . (After Mansoul had fallen under Diabolus) he was much degenerated
from his former king . . . but . . . he would now and then
think upon Shaddai, and have dread of his law upon him,
and then he would speak with a voice as great against Diabolus as when a lion roareth; yea, and would also at certain
times when his fits were upon him—for you must know that
sometimes he had terrible fits—make the whole town of
Mansoul shake with his voice . . . his words . . . were like the
rattling thunder, and also like thunder-claps. . . .[10]

In due course Emmanuel, the king's son, broke through Ear-
gate and sent Captains Boanerges, Conviction, and Judgment,
to take possession of Mr. Recorder's house, an event which
shattered the old gentleman and drove him almost to despair;
but in due course Emmanuel made him the messenger of "a
large and general pardon" to the townspeople, and put him
into office as a preacher, to inculcate the moral law, and with it
all that he had learned, or in future might learn, from "the
Lord Secretary" (the Holy Spirit) concerning the will of Emmanuel's Father.

Here, finally, is William Fenner, in *A Treatise of Conscience*, elaborating this last thought of conscience as a preacher.

> It is a preacher also to tell us our duty both towards God and towards man; yea, it is a powerful preacher; it exhorteth, urgeth, provoketh; yea, the most powerful preacher that can be; it will cause the stoutest and stubbornest heart under heaven to quake now and then. . . . Conscience is joyned in commission with God's own spirit to be an instructor unto us in the way we should walk; so that the spirit and it are resisted or obeyed together, grieved or delighted together. We cannot sinne against conscience but we sinne also against God's spirit; we cannot check our own conscience but we check and quench the holy spirit of God.[11]

Such then, was conscience as the Puritans conceived it.

The Place of Conscience in Puritan Christianity

To bring out the significance of conscience in the Puritan theological scheme, we shall now set it in relation to some of the other major topics on which the Puritans dwelt, and show how some of their most characteristic emphases were bound up with their view of conscience and reflected in their teaching about it.

1. This teaching reflects the Puritan view of *Holy Scripture*.

God, said the Puritans, must control our consciences absolutely. "The conscience . . . must be subjected to him, and to him alone; for he alone is Lord of the conscience. . . . Conscience is God's deputy, and must in the exercise of this office confine itself to the orders and instructions of the sovereign Lord."[12] Hence follows an imperative need to get our consciences fully attuned to the mind and will of God. Otherwise, we cannot help going wrong, whatever we do; for flouting conscience, and following an erring conscience, are both sin. "If you follow it," Baxter explains, "you break the law of God in doing that which he forbids you. If you forsake it, and go against it, you reject the authority of God, in doing that which you think he forbids you."[13]

In his twenty-seventh direction "for faithful serving Christ, and doing good," Baxter warns against the idea that conscience, as such, is an ultimate standard. "Make not your own judgments or consciences your law, or the maker of your duty; which is but the discerner of the law of God, and of the duty which he maketh you, and of your own obedience or disobedience to him. There is a dangerous error grown too common in the world" (it is commoner still today) "that a man is bound to do every thing which his conscience telleth him is the will of God; and that every man must obey his conscience, as if it were the lawgiver of the world; whereas, indeed, it is not ourselves, but God, that is our lawgiver. And conscience is . . . appointed . . . only to discern the law of God, and call upon us to observe it: and an erring conscience is not to be obeyed, but to be better informed. . . ."[14]

But how can God's will be known? Can we tell His requirements with certainty and exactness? Is there any way out of the fogs of pious guesswork on this point into the clear light of certainty? Yes, said the Puritans, there is; the way out is to harness our consciences to the Holy Scriptures, in which the mind of God is fully revealed to us. To them, Scripture was more than the fallible and sometimes fallacious human witness to revelation which is all that some moderns allow it to be; it was revelation itself, the living Word of the living God, divine testimony to God's own redemptive acts and plans, written by the Holy Ghost through human agents in order to give the Church of every age clear direction on all matters of faith and life that could possibly arise.

But, it might be said, such a formula is unrealistic and empty. The Bible is, after all, a very old book, the product of a now long-vanished culture. Most of it was written for people in an utterly different situation from our own. How can it throw clear and direct light on the problems of life today? It can do so, the Puritans would reply, because the God who wrote it remains the same, and His thoughts about man's life do not change. If we can learn to see what principles He was inculcating and applying in His recorded dealings with Israel and the early Church, and to reapply them to our own situation, that will constitute the guidance that we need. And it is to help us to do this that the Holy Spirit has been given.

Certainly, seeing the relevant principles and applying them correctly in each case is in practice an arduous task; ignorance of Scripture, and misjudgment of situations, constantly lead us astray, and to be patient and humble enough to receive the Spirit's help is not easy either. But it remains true nonetheless that in principle Scripture provides clear and exact guidance for every detail and department of life, and if we come to Scripture teachably and expectantly God Himself will seal on our minds and hearts a clear certainty as to how we should behave in each situation that faces us. "God hath appointed means for the cure of blindness and error," wrote Baxter. "Come into the light, with due self-suspicion, and impartiality, and diligently use all God's means, and avoid the causes of deceit and error, and the light of truth will at once show you the truth."[15]

The Puritans themselves sought clear certainty as to God's truth in its practical bearing, and believed that they had been given it. Their very quest sharpened both their moral sensibilities and their insight into the Bible. They would not have been interested in vague moral uplift; what they wanted was to grasp God's truth with the same preciseness of application with which they held that He had revealed it. Because of their concern for preciseness in following out God's revealed will in matters moral and ecclesiastical, the first Puritans were dubbed "precisians." Though ill-meant and derisive, this was in fact a good name for them. Then as now, people explained their attitude as due to peevish cantankerousness and angularity or morbidity of temperament, but that was not how they themselves saw it.

Richard Rogers, the Puritan pastor of Wethersfield, Essex, at the turn of the sixteenth century, was riding one day with the local lord of the manor, who, after twitting him for some time about his "precisian" ways, asked him what it was that made him so *precise*. "O sir," replied Rogers, "*I serve a precise God.*"

If there were such a thing as a Puritan crest, this would be its proper motto. A precise God—a God, that is, who has made a precise disclosure of His mind and will in Scripture, and who expects from His servants a corresponding preciseness of belief and behavior—it was this view of God that created and controlled the historic Puritan outlook. The Bible itself led them to it. And we who share the Puritan estimate of Holy Scripture cannot excuse ourselves if we fail to show a diligence and conscientiousness equal to theirs in ordering our going according to God's written Word.

2. The Puritans' teaching on conscience reflected their view of *personal religion.*

Godliness, to the Puritans, was essentially a matter of conscience, inasmuch as it consisted in a hearty, disciplined, "considerate" (thoughtful) response to known evangelical truth, and centered upon the getting and keeping of a good conscience. As long as a man is unregenerate, his conscience oscillates between being bad and being asleep. The first work of grace is to quicken his conscience and make it thoroughly bad, by forcing him to face God's demands upon him and so making him aware of his guilt, impotence, rebelliousness, and alienation, in God's sight. But the knowledge of pardon and peace through Christ makes his bad conscience good. A good conscience is God's gift to those whom, like Bunyan's pilgrim, He enables to look with understanding at the cross. It is maintained through life by seeking to do God's will in all things, and by constantly keeping the cross in view. Let Fenner explain this.

> Suppose a man have peace of conscience, what must he do to keep and maintain it? I answer,
>
> First, We must labour to prevent troubles of conscience by taking heed that we do nothing contrarie to conscience. . . . Nothing that we get in any evil way will chear and comfort us in a time of need. . . . Wretched is he that alloweth himself in any course which his conscience findeth fault with. It is a good rule the Apostle giveth. *Blessed is he that condemneth not himself in that which he alloweth* (Rom. 14:22): that is, Blessed is he that hath not a condemning conscience. . . .

Secondly, If we will maintain our peace, we must labour to have our hearts grounded in the assurance of the love of God. . . .

Thirdly, We must use the assurance of faith in applying the blood of Christ; we must labour to purge and cleanse our consciences with it. If we find that we have sinned, we must runne presently (i.e., at once) to the blood of Christ to wash away our sinne. We must not let the wound fester or exulcerate, but presently get it healed. . . . As we sinne dayly, so he justifieth dayly, and we must dayly go to him for it. . . . We must every day eye the brazen serpent. Justification is an everrunning fountain, and therefore we cannot look to have all the water at once. . . . O let us sue out every day a dayly pardon. . . . Let us not sleep one night without a new pardon. Better sleep in a house full of adders and venomous beasts than sleep in one sinne. O then be sure with the day to clear the sinnes of the day: Then shall our consciences have true peace."[16]

A good conscience, said the Puritans, is the greatest blessing that there is. "Conscience," declared Sibbes, "is either the greatest friend or the greatest enemy in the world."[17] There is no better friend than a conscience which knows peace with God; for, says Fenner,

"First . . . it is the very head of all comforts. A worthy divine calls it *Abrahams bosome to the soule.* . . .

Secondly, A quiet conscience maketh a man to tast(e) the sweetness of things heavenly and spirituall: It maketh the word to be to him, as to David, *Sweeter than hony.* . . . *I have not departed from thy judgment, O Lord,* saith he (thus saith his conscience) now what followeth next? *How sweet are thy words unto my tast! yea, sweeter than hony unto my mouth* (Ps. 119:103). A good conscience maketh a man tast sweetnesse in prayer . . . in a Sabbath . . . in the Sacraments. . . . What is the reason so few of you tast sweetnesse in these things? The reason is this: Because ye have not the peace of a good conscience. . . .

Thirdly, A good quiet conscience maketh a man tast sweetnesse in all outward things, in meat, in drink, in sleep, in the company of friends. . . . The healthy man onely can take pleasure in recreations, walks, meats, sports, and the like: they yield no comfort to those that are bedrid, or half-dead. But when the conscience is at peace, the soul is all in good health; and so all things are enjoyed with sweetness and comfort.

Fourthly, It sweetneth evils to a man, as trouble, crosses, sorrows, afflictions. If a man have true peace in his conscience, it comforteth him in them all. When things abroad do disquiet us, how comfortable it is to have something at home to chear us? so when troubles and afflictions without turmoil and vex us and adde sorrow to sorrow, then to have peace within, the peace of conscience, to allay all and quiet all, what a happiness is this? When sicknesse and death cometh, what will a good conscience be worth then? Sure, more than all the world besides. . . . The conscience is God's echo of peace to the soul: in life, in death, in judgement it is unspeakable comfort."[18]

A man with a good conscience can face death with equanimity. In his famous account of the crossing of Jordan, Bunyan tells us how "Mr. *Honest* in his life time had spoken to one *Good-conscience* to meet him there, the which he also did, and lent him his hand, and so helped him over."[19] It is through the gift of a good conscience that God answers the prayer, "Lord, now lettest thou thy servant depart in peace" (Luke 2:29).

A good conscience is a tender conscience. The consciences of the godless may be so calloused that they scarcely ever act at all; but the healthy Christian conscience (said the Puritans) is constantly in operation, listening for God's voice in His Word, seeking to discern His will in everything, active in self-watch and self-judgment. The healthy Christian knows his frailty and always suspects and distrusts himself, lest sin and Satan should be ensnaring him unawares; therefore he regularly grills himself before God, scrutinizing his deeds and motives and ruthlessly condemning himself when he finds within himself moral deficiency and dishonesty. This was the kind of self-judging that Paul urged upon the Corinthians at Communion time (1 Cor. 11:31).

The degree of sharp-sightedness which our consciences show in detecting our own real sins (as distinct from the imaginary ones on which Satan encourages us to concentrate) is an index of how well we really know God and how close to Him we really walk—an index, in other words, of the real quality of our spiritual life. The sluggish conscience of a "sleepy," "drowsy" saint is a sign of spiritual malaise. The healthy Christian is not necessarily the extrovert, ebullient Christian, but the Christian who has a sense of God's presence stamped deep on his soul, who trembles at God's Word, who lets it dwell in him richly by constant meditation upon it, and who tests and reforms his life daily in response to it. We can begin to assess our real state in God's sight by asking ourselves how much exercise of conscience along these lines goes into our own daily living.

3. The Puritans' teaching on conscience was reflected in their view of *preaching*.

The most characteristic feature in the Puritan ideal of preaching was the great stress laid on the need for searching applications of truth to the hearers' consciences. One mark of a "spiritual," "powerful" preacher, in the Puritan estimation, was the closeness and faithfulness of application whereby he would "rip up" men's consciences and make them face themselves as God saw them. The Puritans knew that sinful men are slow to apply truth to themselves, quick though they may be to see how it bears on others. Hence unapplied general statements of evangelical truth were unlikely to do much good. Therefore (said the Puritans) the preacher must see it as an essential part of his job to work out applications in detail, leading the minds of his hearers step by step down those avenues of practical syllogisms which will bring the Word right home to their hearts, to do its judging, wounding, healing, comforting, and guiding work. "Because of (this) slownesse in men to . . . apply," declared Ames, "there is a

necessity laid on all Ministers, not only to declare God's will generally, but likewise so farre as they are able, to helpe, and further
both publicly, and in private, the application of it."[20]

Application is the preacher's highway from the head to the
heart. This applicatory part of preaching, says the Westminster
Directory, "albeit it prove a work of great difficulty . . . requiring
much prudence, zeal, and meditation, and to the natural and
corrupt man will be very unpleasant; yet he (the preacher) is to
endeavour to perform it in such a manner, that his auditors may
feel the word of God to be quick and powerful, and a discerner
of the thoughts and intents of the heart; and that, if any unbeliever or ignorant person be present, he may have the secrets of
his heart made manifest, and give glory to God." The Word must
thus cut into the conscience if it is ever to do men good.

Effective application presupposes that the truth applied has
first been shown to be a genuine word from God, and not just a
bright idea of the preacher's. This means that it must have been
drawn out of the preacher's text, in such a way that "the hearers
may discern how God teacheth it from thence" (Westminster Directory), and thus be forced to realize that it comes to them with
the authority of God Himself. Fenner stresses this in connection
with his point that "God's law is the absolute and supreme bond
of conscience."[21]

Whence comes the skill to apply God's truth appropriately in
preaching? From the experience of having God apply His truth
powerfully to oneself. Ordinarily, said the Puritans, it is those
whose own consciences are most deeply exercised by God's truth
who have most power to awaken the consciences of others by pru-
dent and piercing applications. This was part of what John Owen
meant when he laid it down that "if the word do not dwell with
power *in* us, it will not pass with power *from* us."[22] And the Puritans would no doubt have said that this was part of the true meaning of Anselm's assertion, that it is the heart (*pectus*) that makes
the theologian.

It may be asked, Does not this stress on the searching of conscience produce a morbid and introspective type of piety? Does
not this emphasis on constant self-suspicion and self-examination

actually weaken faith, by diverting our gaze from Christ in His fullness to ourselves in our emptiness, so leading us to spiritual despondency and depression? No doubt it would if it were made an end in itself; but, of course, it never was. The Puritans ripped up consciences in the pulpit and urged self-trial in the closet only in order to drive sinners to Christ and to teach them to live by faith in Him. They plied the law only to make way for the gospel, and for the life of dependence on the grace of God. Morbidity and introspectiveness, the gloomy self-absorption of the man who can never look away from himself, is bad Puritanism; the Puritans themselves condemned it repeatedly. A study of Puritan sermons will show that the preachers' constant concern, in all their detailed detecting of sins, was to lead their hearers into the life of faith and a good conscience; which, they said, is the most joyous life that man can know in this world.

The Puritan Conscience in Action

The Puritan concern for a good conscience lent great ethical strength to their teaching. Of all English evangelicals from the Reformation to the present day, the Puritans were undoubtedly the most conspicuous as preachers of righteousness. They were in truth the salt of society in their time, and on many points they created a national conscience which has only recently begun to be eroded. A demand for the sanctification of the Sabbath; plain speaking against demoralizing amusements (bawdy plays, promiscuous dancing, gluttony and drunkenness, salacious fiction); abhorrence of profanity; insistence on a faithful discharge of one's calling and station in life—these were emphases which are still remembered (sometimes applauded, sometimes ridiculed) as "Puritan." Just as Laud had a policy of "thorough" in ecclesiastical affairs, so the Puritans had a policy of "thorough" in the ethical realm; and they went to great pains to give detailed guidance on the duties involved in the various relationships to God and man in which the Christian stood. Among the memorials of their work in this field are the many printed expositions of the ten

commandments; major works like Richard Rogers's *Seven Treatises
. . . the Practice of Christianity* (1603), Perkins's and Ames's volumes
on conscience and casuistry, and Baxter's *Christian Directory*
(1670); and countless small vade-mecums on the Christian life,
from Arthur Dent's *Plain Man's Pathway to Heaven* (1601); to
Thomas Gouge's *Christian Directions Shewing how to walk with God
All the Day long* (1688).

Was all this detailed teaching on Christian conduct a lapse
into a new legalism, and curtailing of Christian liberty? Does it
mark a decline into Pharisaic ways? No; for, first, all this ethical
teaching was evangelically based, as that of the New Testament is.
The supreme ethical motives in Puritanism were gratitude for
grace received, and a sense of responsibility to walk worthy of
one's calling, and there was not the least room in Puritan teaching for self-righteousness; for not only was it constantly stressed
that the Christian works *from* life, not *for* life, but it was also repeatedly emphasized that our best works are shot through with
sin, and contain something that needs to be forgiven.

Then, second, this ethical teaching was all given (again, just
as in the New Testament) not as a code of routine motions to go
through with mechanical exactness, but in the form of attitudes
to be maintained and principles to be applied, so that however
much teaching and advice a man received, he was always left to
make the final decisions and determinations (whether to follow
his pastor's advice; how to apply the given principles in this or
that case; etc.) on his own initiative, as spontaneous, responsible
acts of his own conscience in the sight of God.

Third, Puritan ethical teaching was not authoritarian; it was offered as exposition and application of Scripture, and was to be
checked against Scripture by those who received it, according to the
Protestant principle of the duty of private judgment. The Puritans
did not wish men's consciences to be bound to their own teaching,
as such, but to the Word of God only, and to Puritan teaching only
so far as it was demonstrably in accord with the Word of God.

Fourth, Puritan ethical teaching took the form of a positive
ideal of zealous and wise godliness, at which Christians must always be aiming even though they never fully reach it in this world;

and unattained positive ideals are the death of the legalistic spirit, which can only flourish in an atmosphere of negative restriction where abstinence is regarded as the essence of virtue. In reality, nothing less legalistic in spirit and content than the ethical teaching of the Puritans can well be imagined.

But, it may be said, did not their habitual attention to the minutiae of righteousness, however evangelically motivated, impair their sense of proportion, and make them scrupulous about small matters in which no issues of principle were involved, and which therefore they should have taken in their stride? This was a constant accusation in the Puritans' own day, especially with regard to their insistence that the worship of the Church of England needed to be purified further than had been done in the Elizabethan settlement. The Puritan objections to the surplice, the wedding-ring, the cross in baptism, and kneeling at communion were put down to a "peevish humour" rationalizing itself in an adverse judgment. Again, in 1662, it seemed to many that Richard Baxter and those clergy who shared his views (the majority, it seems, of the ejected) had really no sufficient reason for taking exception to the terms of the Act of Uniformity. In the present tercentenary year of the Great Ejection, it is worth looking at this suggestion to see if there is any substance in it.

Of the poignancy of the choice which Baxter and his friends made there can be no question. They believed in the idea of a national Protestant Church of England; they regarded themselves as already ministers of that Church, and only wanted to continue as such. They were not divine-right Presbyterians; they had no objection to a fixed liturgy (provided it was scriptural), nor to episcopacy (provided it was not prelatical); they accepted the ideal of a national uniformity of religion. Yet they felt bound to refuse the Caroline settlement, and to withdraw, either into silence, or into surreptitious, sectarian forms of church life—two alternatives both of which were to them intensely undesirable, quite apart from the persecution to which the second would expose them. It was a terribly painful decision. Why did they feel bound to take it?

They had four main reasons. First, they could not conscientiously declare "unfeigned assent and consent" to the 1662 Prayer

Book, as the Act of Uniformity required them to do. Not only did that book still retain the ceremonies to which Puritans had been objecting for a century, on the grounds that (a) being tainted with superstitious associations, they were undesirable, and (b) not being scriptural, they should not be made obligatory; it also retained phraseology to which the Puritan spokesmen at the Savoy Conference had definitely objected, such as the declaratory assertion of regeneration in the baptism service, the strong absolution in the Visitation of the Sick, and the reference to the dead man as a brother in the Lord in the funeral service. Even so, had they merely been asked by the Act to assent to the book in the sense of accepting it for regular use, they might have felt free to do so (after all, it was virtually the same book that earlier Puritans had used, many of them without any deviations, up to 1640). But what the Act required was a public declaration of "unfeigned assent *and consent*"; and this seemed to them to imply a degree of approval which they dare not undertake to give, lest they involve themselves in the guilt of perjury.

Second, the Act required them to abjure the Solemn League and Covenant of 1645 (an undertaking to further the work of reforming the English Church so as to bring it closer into line with other Reformed churches, especially the Church of Scotland, and to extirpate the traditional Anglican ecclesiastical hiearchy). But many of the Puritans, even those who did not believe that the New Testament prescribes a thorough-going Presbyterianism, felt unable to renounce the Covenant as an "unlawful oath": neither constitutionally nor theologically could they see anything that was demonstrably unlawful about it. Again, therefore, rather than risk perjury, they declined the abjuration.

Third, they objected to the demand that English clergy who had not hitherto received episcopal orders should be episcopally ordained forthwith. To accept this demand, they held, would be not merely to condemn as invalid their own previous ministrations, but also to condemn by implication all the non-episcopal ministries of Protestant Christendom throughout the world; and this they could not do.

Fourth, these Puritan clergy were prevented from trying to

stretch their consciences by the sense that the eyes of their own flocks—indeed, of all Englishmen—were upon them, and that they could not even appear to compromise principles for which they had stood in the past without discrediting themselves, their calling, and their previous teaching. Calamy records a contemporary comment which focuses their fear—"had the ministers conformed, people would have thought there was nothing in religion." The Puritan clergy held that they should be ready to confirm what they had publicly maintained as truth by suffering, if need be, rather than risk undermining their whole previous ministry by what would look like time-serving abandonment of principle. Therefore, once they had become clear that the terms of the Act of Uniformity were *prima facie* intolerable, they did not expend any energy on trying to find ways and means of wriggling around them. Rather than appear to be trifling with truth, they withdrew into the wilderness.

Was this scrupulosity? Was their attitude one of a mere rationalized peevishness? Surely not. It is, rather, the supreme illustration of the Puritan conscience in action. Two ruling axioms of Puritan casuistry were (a) that no known truth must be compromised or denied in practice and (b) that no avoidable sin must be committed, however great the good to which such compromise and sin might lead. Expediency is no warrant for unprincipled action; the end does not justify the means. Whether Baxter and his friends were right in their verdict on the Restoration settlement we need not now discuss, any more than we need pass judgment on the action of men like Gurnall and Trapp, who conformed; Reynolds, who became Bishop of Norwich; and Leighton, who received both episcopal ordination and consecration to become a Bishop in Scotland. All we wish to do here is to display the action of Baxter and his friends as an instance of costly conscientiousness. The suggestion that—to put it bluntly—the root of their nonconformity was cussedness, wounded pride, and an obstinate refusal to climb down, is simply ridiculous. Perjury, and reformation, and the sufficiency of Scripture, and the dispensability of bishops, were matters of theological principle as far as they were concerned; and they kept a good conscience in the only way open to them, or to any Christian—by following truth as it appears from Scripture, and refusing to sell it, or betray it, for any consideration in the world.

So the conclusion I would draw is simply this: that such conscientiousness as marked all Puritan religion, and was supremely manifested in the ejection of 1662, is a necessary Christian virtue at all times. It is man's proper response to God's immutable revealed truth. It may be costly, as it was in 1662; but without it, churchmanship becomes irreligion, a Christian profession becomes an insult to God. These are compromising days in the Church's life; that, perhaps, is only to be expected when the very existence of revealed Truth is so widely doubted or denied. But if we believe that God has spoken in His Son, and the Bible is His own Word of testimony to that revelation—if, in other words, we hold the Puritan view of Scripture—then, as we said earlier, the uncompromising fidelity to Bible truth which marked the Puritans should mark us also. May God give us light to see His truth, consciences to apply it and live by it, and conscientiousness to hold it fast, whatever the cost, in these Laodicean days.

14

THOMAS BOSTON OF ETTRICK

D. J. Innes

Some of the great Scottish divines of past generations have been "rediscovered" of recent years; others remain in comparative obscurity. Boston of Ettrick, unfortunately, belongs to this latter group. And yet, I verily believe, he was one of the greatest, one of the saintliest, men who has ever adorned the Church in Scotland. His life was characterized by a most close and intimate walk with God; his ministry, in often difficult, sometimes heartbreaking, circumstances, was mightily owned of God; and his potent influence for Christ and the gospel of His saving grace continued, through his writings, for generations after he himself had gone to his reward.

Many, through the years, have borne witness to the worth of Boston, the power of his ministry, and the amazing influence of his written works. The late Dr. Alexander Whyte, recommending the new edition of Boston's autobiography, which appeared in 1899, had this to say: "His sound and commanding common sense, his immense industry, his great learning, attained to amid

259

unparalleled difficulties, his sometimes Shakespearean style, his life of faith and prayer and pastoral efficiency and success, all combine to make Boston's *Memoirs of his Life, Time and Writings* a book to be always at hand in every Scottish manse, as well as in every well-read, patriotic, and pious Scottish home." His biographer, Dr. Andrew Thomson, one-time minister of Broughton Place, Edinburgh, says, "The assertion is not likely to be challenged that, if Scotland had been searched during the earlier part of the eighteenth century, there was not a minister of Christ within its bounds who, alike in his personal character and in the discharge of his pastoral functions, approached nearer to the apostolic model than did this man of God. It is a fact that, even before he died, men and children had come to pronounce his name with reverence. It had become a synonym for holy living." In other words, what Robert Murray McCheyne was to early nineteenth century Scotland, Thomas Boston was to early eighteenth century Scotland.

Witness has been borne not only to the greatness of the man, but also to the influence of his message, as it has been communicated to men of many generations through his written works. H. G. Graham, the author of *Social Life of Scotland* (1901), who was in no way sympathetic to the evangelical faith, has to admit that, in his *Fourfold State*, Boston "moved the hearts and expressed the faith of a large proportion of the people." Dr. Thomas McCrie, that great authority on Scottish life and letters, himself born in the same town as Boston, asserted that the *Fourfold State* was a book that had "contributed more than any other work to mould the religious sentiments of the Scottish people." Certainly it was to be found, along with the Holy Scriptures, and Bunyan's glorious dream, in virtually every humble cottage and stately home over a large part of Scotland, in the eighteenth century. Jonathan Edwards, in a letter of 1747 to his Scottish correspondent, Thomas Gillespie (who was a convert of Boston's ministry), expresses the opinion that the *Fourfold State* showed "Mr. Boston to have been a truly great divine."

Is it not time that those who seek to live with God, and live for God, in the twentieth century—an age, in some ways, not unlike the age of Boston, when the love of many has grown cold—should turn back to ponder anew the lessons that they might learn from the life and ministry, the trials and the triumphs of Thomas Boston of Ettrick?

Life and Times

As you will know, the Restoration of Charles II in 1660 brought great and grievous changes in the ecclesiastical affairs of Scotland. "In the latter end of March the parliament did rescind all the acts approving the National Covenant, the Solemn League and Covenant, and the abolishing of bishops in Scotland; and they rescinded all acts for presbyterian government during the king's pleasure."[1] Thus, the Glasgow and Westminster assemblies, Cromwell and the Long Parliament, the Confession of Faith, the Solemn League and Covenant, were all blotted out. Furthermore, on September 6, the Presbyterian system was summarily set aside when the obsequious Scottish Council ordained the Lyon King-at-Arms "to pass to the Market Cross, and make publication of his majesty's pleasure for restoring the kirk to the right government of bishops," "and to require all his subjects to compose themselves to a cheerful acquiescence and obedience to the same . . . commanding all, if they find any failing in their obedience thereto . . . that they commit them to prison. . . ." About 400 of the best ministers in Scotland were ejected from their charges; and there followed the classic covenanting period—a reign of terror; the murder of Archbishop Sharpe on Magus Muir (1679); and the Killing Times.

It was during this period—in the year 1676—that Thomas Boston was born in Duns, an important little town in Berwickshire. His parents were godly folk, who refused to bend to prelatic authority, and suffered severely for it. One of Thomas's earliest memories was of being taken to prison, to provide company for his father in his loneliness.

It was James II, the Papist, who, to meet his own case, conceded in 1687 liberty of worship, within certain restrictions, all over the kingdom. Most of the sufferers in Scotland were able to take advantage of the indulgence.

This was very significant so far as Thomas Boston was concerned. For one of those now free to exercise his ministry again unmolested was Henry Erskine, the father of Ebenezer and Ralph. He established himself at Whitsome, only some five miles from Duns. Considerable numbers of the Duns people, weary of the sapless and Christless preaching to which they had been constrained to listen in their native town, and no longer held back by the dread of fine or imprisonment, gladly walked to Whitsome Sunday by Sunday. John Boston took his eleven-year-old son; and it was under Erskine's preaching that Thomas was effectually converted to Christ. He refers to his conversion, in his *Soliloquy on the Art of Man Fishing,* in these terms: "Little was thou thinking, O my soul, on Christ, heaven, or thyself, when thou went to the Newtoun of Whitsome to hear a preaching; when Jesus Christ first dealt with thee thou got an unexpected cast." Thereafter, Erskine's ministry continued to be richly blessed to Boston, so that he would walk those five miles come wind come weather—even when he had to go it alone—to obtain food for his soul and refreshment for his spirit. It is interesting, and not surprising, to learn that Boston's first sermon—preached when he was twenty-one—"recalled the powerful ministry of Erskine to at least one of his hearers, who spoke contemptuously of him as 'Mr. Henry Erskine's disciple.'"

James II did not last long; and in 1688 came William of Orange and the Revolution Settlement. This meant much for the Church in Scotland. Presbyterianism was reconstituted; the 1699 Act of Supremacy was abolished; the ejected ministers were restored; and the Church was re-established on the basis of the Confession of Faith and Presbyterian polity. But the settlement was not made by John Knox or Andrew Melville, but by William Carstares—and there were elements of compromise in it: e.g., a middle measure was adopted with regard to patronage. The voice of the people was recognized as a potential element in the settlement of ministers, but the right of nomination was conferred on the heritors and elders. And again, many episcopal incumbents, found willing to submit to the new order of things, were allowed to continue in their charges. Bishop Burnet says of them that they "were ignorant to a reproach, many of them openly vicious, and the worst preachers he ever heard." Many see in them the roots of the moderate party, which came to dominate the Church of Scotland in the eighteenth century.

This, briefly sketched, was the state of the Church into the ministry of which Boston was in 1697 licensed (aged twenty-one), and in 1699 ordained. The situation with regard to patronage explains why he had such a long and trying period of waiting before he was settled in his first parish. Boston would not curry favor with patrons and heritors: he believed that God would clearly overrule and set him in the place of His appointment. Thus it was that in no less than seven parishes, where the people would have called, hostile forces intervened and prevented his settlement.

From the Revolution until 1715 the difficulties of the Church of Scotland were mainly connected with its relations to the state, to the Dissenters, and to Prelatists. After 1715 its difficulties for many years were internal, and rose out of questions of doctrine and administration.

Both of these periods are reflected in the life and experience of Boston. The former may be illustrated by two facts. Firstly, Boston was a non-juror, i.e, he refused to take the "Oath of Abjuration" which Queen Anne's Parliament sought to lay upon every minister of the Church. It was a startling and arbitrary measure—unnecessary as a pledge for the loyalty of men who, on their entrance to the ministry, had taken the oath of allegiance to the crown; and in terms so vague and ambiguous as to be perplexing to men of tender conscience. Even later, when it was made more palatable by the addition of modifying clauses, Mr. Boston stood firm, prepared to suffer the loss of all things rather than sin, and openly declaring in characteristic words that "the oath could not be cleansed, and that, like the leper's house, it needed to be taken down."

Second, in Ettrick, in Boston's earlier years there—he was inducted there on the same day as the Act of Union came into force, May 1, 1707—there was a Mr. McMillan, minister and leader of a party among the Presbyterians who had refused to go in with the Revolution Settlement, or to swear allegiance to the new dynasty. Their presence, and constant agitation of points of difference in which he was the frequent object of attack, tried Boston's sensitive nature, while malcontents and fugitives from discipline were apt to seek refuge in the hostile camp. Boston never entertained separatist principles. In his famous sermon on "The evil and danger of schism," preached at Ettrick in 1708, he argued strongly against the Cameronian position, and pled for the unity and peace of the Church. "There are no corruptions among us, whether real or pretended, which the church obligeth them to approve or join in the practice of, as terms of communion with her," etc.

The latter period is also illustrated by two facts from Boston's life—points to which we shall give more attention later: the part he played in the "Marrow Controversy" of 1717–22, and the protest he lodged against the sentence passed on Professor Simson by the Assembly of 1729.

The first Original Secession Associated Presbytery was constituted in December 1733. The first presbytery of the Relief church came into being in 1752. Thomas Boston did not live long enough to witness either secession. He died on May 20, 1732, aged fifty-six, having been minister of Simprin, 1699–1707, and of Ettrick, 1707–32. His son, who became minister of Jedburgh, joined Mr. Gillespie in the first Relief Presbytery.

The Saint

The outstanding characteristic of Thomas Boston was his saintliness; he was a man separated unto God, a holy man. We are reminded of the words of Robert Murray McCheyne: "How awful a weapon in the hand of God is a holy minister." Thomas Boston was such a one. Robert Chambers, writing in 1834, states that Boston's name was still held in great reverence by the people of the south of Scotland. "Who was the best man that ever lived?" was a question which passed among the boys of Peebles. "Mr. Boston, minister of Ettrick," was the answer.

I would like us to look a little closer at three aspects of
Boston, the saint: namely, his prayer life, his humility, and his afflictions. They are in fact closely connected and interwoven—but
for the purposes of study we may treat them separately.

His Prayer Life

Innumerable quotations could be produced to illustrate this.
A few, which particularly struck and challenged me, must suffice.
In his student days his habits were eminently devotional. While at
Kennet, as tutor to Colonel Bruce's stepson, he had what he described as a "thriving time for his soul." He set aside times for fasting, which did not however so much consist in partial abstinence
from food as in temporary isolation, in which he gave himself
with mingled prayer to self-examination, especially with reference to heart sins. He had also his seasons of prolonged secret
devotion, in which "prayer overflowed its banks like Jordan in the
time of harvest." The same was true of his years as a probationer,
while he waited for God's call to God's place to come.

His biographer records, "We notice in this trying period of
his life the same abounding in prayer, and severe heart-searching
and striving against heart sins, which no eye could see but God's,
as we remarked in his student life. Again and again we meet with
such exclamations as 'Oh, how my heart hates my heart!'" And,
as you read his memoirs, recounting the whole course of his ministry—there is hardly a page where he does not refer to his retir-
ing into his closet to lay some matter before the Lord. "In every
condition he found an errand to the heavenly mercy seat. For
comfort in affliction, guidance in perplexity, help to repel temptation, strength for hourly duties and double strength for sacred
work, he hastened with his empty vessel to the fountain of life;
sometimes, when accusing himself of spiritual decay, or dreading
the thought of divine desertion, 'wrestling for the blessing until
the dawning of the day.'"

It is impossible to labor this point too much: it was the fundamental secret of both the man and his ministry and authorship
in the highest forms of blessing, to this one holy habit, in which
he laid hold on omnipotence! The same outward action would

have been powerless and fruitless without this wrestling devotion, which said, "I will not let Thee go, except Thou bless me." Boston's memoirs remind me of nothing so much as of Brainerd's *Journals* and of Andrew Bonar's *Diary*. The primary secret of these men's mighty ministries is to be found in their secret lives with God.

Boston wrote a *Memorial concerning Personal and Family Fasting and Humiliation*—and I would like to close this section with a couple of quotations from that work. A word of comfort—"The laying over of a matter on the Lord, believing in prayer, gives great ease to a burdened heart; it turns a fast sometimes into a spiritual feast." And a word of warning—"Lay no weight on the quantity of your prayers—that is to say how long or how many they are. These things avail nothing with God, by Whom prayers are not numbered but weighed." Oh for men of prayer in the work of the ministry today!

His Humility

This, of course, is inseparably linked with the previous section: prayer and pride just don't go together! And if the text for the previous section was "men ought always to pray and not to faint," the text for this section must be "seekest thou great things for thyself? Seek them not." For this is the particular aspect of Boston's humility to which I think we should give our attention here.

Boston was an extremely able man—linguist, theologian, and scholar. And he was an outstanding and mighty preacher. Yet he was content to pass his days in two comparatively small country parishes, faithfully shepherding his flock. He believed that God had sent him there, and he was content. He never sought the limelight, though he was prepared fearlessly to take his stand for truth and righteousness, when he felt that laid upon him.

I suppose the outstanding example of Boston's humility was his readiness to accept the call to Simprin. Simprin was an unattractive place. The parish was of the smallest, having only 88 examinable persons. The stipend was meager in the extreme. He disliked the idea of settling in such a mean place where he would be buried out of sight. But, on reflection, he knew that God was calling him there—and he went. And we may well ask what would have happened to him, and to his ministry, had he refused.

His Afflictions

Here I believe we find one of the outstanding lessons of Boston's life and ministry. Jesus said: ". . . every branch (in Me) that beareth fruit, he purgeth it, that it may bring forth more fruit." Are we, like Boston, seeking to go all the way with God? Then we must not be surprised when the heavenly Husbandman's sharp pruning knife cuts us to the quick—and leaves us bleeding and mystified. His ways are not our ways; indeed His ways are passing strange.

The sum of Boston's afflictions can be told in few words; but don't gloss over their implications—the accompanying desolation, anguish, pain, and sorrow. He lost both his parents comparatively early—his mother in 1691, when he was only fifteen (and this event threatened for a time to put an end to his hopes of entering the ministry); and his father in 1701, when he was not yet twenty-five and recently settled in Simprin. Obviously a loving and devoted father himself, he had the sad experience of laying six of his own bairns in the grave—two while he was still at Simprin, and four at Ettrick. He himself was often ill, suffering from much pain and weakness, physically. And, as though this were not enough, his last twelve years were clouded by a great and grievous domestic grief. In the summer of 1720 his wife, to whom he was deeply devoted, began to show unmistakable symptoms of insanity. To quote his own words: "her imagination was vitiated in a particular point, to her great disquietment, accompanied with bodily infirmities and maladies exceeding great and numerous." And this dark eclipse of the spirit, though sometimes diminished, seldom wholly passed away. Indeed, in later years, the gloom became darker still. It touched Boston on his tenderest point. At length the dear sufferer was confined to one apartment, which her husband touchingly called "the inner prison," and there she spent months and years, the subject of a mental malady which no science or human device could even mitigate. Allusions to this great sorrow appear again and again in Boston's diary, and, as we read them, we seem to hear his groans and sighs.

God, in His wisdom, permitted these afflictions, and used them to mellow Boston's character and enrich his ministry. Two tiny glimpses of the way that suffering was blessed to him must suffice here. The first comes from his closet. At a time of great bodily suffering, he says, "My heart was made by grace to say, Welcome, welcome; and kissed the rod, for the sake of Him Who groaned and died on the cross for me; and I was even made to weep for joy in His dying love to me." Thus, his own pain gave him a greater appreciation of his Savior, and a deeper love for Him who had suffered so unspeakably on behalf of sinners.

The second is that, next to his *Fourfold State*, his series of sermons published under the title of *The Crook in the Lot* have been the most widely read, and the most greatly blessed of God, of all his writings. The subtitle of that series was "The sovereignty and wisdom of God in the afflictions of men, together with a Christian deportment under them." The foundation truths which he sought to expound were (1) that whatever crook there is in anyone's lot, it is of God's making; (2) that whatever God sees meet to mar, no one will be able to mend in his lot; and (3) that the considering of the crook in the lot as the work of God—that is, of His making—is the proper means to bring one to a Christian deportment under it. Thus we see how suffering gave Boston an understanding of affliction, and ability to help and comfort his fellows in it, which he could not have gained in any other way.

The Minister

At an early age Boston felt called to the work of the ministry; and through years of preparation—in a notary's office in Duns, at college in Edinburgh, and in practical training at Dumfries and Kennet—he looked forward to that work, with a mixture of apprehension and keen anticipation. He knew increasingly that God had laid His hand upon him to this end.

The Call to a Charge

Boston was sorely tried on this issue three times in the course of his life: during the long period of waiting for a first charge; when the call to Ettrick came to him; and later, while at Ettrick, when a call was sent to him by the people of Closeburn. To ponder the sections of his memoirs recording these different crises is, I believe, to learn some very significant lessons. May I pick out two or three?

Boston *was never in a hurry*: he certainly did not commit himself to the first suggestion made. It was 2¼ years after his licensing before he was settled in Simprin. Toward the end of that period he recorded that "he had now reached the full sea-mark of his perplexing circumstances. He felt like one standing in the dark, and not knowing what his next step should be." Again, a long time elapsed between the first suggestion that Boston move to Ettrick, and his actual induction there. During that time he weighed the whole matter up most carefully, sought the advice of friends, and above all sought the mind of the Lord. You can read all about it in his memoirs; it goes on for pages! He himself testifies that the word, "He that believeth shall not make haste," was helpful to him.

Boston *never took the initiative*, and, when an invitation was extended to him, he made his own position abundantly plain to those inviting him. This was no easier in his day than it is in ours. Much could be said on this subject—but I think it is best summed up by a quotation from his *Soliloquy*. There, among the "rules of carnal wisdom," he sets down these: "Labour to get neat and fine expressions, for that doth very much commend a preaching to the learned, and without these they think nothing of it. Endeavour to be somewhat smooth in preaching and calm, and do not go out upon the particular sins of the land, or of the persons to whom thou preachest. Be but fair especially to them that have the strike in parishes, till you be settled in a parish to get stipend."

It need hardly be added that Boston *was never swayed by other than the highest motives*. The two considerations which perhaps weighed most in taking him to Ettrick were, first, that the call had come unsought; and, second, the great need that he saw to exist in that parish. When it came to the Closeburn call, in 1716–17, promising higher emolument and increased social prestige, Boston increasingly felt that it was not of the Lord; and eventually pled most movingly, before the Commission of Assembly, for his retention in Ettrick. How many men, in the Church of Scotland today, one wonders, would be prepared to do that?

The Preaching of the Word

Boston was preeminently and outstandingly a preacher of the Word. Perhaps we have taken too long to get to this central point? But no: for I believe that, behind the public power, there is always the private price; and how great that price is in many cases God alone fully knows.

As a probationer Boston was greatly used in the preaching of the Word. Wherever pulpits were thrown open to him, testimonies were received of the highest forms of blessing which multitudes had derived from his ministry. It was a frequent experience to be told by some who came to him with streaming eyes that his words had been to them the seeds of a new and heavenly life; while others would be found waiting at the church gates to tell him, with mingled wonder and gratitude, how, while unknown to him, he had seemed by his searching representations to have been reading their history and their hearts.

Boston's power and usefulness as a preacher increased as the years went on. In the earlier years of his Simprin life, he had frequent difficulty in fixing on a text. Sometimes even more time was consumed in finding a text that suited his present state of mind than was usually occupied in the composition of a sermon. But in his later years at Simprin, it was his custom to select large paragraphs of Scripture, which in their succession of verses, supplied texts for many sermons. We find him, for instance, lingering over the few verses of the epistle to the church at Laodicea from January to the end of May, and apparently loath to leave the passage even then. In his mid-week service he preached from the Song of Solomon for nearly three years, 1704–07!

Each Lord's Day he preached forenoon and afternoon, and in the evening he expounded the Shorter Catechism. He instituted a weekly service on Thursday, and on Tuesday evening presided at the weekly meeting for conference and prayer. He began his work at Simprin by preaching "the doctrine of man's natural state, judging the sight and sense thereof to be the foundation of all real religion." He followed this up by preaching on "Christ the remedy," and then on "the application of the remedy." His power lay in his strenuous and persuasive declaration of the love of God in Christ to sinners of mankind. His fine sermon from the text "Compel them to come in" begins: "And are they not happy that are in? And why will ye not come in too? Christ's house is not yet filled. Many have come in, but there is room for more. And we are sent to compel you to come in . . . ," etc. He once exclaimed, in the context of the controversy raging in the kirk in his later years, "Our great business (is) to preach Christ, if we could get leave to do it for our divisions. . . . Oh, sirs, what would come of the many perishing souls up and down Scotland, that are strangers to Christ and their own soul's state, if, as these men would have it, all should leave us, and we be left to preach to the empty walls, or hold our tongues?"

So much could be said about Boston's preaching ministry, and the thousands who attended on it—especially in his later years. But I must desist; and you must read it for yourselves.

The Work of Visitation

Boston was obviously not only a mighty preacher, but also a faithful pastor—and he related the one to the other, applying the preaching in the homes, and gaining suggestions for future sermons from the homes. It is when we see these two parts of his ministry combining and cooperating, preaching and pastoral visitation, and all of course conjoined with prayer, that we can the more easily account for that rich harvest of souls which he was again and again called upon to reap. The living sympathy of the man watered the good seed of the Word which had been sown. And those home visits, winning the affection and the confidence of the people, invested his preaching with a double power, and opened the way for the entrance of the Word. Boston visited each of his families at least once a year, in Ettrick—until increasing infirmity no longer made it possible. Paragraphs such as this—actually taken from his Simprin ministry—are not infrequent in the memoirs: "Being with E. P. the night before she died, I had no satisfaction in converse with her; which affected me exceedingly. Thereupon I came in to my closet, and set myself to wrestle with God on her account; and then went to her again, and was much comforted in her; so that my spirit was more than ordinarily elevated. She said she fixed on that word, 'Thou hast played the harlot with many lovers; yet return again to Me, saith the Lord.' "

The Courts of the Church

It is clear that Boston adhered to his ordination oaths, and played a faithful and not ineffective part in the work of presbytery, synod, and general assembly. In October 1702, Boston was chosen for the important office of clerk to the synod of Merse and Teviotdale; and he held that office until 1711. He fulfilled his duties in this post in an exemplary manner, gaining not only the approval, but also the praise, of not a few. For example, Lord Minto, an eminent statesman, who had also been a judge, went so far as to say that "Mr. Boston was the best clerk he had ever known in any court, civil or ecclesiastical."

The Controversialist

Boston came into greatest prominence in the General Assembly of the Church, first in the course of the Marrow Controversy, 1717–22; and then over the case of Prof. Simson of Glasgow. He was not by nature a contentious or a bellicose man; nor did he desire to attract public attention. But in both these significant cases he felt in duty bound to take his stand openly on the side of what he considered to be truth and righteousness.

The Marrow Controversy

The *Marrow of Modern Divinity* was first published in London, in 1645; and it was one of the books specifically commended by the Westminster Assembly of divines. In substance it was "an exposition of the federal theology—the difference between the covenant of works and the covenant of grace being carefully explained." Thus, its says: ". . . the law of Christ in regard of substance and matter, is all one with the law of works. Both these laws agree in saying, Do this. But here is the difference. The one saith, Do this and live: and the other saith, Live and do this. The one saith, Do this for life; the other saith, Do this from life." Extracts from Reformed and Puritan divines, along with some original material, were woven into a conversation in which Evangelista, the champion of the true gospel way, disposes of all his opponents.

In 1700 Boston, who had at the time no clear views on the doctrine of grace and was concerned to get the claims of God's law and the relation of a child of grace thereto satisfactorily adjusted, found a copy of the first part of the *Marrow* in one of the houses in his parish. "What time, precisely, this happened, I cannot tell," he records, "but I am very sure that, by the latter end of the year 1700, I had not only seen that book, but digested the doctrine thereof in a tolerable measure; since by that time I was begun to preach it, as I had occasion, abroad." "I rejoiced in it as a light which the Lord had seasonably struck up to me in my darkness."

Some fifteen years after Boston had discovered the *Marrow*, increasing conflict arose within the Church as a whole concerning the nature of the covenant of grace, whether it was absolute or conditional. The charge of Arminianism, for example, was brought against Prof. Simson of Glasgow. And during an assembly debate in 1717, Boston told John Drummond of Crieff of the *Marrow*, and of what it had come to mean to him. Drummond followed this up, succeeded in obtaining a copy, and told James Webster of Edinburgh about it. He, in turn, brought it to the attention of James Hog of Carnock, who, in 1718, reissued it. At about the same time the assembly debate concerning the action of the presbytery of Auchterarder further charged the atmosphere. This presbytery, concerned for the doctrine of free grace, was requiring students applying for license to sign certain propositions, one of which read, "I believe that it is not sound and orthodox to teach that we must forsake our sins in order to our coming to Christ." The sinister look of this proposition led to its condemnation by the assembly. But the fault of the proposition was in its wording rather than in its meaning and intention. And the assembly's action seemed to Boston and his friends to be a direct blow at the doctrine of free grace.

Into this confused atmosphere of disagreement and debate came the new edition of the *Marrow*. It was immediately hailed by one party with opprobrium, and by the other with delight. Its wealth of paradoxical language, and what some regarded as "excessive Paulinism," gave Principal Hadow of St. Andrews, Alan Logan, of Culross, and Robert Wodrow, the historian, opportunity to proceed against it. They succeeded in convincing the Assembly of 1720 that it taught such heresies as a universal atonement, that assurance is of the essence of faith, that holiness is not necessary to salvation, and that the believer is not under the moral law as a rule of life. The accusers of the *Marrow*, who, it should be noted, were a mixture of logical, or hyper-Calvinists (like Hadow), and Moderates of the later type, undoubtedly feared that it would fortify antinomianism. But its champions, like Boston, Gabriel Wilson, and Ebenezer Erskine, were what we might call religious Calvinists, persuaded that it taught the pure doctrine of free grace, and that it would be an antidote against "neonomian" or "Baxterian" propaganda.

To take but one example. One of the most fruitful phrases which the *Marrow* bequeathed to Scottish religion was "the deed of gift and grant to mankind lost." The assembly divines held that this phrase implied a universal atonement, whereas the Confession taught that Christ died for the elect alone. The Marrowmen, who also believed in a limited atonement, replied that though "the purchase and application of redemption is peculiar to the elect . . . yet the warrant to receive Him is common to all." The *Marrow* phraseology may appear "to look like a cheat upon mankind to assert the one and yet to teach the other," as John Grant of Auchenlek suggested in a letter to Wodrow. But this is the point: the Marrowmen defied logic, and kept their grip on "the deed of gift and grant to mankind lost." How else could they take seriously the command to preach the gospel to every creature? The missionary passion, which, a century later, began to possess the Church, owed much to their unswerving tenacity.

In the Assembly of 1721 Boston, along with eleven of his brethren, laid before the assembly "The Representation," remonstrating against the condemnation of the *Marrow,* and the prohibition imposed on ministers, forbidding them to preach, write, print, or circulate anything in its favor. This "Representation" was written with fearless candor, and yet in a respectful and conciliatory spirit. It was condemned, and its twelve supporters— the Marrowmen—were rebuked at the bar of the assembly. In his diary Mr. Boston has this record: "I received the rebuke and admonition as an ornament put upon me for the cause of truth."

The Simson Controversy

As we have already had occasion to notice, in 1714–17, Professor Simson of Glasgow was accused of teaching Arminianism. He was following the "Baxterian" or "neonomian" line of teaching; that is, that the gospel is a new law, whose saving benefits the sinner may obtain by fulfilling the divine conditions of repentance and faith. It claimed to be strictly orthodox, but men like Boston, Webster, and Hog believed that such a theology, conceding a saving initiative to the corrupt will of the sinner, must be disruptive of the doctrine of sovereign grace. The mild rebuke which the assembly gave to Simson, in 1717, was in reality a tacit admission that neonomianism, in some form or other, had come to stay.

Simson's mind then turned to speculation on the doctrine of the Trinity; and for three years (1727–29) the presbytery of Glasgow and the General Assembly, with the whole nation as intensely interested auditors, sought to discover whether Simson really taught his students heretical, Arian doctrine. What Simson appears really to have been doing was that he was including in the special properties of the Father, incommunicable to the Son and to the Holy Spirit, certain attributes, such as necessary existence which are essential qualities of true deity.

Eventually, the assembly acted. But, when it did, it was only to suspend Simson from teaching and preaching, and to leave him in possession of all the emoluments of his office. Boston felt that this sentence was "not adequate to the offence"—and rose in the assembly of 1729 to make a lone protest. "I cannot help thinking," he began, "that the cause of Jesus Christ, as to the central and supreme point of His deity, has been at the bar of the assembly requiring justice; and, as I am shortly to answer at His bar for all I do or say, I dare not give my assent to the decision of this Act. . . ." He stood alone, though friends, not members of that year's assembly—like Gabriel Wilson, Thomas Hog, and the Erskines—supported his stand. It must have taken very considerable moral courage, especially in an aging and sorely tried man.

The Scholar

In conclusion, we must not overlook the genuine scholarship, and the literary labors, of Thomas Boston.

He was an able linguist. He left school at the age of thirteen; and by then he knew Latin well, so that he could translate any author at sight. It may be comforting to you to know, however, that he does make this comment about his studies in Edinburgh: "I was also for a while at that time, I suppose, with Mr. Alexander Rule, Professor of Hebrew; but remember no remarkable advantage I had thereby!" But the comfort turns to wonder as we learn that at Simprin he acquired French and Dutch, and made progress in Hebrew. And in 1710, he became the proud possessor of a Hebrew Bible, and "plied the original close." This became his darling study. Indeed, he not only wrote an essay of considerable length on the divine origin and authority of the Hebrew accents, but he also translated it into Latin, which in those days of course was the common language of learned divines. His solid learning, and the ingenuity of his reasonings, along with his modesty and outshining piety, were recognized by all—and his work had a considerable circulation.

He was a thorough theologian. One example, over and above the outstanding example provided by his *Fourfold State*, must suffice. From time to time it happened, especially in his early years at Simprin, that in the course of his Sunday preparation he came across questions which at one and the same time perplexed and interested him. They were theological problems which were new to him, and required more of thought and reading and prayer satisfactorily to answer than he could give at the moment. He did not cast them aside, but carefully noted them, that he might turn back to them for concentrated study when the opportunity arose. In a large volume, which he called his *Miscellanea*, he stated the subject in the form of queries, leaving an ample number of blank pages for recording the answer when the knot of difficulty had been untied, and for stating the reasons by which his conclusions had been reached.

He was an influential author. We have had occasion to refer to most of his major publications already. They reflect pretty accurately the different aspects of Thomas Boston—the man and his ministry. The first place must, of course, be given to the *Fourfold State*, which shows us Boston the theologian and preacher. Then his early work, *A Soliloquy on the Art of Man Fishing*—written when he was still a probationer—shows us Boston the evangelist. *The Crook in the Lot* shows us Boston the tender pastor, able to comfort the afflicted from his own deep experience of affliction. And, published in the last year of his life, his *Memorial concerning Personal and Family Fasting and Humiliation* shows us Boston the saint. There were other works published posthumously—his exposition of the Shorter Catechism, edited by his son; series of sermons, notably his communion sermons; and, last but not least, his memoir of himself, his life, time, and writings—written primarily for his children, and dedicated to them.

The *Fourfold State* was one of those books by which God has chosen to work, and work mightily; and a little more must be said of it. The writing of it took Boston much time, and perhaps even more prayer. For years he hesitated to launch it on the uncertain sea of public opinion. It was eventually published in 1720—although it had first been suggested to him by his friend Dr. Trotter in the Simprin days. Its full title informs us briefly of its content: "Human nature in its fourfold state of primitive integrity, entire depravity, begun recovery, and consummate happiness or misery." In other words, it is really a miniature systematic theology. But Boston's aim was, while presenting Christian truths in systematic form and seeking to show their mutual relationship and dependence, to adapt his language to the general capacity of his readers and to bring the whole to bear upon their greatest needs and their eternal well-being. In fact, by means of the *Fourfold State*, Boston preached the gospel of heaven's great love, not only to his people in Ettrick, but to the whole of the south and southeast of Scotland. It was read by multitudes, and literally thousands were converted through it. Indeed, we find him mentioning in the last chapter of his diary that he had received a comfortable account of its acceptableness and usefulness in places far more distant, particularly in the highlands.

The late Dr. Young of Perth has this to say about Boston's work in the *Fourfold State*. "He took the bewildered child of trespass familiarly by the hand, and descending to the level of his untutored capacity, gave him a clear and consecutive view of the innocence from which he had fallen, the misery in which he was involved, the economy of restoration under which he was situated, and the hope which, by submitting to that economy, he might warrantably entertain. His eye, as he wrote, was upon the unawakened sinner, that he might arouse him from his dangerous lethargy; upon the anxious enquirer, that he might guide his steps into the right way; and upon the young convert, that he might guard him against devious paths and perilous delays. He never failed to show the bearing of Christian doctrine upon the conscience, the affections and the life, and to mingle with the light of systematic arrangement beseeching tenderness and practical appeal." That surely is eloquent testimony to any work.

Now, to conclude our paper, let Boston speak again the closing words of his autobiography: "Upon the whole, I bless my God in Jesus Christ, that ever He made me a Christian, and took an early dealing with my soul; that ever He made me a minister of the gospel, and gave me some insight into the doctrine of His grace; and that ever He gave me the blessed Bible, and brought me acquainted with the originals, and especially with the Hebrew text. The world hath all along been a step-dame to me; and wheresoever I would have attempted to nestle in it, there was a thorn of uneasiness laid for me. Man is born crying, lives complaining, and dies disappointed from that quarter. 'All is vexation and vanity of spirit'—'I have waited for Thy salvation, O Lord.'" We, too, would bless the Lord for such a faithful soldier of Jesus Christ, and seek to follow in his steps.

15

JOHN OWEN'S DOCTRINE
OF CHRIST

F. R. Entwistle

Before we turn to our subject, may I remind you who John Owen was. He lived from 1616 to 1683, and so may be called a later Puritan. He entered Oxford at the age of twelve and was noted for his academic diligence. During his later years at the University, the Holy Spirit began a work of grace in his heart, and he left Oxford at the age of twenty-one on account of Laud's statutes. He cast in his lot with Parliament at the outbreak of Civil War. He removed to London where his spiritual troubles were settled by an unknown preacher. In 1642 he published his first work, *A display of Arminianism*. In 1643 he was appointed to the living of Fordham and in 1646 to Coggeshall. About this time his ecclesiastical views changed from Presbyterianism to modified Congregationalism. He preached before Parliament, and in 1649 was taken by Cromwell to Ireland and

in 1650 to Scotland. In 1651 he was appointed Dean of Christ
Church, Oxford, and in 1652 Vice-Chancellor of the University.
After a period of valuable service to the University he was removed from his post in 1658, and in 1660, on the Restoration,
he lost the deanery.

Throughout this period, in spite of many administrative
and advisory duties, he continued both to preach and to publish. After the Restoration we find him being indicted for holding religious assemblies in Oxford, but later, in 1673, he was allowed to preach to an Independent congregation in London.
He continued to publish throughout these later years, and
many of his most valuable works date from this period. He died
in 1683.

The *Dictionary of National Biography* says of him, "Owen
ranks with Baxter and Howe among the most eminent of Puritan divines. A trenchant controversialist, he distinguished himself no less by temperateness of tone than by vigour of polemic.
His learning was vast, various and profound, and his mastery of
Calvinistic theology complete." To some aspects of that theology we must now give our attention.

We are dealing with only *some aspects* of Owen's doctrine of
Christ. No apology for this is needed when we are dealing with
an author so voluminous as John Owen and a subject so central
and complex as the Person and Work of Christ. As to sources,
it has been necessary to limit ourselves to four major treatises
of Owen's: his *Salus Electorum;* or, *the Death of Death in the Death
of Christ* (1648); *Of Communion with God, the Father, the Son and
the Holy Ghost* (1657); CHRISTOLOGIA, *or a Declaration of the Glorious Mystery of the Person of Christ—God and Man* (1679); *Media-
tions and Discourses on the Glory of Christ* (1684–96). Our sources
thus range from Owen's second major treatise to "his dying testimony to the truth."[1] In deciding what to include and what to
omit, we have had two aims in mind; first, to include enough to
indicate the main lines of Owen's thought, and second, to give
particular attention to those points at which his teaching is important for guiding our own thought at the present time. Our
aim, then, is to let John Owen speak today.

Theological Method

Owen has something of value to say, first, to our theological method. Here two matters require our attention.

The Foundation of Owen's Thought

It is immediately apparent that Owen's great concern in his theological writing is to set out and explain what the Scripture teaches. This he conceives to be his great duty as theologian and as pastor. It is no exaggeration to say that his theological method is the exegesis of Scripture. In writing his treatises he is accustomed to state a proposition, which he believes summarizes and expresses the teaching of Scripture, and then he confirms it with vast quantities of scriptural quotation. The authority of Scripture is final and absolute and never called into question, for what the Scripture says, God says. From his use of Scripture we may learn at least three things:

1. Owen gives the lie to the common impression that a careful and critical use of texts was virtually unknown before the nineteenth century. Owen is extremely careful in his use of texts. He has regard to the context, and treats each text in its setting not only in the Bible but in the whole body of biblical truth. It is true that he is prepared to make more use of the Old Testament in discussing the Person and Work of Christ than most modern writers do, but his quotations are taken from Messianic psalms, or prophetic Messianic passages, such as the Servant Songs of Isaiah, or from passages dealing with the Wisdom or the Word of God; very often from passages which the New Testament itself applies to Christ. In doing this, Owen is doing no more than follow the two New Testament principles that the Old Testament does speak of Christ, and that in studying the inspired Scriptures we must give attention to the individual words if we are to understand the whole. A little more hesitancy may be felt about some passages in which Owen bases a detailed exposition of the Person of Christ upon verses from the Song of Solomon (e.g. *Of Communion with God*);[2] but if we were to express that hesitation to Owen he might well reply that he was following the analogy of Scripture, and the principle that we must study the words if we are to un-

derstand the meaning. There may be occasional exceptions, but in general we can say that Owen was most careful in his use of texts.

2. Owen gives the lie to the accusation which is still sometimes heard, that Calvinist theologians tend to be ruled by a narrow logic, which they impose upon Scripture, rather than by Scripture itself. Of no doctrine is that accusation made with more vehemence than the doctrine of definite or particular redemption. Yet with regard to Owen, at any rate, the charge is quite groundless. His main argument in *The Death of Death*, in which he is concerned with this subject, is not a logical one at all, but a scriptural one. He argues that the Scriptures teach particular redemption; that in fact the scriptural terminology of redemption is evacuated of meaning if we understand it to teach anything less than the definite, effective redemption of God's elect. Other views of the atonement are condemned not because they are logically inconsistent in themselves, but because they are neither taught in Scripture nor consistent with scriptural teaching. There is order and system in Owen's writing, but it is there with a view to displaying the teaching of Scripture. It is governed by his biblical exegesis.

3. Owen's use of Scripture serves as a healthy corrective in the present century, when some treatments of the Person and Work of Christ have been rather preoccupied with intellectual problems—problems of philosophy and psychology—rather than with the submissive exegesis of Scripture. Owen, with his careful and acute analysis, is the last person to be opposed to an accurate and full doctrinal understanding; indeed, he sees the development of such an understanding as part of our increase in the knowledge of God. But he is never content with mental accuracy in either himself or his readers. His object in writing is always practical and pastoral. In the Preface to his treatise on *The Person of Christ* he describes the knowledge of Christ which he is concerned to promote:

> . . . the principal design of their whole lives unto whom he
> is thus precious, is to acquaint themselves with him—the

mystery of the wisdom, grace, and love of God, in his person and mediation, as revealed unto us in the Scripture, which is "life eternal"; (John 17:3)—to trust in him, and unto him, as to all the everlasting concernments of their souls—to love and honour him with all their hearts—to endeavour after conformity to him, in all those characters of divine goodness and holiness which are represented unto them in him. In these things consist the soul, life, power, beauty and efficacy of the Christian religion; without which, whatever ornaments may be put upon its exercise, it is but a useless, lifeless carcass.[3]

There are, and there have been, he says, many errors in the Church concerning the Person and Work of Christ. But we must look for more than doctrinal correction: "The re-enthroning of the Person, Spirit, Grace and Authority of Christ, in the hearts and consciences of men, is the only way whereby an end may be put unto these woeful conflicts."[4]

This practical and pastoral concern is something from which we can learn today. He is prepared to write volume after volume with the simple object of expounding and teaching all that the Scriptures teach about these doctrines, because he believes that it is the teaching of Scripture which his readers need to know and believe for their salvation.

The Trinitarian Framework of Owen's Thought

The second aspect of Owen's theological method which requires our attention is this—Owen's exposition of scriptural truth takes a Trinitarian form. In giving this form to his thought Owen is not simply adopting a framework because it is neat, nor is he placing himself in bondage to a system, as a sort of Protestant scholastic. The great theme of all his writings is redemption, for that is the theme of Scripture. Owen therefore gives his work a Trinitarian form because the Scripture reveals a Trinity, working for our salvation. The foundations of this Trinitarian framework are thus twofold: first, in the exegesis of Scripture, from which as we have seen Owen seeks to quarry all his theology, and second, in the nature of God, the essential Trinity Whom Scripture reveals. Two quotations may illustrate this.

In his treatment of the agent of redemption in *The Death of Death*, book 1, Owen discusses in turn the work of the Father, the Son, and the Spirit, and prefaces his discussion with these words:

> The agent in, and chief author of, this great work of our redemption is the whole blessed Trinity; for all the works which outwardly are of the Deity are undivided and belong equally to each person, their distinct manner of subsistence and order being observed. . . . In the several persons of the Holy Trinity, the joint author of the whole work, the Scripture proposeth distinct and sundry acts or operations peculiarly assigned unto them; which, according to our weak manner of apprehension, we are to consider severally and apart.[5]

In his treatise *Of Communion with God*, one of his fundamental positions is "that the saints have distinct communion with the Father, and the Son, and the Holy Spirit (that is, distinctly with the Father, and distinctly with the Son, and distinctly with the Holy Spirit)."[6] Owen proceeds to demonstrate this from Scripture, and organizes his whole treatise on the basis of this threefold distinction. He clarifies his position on this matter as follows:

> Now the works that outwardly are of God (called "Trinitatis ad extra"), which are commonly said to be *common and undivided*, are either wholly so, and in all respects, as all works of common providence; or else, being common in respect of their acts, they are distinguished in respect of that principle, or next and immediate rise in the manner of operation: so creation is *appropriated* to the Father, redemption to the Son. In which sense we speak of these things.[7]

Scripture speaks of the work of three Persons, Father, Son, and Holy Spirit: Owen therefore will speak of them too.

Frequently, where Scripture leads him, Owen carries this distinction into the discussion of detailed aspects of doctrine. Thus, with regard to the *coming* of Christ into the world for our redemption, "The Father loves the world, and sends his Son to die"; the Son takes flesh; and the Spirit co-operates in over-shadowing the Virgin and in filling Christ until "he was thoroughly furnished and fitted for his great undertaking."[8] Again, with regard to the *oblation* of Christ, the Father laid upon Christ the punishment of sins;[9] Christ voluntarily gave Himself up as an oblation and a sacrifice;[10] and He did so "through the eternal Spirit."[11] And third, with regard to the *resurrection, ascension, and heavenly mediation* of Christ, the Father "crowns Him with glory and honour";[12] the Son now appears in the presence of God as our Advocate;[13] and both His resurrection and His presentation of Himself in heaven are through the Holy Spirit.[14]

The Trinitarian framework of Owen's thought, in which his Christology is set, contrasts with some modern theology which makes much of Christocentricity. The great difference between Owen and some of our contemporaries lies of course in their ideas of revelation. Owen believes that God has revealed Himself through truths about Himself conveyed through the words of Scripture, and this belief leads him to a thoroughgoing Trinitarianism. Some modern theology tends to regard belief in the revelatory significance of Christ as an alternative to such a view of Scripture, and hence to argue analogically from the Person of Christ rather than directly from the Bible. Owen's Trinitarianism rests upon his belief in the nature of Scripture, and for that reason will commend itself to those who share that belief.

It is sometimes suggested that this modern, Christological theology is more honoring to Christ than the older Trinitarianism, and in such a suggestion lies its appeal to the Christian. But this is not so. Owen's full Trinitarianism is not less honoring to Christ: to give glory to the Father and the Spirit does not detract from the glory of the Son. On the contrary, Owen can only do justice to the Scripture teaching about Christ, by being thoroughly Trinitarian when he is discussing it. And we shall see that his biblical Trinitarianism leads him to a theology which is wonderfully Christocentric and Christ-exalting.

The Person of Christ

Owen has much of value to say, second, to our doctrine of the Person of Christ. The foundation of his doctrine is his view of the constitution of the Person of Christ, His human and divine natures. Owen's doctrine here is the orthodox Christian one, and his contribution lies in the clarity of his thought, the accuracy of his definitions, and the rich, scriptural way in which he expounds the doctrine, rather than in anything strikingly original. He deals with this matter under four heads.

> I. The assumption of our nature into personal subsistence with the Son of God. II. The union of the two natures into that single person which is consequential thereon. III. The mutual communication of those distinct natures, the divine and human, by virtue of that union. IV. The enunciations or predications concerning the person of Christ, which follow on that union and communion.[15]

Christ became Incarnate, he says, by taking our nature into His: "He could no otherwise . . . be made flesh, or made of a woman, but in that our nature was made his by his assuming it to be his own. The same person—who before was not flesh, was not man—was made flesh as man, in that he took our human nature to be his own."[16]

From this assumption follows the union of the two natures of the same person, or the hypostatical union; "that is, the union of the divine and human nature in the person of the Son of God, the human nature having no personality nor subsistence of its own."[17] This union is different from all other unions. It is different from the union of the Trinity: that is a unity of three Persons in one nature, this of two natures in one Person. It is different from the union of soul and body: soul and body together constitute one entire nature, this is a union of two complete natures which remain two complete natures; soul and body united constitute a new individual person, while Christ did not become a new person by taking humanity into Himself. It is certainly not a mixture of two natures to produce a third, nor is it the conversion of one into the other. It is different from the spiritual union between Christ and believers: to use this analogy is to divide the Person of Christ, in Nestorian fashion.

From the union of the two natures follows their interrelationship. Thus the divine nature gives to the human its subsistence, that fullness of grace which belongs to divinity, and worth and dignity in its official actions. In this interrelation of the two natures, each nature preserves its own natural, essential properties; the divine nature is not made finite or limited, nor is the human nature made infinite and omnipotent. "Unless this be granted, there will not be two natures in Christ, a divine and a human; nor indeed either of them, but somewhat else, composed of both."[18] Moreover, each nature operates in Christ according to its essential properties: "The divine nature knows all things, upholds all things, rules all things, acts by its presence everywhere; the human nature was born, yielded obedience, died and rose again. But it is the same person, the same Christ, that acts all these things—the one nature being his no less than the other."[19]

From this last point it follows that the work of Christ, in every act of his mediatory office, is the act and work of the whole Person. In all that Christ did as King, Priest, and Prophet of the Church—in all that He did and suffered and continues to do for us—His work "is not to be considered as the act of this or that nature in him alone, but it is the act and work of the whole person—of him that is both God and man in one person."[20]

This helps us to understand some of the scriptural statements about Christ. Some of the things which Scripture affirms of His Person belong to it with respect to one nature only: His eternal preexistence, His upholding all things by the Word of His power, belong to His Person on account of His divine nature; His being born and suffering, on account of His human nature. Each statement of Scripture needs to be studied carefully in this respect.

It will be important for our subsequent discussion to note here that Owen teaches that the office and work of Christ as Mediator follows not from one or the other of His natures, but from the fact that both are united in Him.

Much modern discussion of the Person of Christ has been concerned with the psychology of His Person, and in emphasizing His humanity has failed to do justice to His divinity. The implications of this in present-day writing with regard to the truthfulness of His utterances and the authority of Scripture are well known to us all. But in fact, as we shall see, the effects of such a tendency are even more far-reaching; it is subversive of the whole of religion and theology. With regard to the psychology of the Person of Christ, Owen does not help us to explain what he regards as beyond explanation, but he does remind us of the range of scriptural concepts upon which our doctrine must be based; he recalls us, in short, to more scriptural views of the Person of Christ.

Owen makes this scriptural doctrine of the Person of Christ, God and man, the foundation of a great body of Biblical Theology. We may summarize some of it under four propositions.

1. *The Person of Christ is the immediate cause of all true religion and worship.* Ultimately religion depends upon taking God to be our God, but it is the manifestation of His Being and excellencies which moves us to worship Him. And the most glorious result of divine wisdom, grace, and power is the constitution of the Person of Christ. It is "that singular expression of divine wisdom, goodness and power, wherein God will be admired and glorified unto all eternity."[21] It must move every true believer to worship.

> Let all vain imaginations cease: there is nothing left unto the sons of men, but either to reject the divine person of Christ—as many do unto their own destruction—or humbly to adore the mystery of infinite wisdom and grace therein. And it will require a condescending charity, to judge that those do really believe the incarnation of the Son of God, who live not in the admiration of it, as the most adorable effect of divine wisdom. . . . This is the

glory of the Christian religion—the basis and foundation that bears the whole superstructure—the root whereon it grows. This is its life and soul, that wherein it differs from, and inconceivably excels, whatever was in true religion before, or whatever any false religion pretended unto.[22]

In these days of minimizing doctrinal statements, when the Person of Christ is assailed by sects outside the Church and, albeit unwittingly, by skeptical theological tendencies within, Owen reminds us of the utter necessity of true and full views of the Person of Christ.

2. *The Person of Christ is the foundation of all the saving purposes of God.* God's purposes for the sanctification and salvation of the Church to His own glory, were all to be effected "in Christ"; their foundation was laid "in and with him."[23] God delighted in these purposes, and in the Person of Christ, "as his eternal wisdom in their contrivance, and as the means of their accomplishment in his future incarnation."[24] His purposes for the sanctification and salvation of the Church are acts of infinite wisdom, goodness, love, and grace, and they were all laid in the Person of Christ. Their origin, of course, was in the divine will and wisdom alone, but their accomplishment was to be in the Person of the Son alone. They were expressed in election, and election is in Christ. "In him we were not actually, nor by faith, before the foundation of the world; yet were we then chosen in him, as the only foundation of the execution of all the counsels of God concerning our sanctification and salvation."[25]

Wrong and defective views of election abound today. It is often a help to those who regard the decree of election as harsh and arbitrary, to be reminded that it is election in Christ of which we speak. It is also a corrective to the view which is still sometimes heard, that the decree of election was based upon the divine foreknowledge of repentance and faith, to remind ourselves that the only ground of election outside the will and purpose of the Father, was the Person of His Son.

3. *The Person of Christ is the great revelation of God and His will.* All religion depends upon a revelation of God and His purposes.

And, says Owen, "This is done perfectly only in the Person of Christ, all other means of it being subordinate thereunto, and none of them of the same nature therewithal. The end of the Word itself, is to instruct us in the knowledge of God in Christ." He therefore seeks to demonstrate "that in the person and mediation of Christ (which are inseparable, in all the respects of faith unto him) there is made unto us a blessed representation of the glorious properties of the divine nature, and of the holy counsels of the will of God."[26] We who believe in propositional revelation, and the importance of doctrinal statements, do well to note what Owen says about the relation between the Scriptures, and the revelation of God in Christ:

> A mere external, doctrinal revelation of the divine nature and properties, without any exemplification or real representation of them, was not sufficient unto the end of God in the manifestation of himself. This is done in the Scripture. But the whole Scripture is built on this foundation, or proceeds on this supposition—that there is a real representation of the divine nature unto us, which it declares and describes. . . . All this is done in the Person of Christ. He is the complete image and perfect representation of the Divine Being and excellencies . . . as God proposeth himself as the object of our faith, trust, and obedience.[27]

What is thus true of the nature of God is true also of His purposes. "Of them all the person of Christ is the sacred repository and treasury—in him are they to be learned. All their efficacy and use depend upon their relation unto him. He is the centre and circumference of all the lines of truth—that is, which is divine, spiritual and supernatural."[28]

Reformed Christians are rightly accustomed to make much of the Scriptures. But let us remember that the Scriptures were given to lead us to Christ. Sometimes our zealous defense of the Scriptures can lead us to overstatement—or rather, on this point, understatement. Let us remember that the purpose of the Scriptures is simply to mediate to us the revelation which God has given us in His Son.

4. *The Person of Christ is the foundation of His work, and hence of our salvation.* Here is a very important point in Owen's thought. We may note two ways in which he works it out. In the treatise *Of Communion with God,* he shows how Christ's Person is the foundation of His work generally as Mediator and Savior.

His *fitness* to save results from the union of the two natures in Him: "The uniting of the natures of God and man in one person made him fit to be a Saviour to the uttermost. He lays his hand upon God, by partaking of his nature, Zech. 3:7; and he lays his hand upon us, by being partaker of our nature, Heb. 2:14, 16: and so becomes a days-man, or umpire between both."[29]

We saw earlier that from the union of the two natures follows their inter-relationship, and that in this relationship the divine nature gives to the human that fullness of grace which belongs to divinity. This, says Owen, constitutes Christ's *"fulness to save."*[30] It pleased the Father that in Him should all fullness dwell, and He received not the Spirit by measure. "Had it been given to Him by measure, we had exhausted it."[31] From these two follows, says Owen, Christ's complete suitableness to all the wants of the souls of men.

In his treatise on *The Person of Christ,* Owen shows how the Person of Christ is fundamental to His threefold office as Prophet, Priest, and King.[32] The Person of Christ was essential, says Owen, for the saving exercise of these offices in general. For we could not have an interest in what He did, He could not be our Representative and Substitute, if He were not human as well as divine. But humanity without deity could not make a Savior any more than vice versa. He could not be the Prophet of the whole Church, before His incarnation, during His earthly ministry, and to the end of time, revealing the mind of God fully, infallibly, and authoritatively, if He were not divine. He could not be the King, ruling over the whole creation for His people's good, and graciously working in the mind, soul, and conscience of every believer, if He were not divine. He could not be Priest, expiating the sins of His whole Church, if He were not divine. Thus the work of Christ utterly depends upon, and arises from, His divine-human Person. Faith in the mystery of His Person is therefore essential if we are to understand or benefit from His offices. The life which we receive through His mediation is the life which is in the Son of God.

So Owen speaks to us of the utter centrality of the Person of Christ in the Christian religion. He shows us that true religion, and salvation, and eternal life, stand or fall by right views of His Person. He calls us to worship His Person, to depend upon Him, to make Him our glory. If ever we thought in preaching to magnify Calvary by minimizing Bethlehem, Owen shows us the utter folly of such a practice. May we learn to live and preach to the glory of the Father, by giving glory to the Person of the Son.

The Office of Christ

Let Owen be our teacher, third, with regard to the office of Christ, for which His Person fits Him and which He discharges in His work. "There is one God, and one mediator between God and men, the man Christ Jesus" (1 Tim. 2:5). The thought of Christ as Mediator is central to Owen's exposition of the Work of Christ. The need of a Mediator is clear:

> In that great difference between God and man occasioned by our sin and apostasy from him, which of itself could issue in nothing but the utter ruin of the whole race of mankind, there was none in heaven or earth, in their original nature and operations, who was meet or able to make up a *righteous peace* between them. Yet this must be done by a mediator, or cease for ever.[33]

We have already seen how in Owen's thought the Person of Christ fitted Him for this office. Now we consider how it actually became His. In His entry upon the office of Mediator, a number of actions may be distinguished. The fact that they are distinguished and listed consecutively does not mean that they necessarily follow each other chronologically. The distinctions are made only so that our finite minds may understand more clearly.

1. *Christ was appointed by God to the office of Mediator.* In this appointment three actions may be discerned: First, the eternal purpose of God. It was eternally established in the mind and will of God, that His incarnate Son should be set apart for this work.

Second, the furnishing of Christ with a fullness of spiritual gifts and graces—all "that might any way be requisite for the office he was to undertake, the work he was to undergo, and the charge he had over the house of God."[34] This fullness is not the natural perfection of Christ's Deity, but "a *communicated* fulness, which was in him by dispensation from his Father, bestowed upon him to fit him for his work and office."[35] It means that "there is no grace that is not in Christ, and every grace is in him in the highest degree." From another aspect, it is this full and unique bearing of the Spirit.

And third, God's entering into covenant with Christ, concerning His work and its fruits. This "covenant of redemption" consisted of a twofold promise. First, the Father promised to protect and assist His Son in the accomplishment and fulfillment of His work:

> The Father engaged himself, that for his part, upon his Son's undertaking this great work of redemption, he would not be wanting in any assistance in trials, strength against oppositions, encouragement against temptations, and strong consolation in the midst of terrors, which might be in any way necessary or requisite to carry him on through all difficulties to the end of so great an employment.[36]

Second, the Father promised the Son success in His work, and the achievement of all that He set Himself to do. What was the content of this promise? Owen tells us, basing his exposition upon the words of the Lord to His Servant in Isaiah 49:

> that he should gather to himself a glorious church of believers from among Jews and Gentiles, through all the world, that should be brought unto him, and certainly fed

in full pasture, and refreshed by the springs of water, all
the spiritual springs of living water which flow from God
in Christ for their everlasting salvation. This, then, our
Saviour certainly aimed at, as being the promise upon
which he undertook the work—the gathering of the sons
of God together, their bringing unto God, and passing to
eternal salvation.[37]

2. *Christ was actually admitted into the office of Mediator.* This may
be said to have taken place in three distinct acts: (1) At His birth,
when God "prepared him a body," and caused the angels to bear
testimony to Him. (2) At His baptism, when God sent the Spirit
visibly to light upon Him: "when He was endued with a fulness
thereof, for the accomplishment of the work and discharge of the
office whereunto He was designed," and the Father bore testimony to Him as His well-beloved.[38] And (3) at His resurrection,
ascension, and sitting down in heaven, when God crowned Him
with glory and honor, and appointed many witnesses.

3. *Christ willingly undertook the office of Mediator.* This He did (1)
in His incarnation, in that He willingly took our human nature into
personal union with Himself; (2) in His oblation, when He voluntarily gave Himself up to be an oblation and a sacrifice; and (3) in
His intercession, when He freely undertook to be our Advocate.

These last points must await development in our next section. But it may be worth making one or two observations about
this doctrine of the office of Christ. The doctrine of Christ as
Mediator in the sense in which Owen taught it is not common
today. May we suggest that this is at least partly because the
Church no longer believes in "that great difference between
God and man occasioned by our sin and apostasy from him." If
the serious consequences of sin are minimized, then the need of
a Mediator is lessened and men pay less attention to the teaching of Scripture on the subject. The incentive to do so is gone.
When, in a day of grace, men are made conscious of divine holiness and human sinfulness and cry, "What must I do to be
saved?", the doctrine of Christ as Mediator will again be cherished by the Church. Second, we can learn from Owen here,

also, in the way in which the work of Christ is seen to arise from the eternal will of God, and the covenant between Father and Son. In this doctrine, and in the doctrine of election, we are able to understand something of how the work of Christ was related to His preexistence, and it is made plain that His work in time is rooted in eternity.

The Work of Christ

In this doctrine, as in the others we have considered, Owen's teaching will be seen to have a number of aspects which are neglected by the Church today, and in which we can learn from him. Owen sees the work of Christ as threefold.

The Obedience of Christ's Life

By this Owen means "the universal conformity of the Lord Jesus Christ . . . to the whole will of God; and his complete fulfilling of the whole of every law of God, or doing all that God in them required."[39] The actual obedience of Christ consisted of two parts: (1) He did whatever was required of us by the law—the law of nature, the moral and ceremonial laws, the righteous judicial laws. "This was that which he owned of himself—that he came to do the will of God; and he did it."[40] (2) He did whatever was required of Him as Mediator, carrying out all His duties which are not for our imitation—such as His dying for us on the cross.

What effect did the obedience of His life have toward our free acceptance with God? His obedience to the law of the Mediator involved His doing what was necessary for the exercise of His office, and of itself does not benefit us. With regard to His actual fulfilling of the law, in doing everything which is required of us, Owen says that three views were held. The first view sees the obedience of Christ as simply preparatory to His death, which is the sole ground of our justification. The second view was that the obedience of Christ was pure obedience, but that insofar as it involved suffering, it was part of His humiliation and so is part of the ground of our justification. The third view regards the obedience of Christ as being *for* us, and therefore reckoned *unto* us as the ground of our acceptance as righteous.

Owen comments on these views as follows: First, all that Christ did (that is, not just His fulfilling of the law of the Mediator), He did as Mediator, and therefore for those for whom He was Mediator. Second, the end of His active obedience cannot be to prepare Him for His death, for He was already fitted to be an offering for sin by virtue of His Person. Third, Christ need not by nature render obedience to the law of nature or to the ceremonial law, or, for example, submit to baptism. The conclusion is that His obedience in such matters must be for us. Fourth, the obedience of Christ is clearly distinct from His sufferings: "Doing is one thing, suffering another."[41] Owen's views on this matter may therefore be summarized under three propositions:

1. The obedience of the life of Christ means His perfect and willing submission to every law that bound any of God's people.

2. "That this obedience was performed by Christ not for Himself, but for us, and in our stead."[42]

3. "Then, I say, this perfect obedience of Christ to the law is reckoned unto us."[43] Life is not to be obtained, says Owen, unless all be done that the law requires. The commandments must be kept, by us or by our surety. The fact that Christ kept them for us should not lead to antinomianism: "we are not freed from obedience, as a way of walking with God, but we are as a way of working to come to him."[44]

Owen recognizes that Romans 5 is central to a discussion of this matter, and gives particular weight here to verses 18–19: "By the righteousness of one the free gift came upon all men unto justification of life: by the obedience of one shall many be made righteous."

The Oblation and Death of Christ

It would be true to say that Owen does not precisely identify the oblation of Christ and His death. His concept of oblation is rather wider and includes the life of Christ viewed from certain aspects:

Now this oblation or offering of Christ I would not tie up to any one thing, action or passion, performance or suffering; but it compriseth the whole economy and dispensation of God manifested in the flesh and conversing among us with all those things which he performed in the days of his flesh . . . all the whole dispensation of his coming and ministering, until he had given his soul a price of redemption for many.[45]

The death of Christ, he says "was the sum and complement of his oblation and that wherein it did chiefly consist," but His oblation includes

his whole humiliation, or state of emptying himself, whether by yielding voluntary obedience to the law, as being made under it, that he might be the end thereof to them that believe, Rom. 10:4, or by his subjection to the curse of the law, in the antecedent misery and suffering of life, as well as by submitting to death, the death of the cross: for no action of his as mediator is to be excluded from a concurrence to make up the whole means in this work.[46]

Owen believes that the scriptural teaching concerning the nature of the death of Christ may be summarized under three propositions.

1. It is a *price*, and its effect is *redemption*. The essence of redemption is deliverance from bondage or captivity through the payment of a price. The price of our deliverance was the blood of Christ. "Free justification from the guilt and pardon of sin, in the deliverance from the punishment due unto it, is the effect of the redemption procured by the payment of the price."[47] Owen recognizes that the language of redemption when it is applied to the death of Christ differs from its usual applications in a number of points. Thus, He Who receives the ransom also gives it: "His love is the cause of the price in respect of its procurement, and his justice accepts of the price in respect of its merit."[48] Again, this re-

demption is not so much a release from the power of God as a bringing into His favor.

2. The death of Christ is a *sacrifice*, and its effect is *reconciliation* and *atonement*. Reconciliation is the renewing of friendship between two parties. Christ thus reconciled God to us, by turning away His wrath from us; and He turned us away from our enmity toward God, by redeeming us and reconciling us to Him.

3. The death of Christ is a *punishment*, and its effect is *satisfaction*. Our debt to God lay in that we were under the curse of the law. Jesus "took away the curse, by 'being made a curse,' Gal. 3:13. He delivered us from sin, being 'made sin,' 2 Cor. 5:21. He underwent death, that we might be delivered from death. All our debt was in the curse of the law, which He wholly underwent."[49] His satisfaction "was a full, valuable compensation, made to the justice of God, for all the sins of all those for whom he made satisfaction, by undergoing that same punishment which, by reason of the obligation that was upon them, they themselves were bound to undergo."[50]

The Intercession and Mediation of Christ

Once again, we must briefly summarize Owen's teaching in a number of propositions:

1. The intercession of Christ stands in the closest relationship to His oblation. They have the same persons in view, and they have the same end in view. Owen is able to describe the intercession of Christ in heaven as "a *continuance and carrying* on of his oblation."[51]

2. Christ by His death secured certain benefits for His people. By His intercession He secures the *application* of those benefits to His people. He appears in heaven "to be our advocate, to plead our cause with God, for the application of the good things procured by his oblation unto all them for whom he was an offering."[52] "The *oblation* of Christ is . . . the foundation of his intercession, inasmuch as by the oblation was procured every thing that, by virtue of his intercession, is bestowed."[53] And so Owen is able to say that Christ is in heaven as the Representative of believers

to *make effectual the atonement* that he hath made for sin. By
the continued representation of it, and of himself as a
"Lamb that hath been slain," he procures the application
of the virtues and benefits of it, in reconciliation and
peace with God, unto their souls and consciences. . . . To
undertake their *protection*, and to plead their cause against
all the accusations of Satan. . . . To *intercede* for them, as
unto the communication of all grace and glory, all sup-
plies of the Spirit, the accomplishment of all the promises
of the covenant towards them.[54]

3. The nature of the intercession is an authoritative presenting Himself in glory.

The very nature of this intercession . . . is not a humble,
dejected supplication, which beseems not that glorious
state of advancement which he is possessed of that sits at
the right hand of the Majesty on high, but an authoritative presenting himself before the throne of his Father,
sprinkled with his own blood, for the making out of his
people all spiritual things that are procured by his oblation, saying, "Father, I will that those whom thou hast
given me be with me where I am," John 17:24.[55]

His intercession, therefore, is not vocal, but real:

. . . it cannot be conceived to be *vocal*, by the way of entreaty, but merely *real*, by the presentation of himself,
sprinkled with the blood of the covenant, before the
throne of grace on our behalf. . . . His intercession there
is an *appearing* for us in heaven in the presence of God . . .
so presenting himself that his former oblation might have
its perpetual efficacy, until the many sons given unto him
are brought to glory.[56]

The End of the Work of Christ

Here we must be brief: to go into this matter in detail would
carry us too far afield. For Owen it is axiomatic that the end

which God sets out to accomplish, and the result which He finally achieves, are one and the same thing. The work of Christ, he says, was effective in achieving its end. "Whatsoever the blessed Trinity intended by them (the oblation and intercession of Christ), that was effected."[57] The supreme or ultimate end is the glory of God, that is "the manifestation of his glorious attributes, especially of his justice, and mercy tempered with justice, unto us."[58] And to that end, His purpose is to bring many sons to glory. Thus the Father sent Christ to die *"for the purchasing of eternal redemption, and bringing unto himself all and every one of those whom he had before ordained to eternal life, for the praise of his own glory."*[59] All the blessings of the gospel flow from our justification, and we are justified by means of the "great exchange," of which there are two parts: "*First*, the laying of our sin on Christ, or making Him to be sin for us . . . *Secondly*, the gracious imputation of the righteousness of Christ to us, or making us the righteousness of God in him."[60] From this peace with God which was obtained for us, everything else flows: grace and faith, salvation and glory:

> A real, effectual and infallible bestowing and applying of all these things—as well those that are the means as those that are the end, the condition as the thing conditioned about, faith and grace as salvation and glory—unto all and every one for whom he died, do we maintain to be the end proposed and effected by the blood-shedding of Jesus Christ, with those other acts of his mediatorship which we before declared to be therewith inseparably conjoined: so that everyone for whom he died and offered up himself hath, by virtue of his death or oblation, a right purchased for him unto all these things, which in due time he shall certainly and infallibly enjoy.[61]

It remains to make one or two brief comments about Owen's doctrine of the work of Christ, and then briefly to sum up the whole. His doctrine of the obedience of the life of Christ as righteousness which is reckoned to us, is the orthodox doctrine, but it is nevertheless one which is much neglected in the Church today.

One often hears the other views of which Owen spoke put forward in our churches and pulpits. Yet here is a thoroughly scriptural doctrine, one which shows the unity of the life and death of Christ in the one work of mediation and justification; and moreover one which does justice to the biblical view of righteousness, as not merely freedom from guilt, but the possession of a status which is positively pleasing to God, and conformed to His will.

Owen's doctrine of the death of Christ, again, has value today as a rich statement of the biblical doctrine. He bases it upon careful and detailed exegesis, and shows a sound awareness of the danger of allowing nonbiblical uses of such ideas as redemption to push our doctrine in nonbiblical directions.

The present writer confesses to hesitations about Owen's doctrine of the heavenly intercession of Christ. On the one hand, and this is good, Owen shows a healthy freedom from the over-pressing of biblical metaphors and the indulgence of the imagination which has characterized some Roman and Protestant writing on the subject. But on the other hand, there seems to be a contradiction between Owen's doctrine of the death of Christ, and his doctrine of His intercession. If the death of Christ has really secured both the ultimate salvation of the "people of God, and all the means to it, including the gift of faith, how can Christ be praying in heaven for the application of the benefits of His death to His people?" [But Owen himself describes the intercession as *not* "vocal, by the way of entreaty, but merely *real* . . . an *appearing* for us in heaven": see above.] To take such a view is to detract, unwittingly, from His death. Owen would have been more biblical had he said that the death of Christ really did secure all things for His people for time and eternity; that the intercession of Christ consists in His session at the right hand of God as the guarantee of our acceptance and of all that flows from it; and that His present work is one of distributing to men the benefits of His passion.

The personal challenge of Owen's work is very real. He calls us to more scriptural views of the Person and Work of Christ; to worship Him and to uphold Him in our life and preaching not, as so many of us do, in one or two aspects, but in all His glory and fullness as He is revealed in the whole counsel of God, as our God and our Savior. He makes us feel how little we know and understand about our Lord Jesus Christ, and even more, how little we know Him. He helps to bring us to the point at which we can say with Paul, "Yea, doubtless, and I count all things but loss for the excellency of the knowledge of Christ Jesus my Lord. . . . I count not myself to have apprehended: but this one thing I do, forgetting those things which are behind, and reaching forth unto those things which are before, I press toward the mark for the prize of the high calling of God in Christ Jesus" (Phil. 3:8, 13–14).

16

PURITAN PERPLEXITIES: LESSONS FROM 1640–1662

D. Martyn Lloyd-Jones

The subject on which I propose to speak is, "Some lessons from 1640–1662." I have four main reasons for calling attention to this subject. The first is, of course, that this does happen to be 1962, and it would be a terrible thing if this conference, of all conferences, did not give some time and attention to the consideration of that great and notable event.

Having already tried to say something about it from the more purely historical standpoint in a lecture I gave under the auspices of the Evangelical Library, I am going to take it for granted on this occasion that we are most of us familiar with the salient facts of that great story. I am concerned rather to draw certain lessons from what happened, not only in 1662 but also from the whole period of 1640 to 1662.

My second reason for dealing with this subject is, that as we have been rightly reminded more than once in this conference already, there was nothing more remarkable about the Puritans than their emphasis upon the conscience. "The Puritan conscience!" There was nothing more characteristic of them. And we have been reminded, very rightly, that they were very scrupulous in this matter. They were scrupulous in their desire to know exactly what the Truth was, not simply that they might have a theoretical knowledge of it, but in order that they might carry it out, and put it into practice whatever might be the cost. That has been emphasized already in this conference, and therefore it is essential that one session at any rate, and perhaps most appropriately the last session, should be given to the application of what we have been considering. This is particularly appropriate this year, for the message of 1662 is one which places emphasis upon the conscience and the importance of translating what we have already understood in theory, and intellectually, into actual practice. That is my second reason.

The third reason is already implied by what I have just said—anyone who knows anything at all about Puritan preaching knows that they had never finished until they came to "application." It is vital, therefore, that we should do this year by year. These men with their pastoral and experimental interest were essentially concerned with application. There is nothing that they more deplored than a mere academic, intellectual, theoretical view of the Truth. It was one of their criticisms of the Caroline preachers, that they contented themselves with that, giving their learned disquisitions with their classical allusions and so on, and were more or less indifferent to the practical application in the lives of the people. The Puritans always put great emphasis upon application. So we must try to apply to our own contemporary situation something of what we have learned of their whole attitude to the Christian faith, and to the Church, and to practical Christian living, and to conscience.

My last reason is this, that concerned as we all are, or at any rate should be, with a true revival of religion, with a manifestation of the power of Almighty God amongst us, with a shaking and a bringing together of the "dry bones," with a demonstration of the power of God and an authentication of His most holy Word—

concerned as we are about that, we must realize that there is nothing more urgently important than that we should examine ourselves. Some kind of reformation generally precedes revival. There are certain conditions in this matter of revival, and God has so ordained it, as history shows us clearly, that before He pours forth His Spirit upon a people, or upon an individual, He first prepares that people or that individual. It is inconceivable that great blessing should be given to a Laodicean, backsliding, or apostate Church without a preliminary work of repentance. It is vital, therefore, that we should address ourselves to this whole problem of the condition and state of the Church in order that we may obey the leading and prompting of the Spirit of God and prepare ourselves for the much longed for and looked for out-pouring of His Holy Spirit.

Those are my four reasons for dealing with this subject. They all come together as you notice, and it would have been wrong of us, as I say, to allow this year to pass without trying to garner for ourselves some fruit from that great and notable event of 1662. That it was a very crucial episode in the religious history of this country is something about which all, I think, will agree. It was a turning point at which the history and the pattern of religion in this country was more or less determined for nearly three hundred years. There is a sense in which that period which led up to 1662 was almost as important as the Protestant Reformation itself, because a final decision was taken at that point with regard to the nature of the Anglican Church.

Puritan Dissatisfaction with the Church

It is vital that we should remind ourselves that from the very beginning of the Protestant Reformation in this country there had not been complete satisfaction in the Church. The group that became known as Puritan was dissatisfied from the very beginning; they had a feeling that the Reformation was incomplete. If we do not lay hold on that we cannot possibly understand this history. There was never a period when they were satisfied.

Some have been trying to say recently that, from about the time of the setting aside of the Cartwright and Marprelate episodes to the arrival of Laud upon the scene, the Puritans and Anglicans "differed very little." That is a statement that simply will not hold water when tested by the facts. The book of the American Professor George and his wife which it is claimed "demonstrates" this, seems to me to be based upon a fallacy—and that is, that they rely almost exclusively upon the sermons of that period and not upon the actual historical facts.

It is true that there were not perhaps the same number of references in the sermons to the dispute during that period, but this was to be explained by the utter discouragement which the Puritans felt as the result of the disappointment of the Hampton Court Conference of 1604, and also to certain repressive measures introduced by James I and Archbishop Bancroft. The result was that the Puritans just went on preaching quietly and positively and were not as active in their protest as they were before, and as they were after. But there are facts, and I have tried to state some of them in that lecture delivered at the Evangelical Library, which make it abundantly clear that there was a continuous and persistent sense of dissatisfaction.

At no period from the time of the Reformation to 1662 were the Puritans satisfied with the state of affairs in the Church. As to the actual period of the early part of the reign of James I, the conclusion arrived at by Dr. S. Barton Babbage in his book *Puritanism and Richard Bancroft*[1] is undoubtedly correct: "His achievements were solid and substantial; however, it is not unfair to say that, in relation to the challenge of Puritanism, the peace which reigned was more apparent than real; the conflict was only postponed and not concluded." But our immediate concern now is that all this came to a head and to a climax in 1662, for then a final decision was really taken.

It is a most remarkable phenomenon. How often have we contemplated this fact—the extraordinary change which took place almost within a matter of a year? I mean this. Look at the period of the Civil Wars and the Interregnum and the Commonwealth under Cromwell. By 1644 the bishops and the various other offices had been abolished, the Prayer Book had been prohibited, and the Westminster Directory had been brought in. The Church of England as she had been known for nearly one hundred years, seemed to be almost entirely defunct; many of her own people, her greatest supporters, thought she was. She seemed to have gone and to have gone forever, and the Puritans of various schools were in control. And yet by 1662 you find a complete transformation; indeed you already see the beginnings of it in 1660. Here in this nation which had beheaded Charles I, and had dealt in that drastic manner with the whole Anglican conception of the Christian Church, you see the transformation that produced the crowds in London acclaiming the return of Charles II on May 29, 1660, and the Presbyterians having a prominent place in the procession of that monarch into the City of London and into Westminster. The thing is a phenomenon; the change truly extraordinary. And it must be examined by us.

I assert again that what happened in 1662 was really a definite turning point in the history of the Church in England. Let me put this point in the words of Dr. Robert S. Bosher in his book *The Making of the Restoration Settlement.*[2] He says that "1662 marks the final refusal to come to terms with the Continental Reformation." Now this statement by Bosher is interesting because he writes from the Anglican standpoint, and his book has been recommended in a Foreword to it by the late Dr. Norman Sykes, a great historian and professor of Church history in Cambridge at one time and later Dean of Winchester in the Church of England. Dr. Norman Sykes says that he feels that Dr. Bosher has established his thesis; and the thesis is that 1662 was a complete victory for the Laudian party in the Anglican Church. It is for that reason that it can be regarded as the final refusal of the Anglican Church to come to terms with the Continental Reformation. The Puritans had hoped throughout the century that the Church of England would be brought into conformity with the Reformation as it had worked itself out on the Continent. They hoped against hope that this could be done. But after 1662 there was no longer any hope. The Laudian view of the Church, according to Dr.

Bosher, was something that was finally established; it was a complete victory for that point of view.

This is something, therefore, that we must consider, and consider very seriously. Dr. Bosher says again, "The ecclesiastical settlement which thus took effect has been rightly regarded as a major landmark in English Church history and remains as a permanent achievement of the Laudian party. The Church of England would continue to be a meeting place of divers traditions, but, broadly speaking, its essential position, and the limits of its comprehensiveness, were finally established by the decision made in 1662. If, a century before, Anglicans had solemnly affirmed that 'the Church of Rome hath erred,' the Laudian triumph resulted in a judgment of equal moment—that the Ecclesia Anglicana was of another spirit than Geneva." "In the Elizabethan settlement," he goes on, "the Reformation had been given a peculiarly English expression, and we may interpret the settlement of 1662 as an equally characteristic version of the counter-Reformation." What happened in 1662 was, therefore, a most important event; it was a very real turning point. The hope of the Puritans was finally dashed to the ground. It was their final defeat, and the exploding of all their longings.

The Importance of 1662

Why is it important that we should look at this matter and examine it? I suggest that it is important for this reason—that if I am not guilty of entirely misreading and misunderstanding the signs of the times—we are today in a position that is more closely similar to the whole state of affairs from 1640 to 1662 than has ever been the case during the intervening three hundred years. What I mean is this. During the period we are examining (1640–1661) everything was in the melting pot as it were. The possibilities were tremendous; it was difficult to prophesy which way they were going to turn. Many of the Puritans believed at one or two points that they really had succeeded at last, and that they had got everything they had wanted; but in the end it all proved to be vain, and everything was in the melting pot again.

Surely today everything is in the melting pot once more. The whole question of the nature of the Church is being raised acutely again. Men are now prepared to think in a more loose and detached manner of their denominational attachments than they have been for three hundred years. Until comparatively recently they have fought for their denomination, the particular denomination to which they belong, with great tenacity, and there has often been much bitterness. All that has practically gone, and men are now apparently prepared to throw the whole situation into the melting pot again and are talking about the emergence of something new.

Well, here is my question: Are we ready for that? Where do we come in at this point? What is our attitude to these possibilities? For I believe they are very real, and I think we shall witness something quite new probably in the lifetime of most of us. So it seems to me that here we have brought before us, as it were providentially, by this tercentenary of 1662, the very thing that we need to give us some guidance. Alas, unfortunately, the lesson, as I see it, of this period is mainly one of warning. God grant that we may turn even that into a source and a means of blessing and of encouragement. We are in a situation in which we must all examine ourselves, and do so very honestly. I predict that we are going to pass through a period in which probably every one of us in this room will have to make as vital and as drastic a decision as did those men of 1662. We shall be forced to decide one way or the other—indeed that is already upon us. It is for that reason, therefore, that I invite you to turn to a consideration of this most extraordinary period.

Causes of the Puritans' Failure

So I start by asking a question: What went wrong? What was it that produced this amazing change from the apparent utter defeat of Laud to the triumph of this cause? You remember that he was impeached and put to death and that all that belonged to that side seemed lost, especially when Charles I was beheaded. It seemed to be in utter defeat; and yet in 1662 here they are victorious. The Laudian party that had seemed to be almost exterminated is back in control again and celebrating a notable victory. What went wrong? What went wrong especially with the Puritans who had been in the ascendancy during most of this period? What were the causes of failure?

I can simply put before you my own analysis of the period, my own idea as to what it was that went wrong. The first cause, I would say, was the admixture of religion and politics. That was the thing that seems to me to bedevil most of their history. It was unfortunate that Laud, in addition to being Archbishop, was a most important political person who as chief adviser to the King had a great deal to do with politics. The result was that it was impossible to disentangle the political grievances and the religious grievances. Finding that the Puritans also had grievances they naturally gravitated together, with the result that you had this—I had almost said unholy—alliance between those who were purely political in their motives and those who were essentially religious, because they seemed to be fighting a common enemy. This meant, of course, that the real issue tended to be confused and men made compromises for the sake of gaining a victory over the common enemy.

The records make it quite clear that there were those on the Puritan side, such as Baxter, who did not really believe in the Solemn League and Covenant, but in order to have the help of the Scots many of them subscribed to it. Thus, the motives became mixed, as they always will become mixed if we begin to confuse and admix politics with our religion.

It is a fact also that about 1640 there were even Royalists who heartily disliked and hated Laud and all his practices. Men, who in 1660 and 1662 were nothing but pure Royalists and supporters of the bishops, had been anti-bishop, because of the excesses of Laud, twenty years earlier. Their dislike of Laud had driven them to work with the Puritans, whose interest was more purely religious, and the result was that there was a great deal of confusion.

I do not want to stop with this, but I put it first because I have always felt that it is the first key to the understanding of the tragedy of what happened in 1662. This is always a danger, this admixture of politics and religion. Surely we need to face it at the present time. I feel certain that every Nonconformist or Free Churchman in this gathering will agree with me when I say that the main cause of the present condition of Nonconformity is to be found in the action of the leaders at the end of the last century and the beginning of this century who were more politicians than religious leaders! If you object to bishops in the House of Lords, I hope you object equally to the preacher-politician who was the curse of the Nonconformist Churches during the second half of the reign of Queen Victoria and indeed right up to 1914. The fire and the zeal and enthusiasm went into social reform and political action, and there was real justification for the saying that Nonconformity was the Liberal Party at prayer as the Church of England was the Tory Party at prayer.

To mix politics with religion in the Church is always a danger. May we learn the lesson of 1640 to 1662 and keep clear of any such worldly entanglements. Let us fight the battle of the Lord with spiritual weapons. That is the first explanation.

The second is a much more tragic one. It is the unfortunate and most regrettable divisions in the ranks of the Puritans. This is what makes the story a real tragedy. Fundamentally, these men were all agreed about doctrine. What is the difference between the Savoy Declaration and the Westminster Confession? It is negligible. They were fundamentally agreed about the great essentials of the faith, of their approach to it, and all it contained. Yet the picture that is presented is one of division, endless divisions almost, in the ranks of the Puritans.

They divided chiefly, of course, on the question of Church government; but there were other matters which also caused division. No one can read the biography of Oliver Cromwell without seeing the way in which that righteous man's soul was vexed by these endless divisions among the Puritans. There is something pathetic in the way in which he wrote in a letter from Bristol on September 14, 1645, "Presbyterians, Independents all had

314 ∞ D. Martyn Lloyd-Jones

here the same spirit of faith and prayer: the same pretence and answer; they agree here, know no names of difference; pity it is they should be otherwise anywhere! All that believe have real unity, which is most glorious, because inward and spiritual in the Body, and to the Head."[3]

I do not want to be unfair to any section, or any one group among them, but I am compelled to say that, taking a detached historical view—and especially for one who has been brought up as a Presbyterian—the really guilty party in all this was the Presbyterian party.

On what grounds do I say that? I do so for this reason, that they were the most intransigent. Not only that, they were always ready to make agreements with the king, whether it was Charles I or Charles II. It is almost incredible, but actually in 1650 the Presbyterians in Scotland came to an agreement with Prince Charles, afterwards Charles II, and brought him over from France. There was that brief war, which fortunately ended in disaster for the Royalist party and their Presbyterian supporters in the Battle of Worcester. But is it not a tragic thing that the Presbyterians should be found in such company, and fighting against the men who on the vitals of the Christian faith were in such entire agreement with them?

And then, later, at the end of the Interregnum or Commonwealth, and the early part of 1660 you come across the character General Monck. What can one say about him? He was the man in many ways who "sold the pass" and made possible the return of Charles II and his Laudian entourage; and it was very largely because of this Presbyterian interest that he did so.

Divisions arose among the Puritans, and, as I say, they were almost endless. You had the Presbyterians, the Independents, the Fifth Monarchy Men, the Quakers, the Diggers and the Levellers, and others. You see the Puritan party divided, almost splintered. And, of course, the Anglicans not only knew this, but they played upon it and took advantage of it. Their policy was, as it has always been the policy of people who stand for any kind of Establishment, "divide and conquer." And it worked out most successfully! The result was that you had eventually the disaster of 1662. While the Puritans were divided and quarrelling among themselves, that brilliant group of Laudians, men who believed in the teaching of Laud, and most of whom escaped to the Continent, were planning and scheming for the restoration of all they held dear.

Bosher brings this out and establishes this fact very clearly. His great thesis, which Professor Norman Sykes, as I say, asserts he has proved to the hilt, is that it was this brilliant Laudian party in exile which produced the extraordinary victory of that party in 1662. They had the aid of the most brilliant politician of the century in many ways, Edward Hyde, afterwards the Earl of Clarendon. They were all there together, and they were the people who immediately surrounded the person of the prince, who eventually became King Charles II. They just went on preparing and scheming and plotting. They just kept on, and in the meantime kept in touch with their agents in this country. While the others were quarrelling among themselves and poor Oliver Cromwell was driven to say that "the new presbyter was as bad as the old priest," here was this party with its cohesion standing together, fighting together, though everything seemed to be hopeless. The result was, in the end, that because of the divisions among the Puritans and their successful exploiting of those divisions, they obtained this their most notable victory in 1662.

That brings us to the third point I would establish—the main cause of the division. And that is none other than the whole question of the State-Church idea. Now let us be clear about this: they all really believed in that. The Presbyterians believed in a State Church quite as much as the Anglicans. There is a sense in which it is perfectly true to say that the same thing applies even to Oliver Cromwell! We need not be surprised at this. After all, this was the situation and the position which they had inherited; they had never known any other situation at all. The Church had always been the State Church. So they started with the position as they found it. They were all essentially Erastian in their standpoint.

The position of Cromwell in this matter is to me particularly interesting. There is a sense in which he was Erastian but it was as Bosher says, "an Erastianism with a difference." Let me quote

Bosher again. He is talking about the anarchy in the National Church during the Interregnum, or during the Commonwealth, and he says: "None-the-less, beneath the anarchy of a National Church based on the merely negative principles of tolerance, a coherent policy can be observed radically different from the old. The clue to the Cromwellian Church is to be found in the vehement 'religiousness' of the new regime, in its profound conviction of the religious character of the State, its endless legislation upon matters of private and public morality. Unlike previous governments, it was utterly non-ecclesiastical and non-clerical in its attitude toward the State Church. The questions of ordination, sacramental administration, liturgy, and ceremonial, which, as the symbols of Church order and unity, had been bones of contention in the past, were now ignored. Every attempt to elaborate a doctrinal basis for the Church beyond the simple requirements of 'faith in God by Jesus Christ' was resolutely opposed by the Protector. To a recalcitrant Parliament he declared that 'whoever hath this faith, let its form be what it will: he walking peaceably, without the prejudicing of others under another form' would be guaranteed full liberty of worship."

I repeat what I said in my lecture at the Evangelical Library—here is the father and the pioneer of toleration and of religious liberty in England. Let us go on with the quotation: "The new conception was unashamedly Erastian, but Erastian with a novel twist." Now comes the important point: "The authority of the State was to be exercised not for regulating religious doctrine and practice, but for preventing any such regulation." That is the exact opposite of the view held before. Previously it had been "to regulate religious doctrine and practice"; as is still the case. But Cromwell was opposed to that. What he wanted the State to do was to put an end to such regulation, and thereby to guarantee toleration and liberty. To go on with the quotation: "To make the Establishment the instrument for enforcing an almost unlimited tolerance of opinion, and for uniting warring groups in a common zeal for godliness was Cromwell's ideal." Thank God for Oliver Cromwell! "Hence," Dr. Bosher continues, "he could regard with equanimity the crazy patch-work of the Commonwealth

Church at the parish level—a spectacle that to Anglican and Presbyterian alike seemed an intolerable nightmare."

We say and quote all that in defense of and to the glory of Oliver Cromwell. Though he took, in a sense, the Erastian view of a State Church and held it and practiced it, his idea was to use the power of the State to guarantee tolerance and variety and liberty, not to enforce particular points of view.

What, then, is our criticism of the other idea? I do not mean the Cromwellian, but the idea that too much controlled thinking both on the Anglican and the Presbyterian side. Is it not that it was too much governed by the existing conditions instead of stopping and asking, "What does the New Testament say about this?" Instead of taking the present position as it was and saying, "What can we do to this?" they should rather have said, "Well now, here is an opportunity for a new start; let us go back and look at the Church as depicted in the New Testament, and start from that." But they did not do so in reality though both claimed to be scriptural. They started, as if it were beyond any need of demonstration or proof, with the fact of a State Church; and the whole point then resolved itself to this—should it be Episcopal, or should it be Presbyterian?

Second, were they not too much influenced by the analogy of the Old Testament and of Israel? Here, it seems to me, was the source of the trouble, that they would persist in taking the analogy of Israel in the Old Testament and applying it to England. Was not that the real error? In the Old Testament and under that Dispensation the State (of Israel) was the Church (Acts 7:38), but the State of England in the sixteenth century was not the Church. In the Old Testament the two were one and identical. But surely in the New Testament we have the exact opposite. The Church consists of the "called out" ones, not the total State. The State and the Church are not coterminus, but the Church consists of those who are "called out" of the world, out of the State, into this peculiar and separate body. Nowhere in the New Testament is a direct connection between Church and State taught. To conceive of the Church of the New Testament in its relationship to the pagan Roman Empire in any other way is just impossible. Moreover the Christian is one who is "delivered out of this present evil world" and exhorted to "come out from among them, and be ye separate" (Gal. 1:4; 2 Cor. 6:14, 17). The called out ones are of all nations, "whether Jews or Gentiles, Barbarians or Scythians, bond or free." So, there, it seems to me, is a large part of the explanation of what led to this ultimate tragedy.

But, furthermore, holding the view they did of the State-Church connection, quite naturally they believed that their particular view should be "enforced." Now let us be perfectly fair to the Anglicans, who were most responsible for that Act of Uniformity in 1662; the others did exactly the same thing when they had the power, and would have done so in 1660–62. The Presbyterians believed, quite as much as the Anglicans, that people should be compelled by Act of Parliament and the power of the State to submit to their particular view of the Church, and in 1644 they enforced their view by the power of the State and by the enactments of Parliament.

This view means, that ultimately these matters depend upon and are determined by the fickleness of the crowd. The result is that the same London crowd that had acclaimed Cromwell is to be seen in 1660 in its gaiety and its buffoonery welcoming back Charles II. The same people! That is what follows when you give this power to legislate and to enforce doctrine to the State. You are left ultimately with the fickleness of the crowd, without stopping to mention the inherent inability and incapacity of the crowd, the irreligious crowd in particular, to have any opinion that is of any value concerning these matters. If we are told in 1 Corinthians 6 that members of the Christian church should not take even matters of private personal disputes to the public Law Courts, how much less should we take matters of doctrine?

It seems clear that both sides were starting with the given position and did not trouble to examine it in the light of the New Testament teaching. In addition to all this, as we have already seen, they also believed that you could enforce a kind of "strict religious behaviour" upon the populace by Acts of Parliament; hence those various Acts they passed with regard to sports and entertainments and certain other things. I am bringing this forward quite deliberately because it is more than likely that there will be a fight about all this in the immediate future, and you and I will be expected to have some kind of attitude with respect to it.

I venture to assert that once more we are dealing with a standpoint which is based upon a fallacy, which is Old Testament thinking again rather than New Testament; and it always leads to trouble. Take that crowd, the London crowd, that had been compelled to live in a given way, and according to a given pattern, during the Commonwealth. It had never believed in what was being forced on it, and had never understood the principles on which it was being enforced. Consequently it got very tired and weary of it. This was one of the main factors in turning people back to Royalty, and to saying that they must have the king back, and that they must get rid of those wretched Puritans who were spoiling life, and so on. That kind of "enforcing" of morals by Act of Parliament instead of by moral and spiritual suasion, it seems to me, is bound to produce a reaction against itself. I believe we are witnessing just that at the present time. We are witnessing a reaction against Victorianism, which was so similar to what was in force during the period of the Commonwealth. This has been described in many books. During the time of Queen Victoria, and even before, as the result of the work of Wilberforce and others, what is called "Victorianism" came into being, and people were compelled by Act of Parliament, as it were, to live a certain kind of life. But that always produces a reaction against itself as it did toward the end of the Commonwealth and in 1660–62.

I am suggesting that if only all these different divisions and factions had stood together when they had a wonderful opportunity, and especially at the return of Charles II—if they had only stood together for a general religious toleration—the whole situation would have been entirely different. But the Presbyterians would not agree to that; it had to be Presbyterianism. And so the forces were divided; and the Anglicans, as I say, with their ability and astuteness and cohesion, and with what is generally described as the astounding "political finesse" of Sheldon, the Bishop of London, afterwards Archbishop, were entirely and completely successful. If the Puritans had but stood together for religious toleration in general rather than any one system, the history at that time and during the subsequent three hundred years would have been very different.

Now that was all that the Independents asked for. The Sectarians, the Independents, simply asked for toleration. They did not go into the discussions at the Savoy and various others places. They were not interested in this "either—or," Presbyterianism or Anglicanism. All they wanted was liberty to worship God in the way they understood the Bible to teach. But, that, unfortunately, was not the view held by all Puritans and because of their divisions about these secondary matters, the whole position was lost. Of course, it was not lost in the sense that these men did not go on preaching. Alas, too late, many of them were forced to see the truth of the position taken by Dr. John Owen and Dr. Thomas Goodwin and others, and they were driven to that position. But by then the damage had been done, and a glorious possibility and opportunity had been missed.

Lessons for Today

There, then, is a kind of analysis of the causes of failure. Let me now attempt in a final section to draw some lessons for ourselves today. The first is this: what is it, according to our Reformed and Puritan view, that really matters? I have tried to show that this central all-important point became obscured for the various reasons I have adduced—the political admixture, and the concern about matters which are not, surely, of primary importance. Well, then, we must ask ourselves the question—what do we regard as of supreme importance? What are we going to put in the center? What are we going to say matters above all else, and which we must never lose sight of? Surely there can be no disagreement among us with regard to the answer. It is the gospel of salvation which is also, "the gospel of the glory of God." It is the thing about which all those Puritans were agreed—the nature, the essence of the gospel. We have looked at it so many times in these Conferences that I need say no more.

Coupled with that, there was their emphasis upon the necessity of having able and good ministers, and the primacy and the centrality of preaching. These were the things about which they were all agreed, and about which, surely, we must also all agree as being the first, the primary, and the most essential things.

What is the gospel? Must we not put this first—that there can be no uncertainty about this? Our consciences must compel us to say this; that we cannot allow any vagueness or uncertainty or indefiniteness about this. Surely our whole position is based upon this, that we say the gospel can be defined, can be stated in propositions. We *do* believe in Confessions of Faith, we *do* believe in Creeds. It is just there that we are differentiated from the majority of people in the Christian Church at the present time. Surely, then, that is something which we must assert and proclaim and defend at all costs—this pure gospel, this pure Word of the gospel. And we will tolerate no compromise with respect to this.

Then second, we are surely compelled by all this to face again our whole view of the Church. That was a question about which the Puritans—and, indeed, for that matter the Anglicans as well at that period—were all agreed as being central. We must praise and commend them all in that respect: they were all concerned about the Church. They did not try to solve their problems by forming movements; every one of them was concerned about the state of the Church. The Anglicans were contending for their view of the Church. The Presbyterians were not content to be just a movement within the Church, they wanted the whole Church to be Presbyterian. The point I am making is that they did not meet the position by just saying, "Well, all right, we will remain Anglicans, but we will have a movement of our own within the church, and we will meet together and have fellowship and carry out activities from time to time"—leaving the Church untouched as it were. That was not their view at all. The same is true of the Independents also. Every one of them was contending for a view of the Church. They were not content to allow the condition of the Church to be chaotic as long as they could meet together in fellowship in their movements. Every one of them was concerned about the state and condition of the Church. The doctrine of the Church was central with all of them.

We need to be reminded of that. Is it not the case that for far too long we as Evangelicals have been divided, and are rendered ineffective, because we do not think in terms of the Church? We have formed movements, and we have not applied what we believe to the Church situation—hence the chaos and the anarchy of our time in almost every department of our life and activity.

That, then, raises the question: What is our view of the Church? What is the New Testament view of the Church? What has the New Testament to say about this whole question of a State Church, and as to the way in which doctrine and practice are to be determined? Surely this question ought to be one of our priorities. These people of 1662 compel us to face that. The movements around us today, the Ecumenical movement in particular, and other factors, I believe, are forcing us to ask this question: What is our view of the Church? And surely at this point we need to learn this great lesson from the Puritans—the all-importance of the purity of the Church, especially in the matter of doctrine.

Implicit in that, of course, is the necessity for discipline. Is it right to tolerate in the same Church people whose views on the essentials of the faith are diametrically opposed? Is it right that we belong to the same company, calling itself a church, as men who deny almost everything we stand for—the Deity of our Lord, the Virgin Birth, His miracles, His atoning sacrificial death, the punitive and substitutionary elements in the atonement, our Lord's literal physical resurrection, the Person of the Holy Spirit, regeneration, justification by faith only, the "blessed hope" of our Lord's return? Is it right in the light of New Testament teaching that we regard such people as "brethren," that we should refer to people who never darken the doors of a place of worship as "lapsed Christians" simply because they were baptized when infants? Is that compatible with the New Testament teaching with regard to the Church, and her purity, and her discipline, and her life? Such questions have got to be matters of prior and primary consideration for us if we really take these Puritans seriously, if we pay any serious regard to their teaching about the conscience, and of the need of being scrupulous, and of honestly carrying out what we believe to be the Truth whatever the consequences.

Another urgent question surely is the freedom of the Church to determine her own affairs. Is there any suggestion anywhere in the New Testament that any body, the State and Monarch included, has any right in that respect save the Church herself? Do we not need to remind ourselves again of "the crown rights of the Redeemer"?

I go on to put a practical question: Can we who are agreed about the vital, fundamental, first, things allow anything of lesser importance to divide us? We have a great lesson in the history of 1640 to 1662 which shows us what happens if we do so. As Evangelicals we are divided among the various denominations, and our efforts are made negatory and nullified; and in the end we count for very little. But is it right, I ask, for us to allow ourselves to be separated and divided by anything which falls short of the great central things we have mentioned? Is it right that we should be more associated in general, and in our total life as Christians in the Church, with people with whom we do not agree, than with people with whom we do agree about these central vital matters?

The next lesson we learn from 1640–62 is the importance of fighting this battle in a spiritual manner, and not with carnal weapons. If 1640 to 1662 teaches us nothing else it teaches us this: that in that kind of ecclesiastical fighting, the ecclesiastics will win every time. They are past masters at it. It is the thing in which they really believe, and while you and I are concerned about doctrine, and the culture and the nurture of the soul, their whole attention is given to practicalities and to the politics of the situation. So the moment we begin to fight with a semi-political, ecclesiastical outlook, the moment we develop a party spirit and begin to think in terms of party advantage, and regard people who really agree with us about the centralities, as enemies almost, and in opposition, the cause is already lost.

There is nothing, it seems to me, that is more offensive, or more removed from the spirit of the New Testament than a party spirit that puts the interests of its own particular point of view upon matters that are not of primary and central importance before those matters that are of primary and central importance. Not only is it wrong but, as I say, the ecclesiastics will always succeed best at that kind of thing. They always have succeeded; they always will succeed. Our only comment upon them is this—"Verily, they have their reward." They are past masters at manipulation, at lobbying, at meeting behind the scenes, and at organizing. And they will stoop to almost anything. Fancy the Presbyterians, during this period we are examining, actually cooperating with Henrietta Maria, the widow of Charles I! They cooperated with her though she was a Roman Catholic who really hated everything for which they stood. They did so in order to get an advantage over the Anglicans. Shame on them!

"The weapons of our warfare are not carnal, but mighty through God to the pulling down of strongholds" (2 Cor. 10:5). But the moment men become animated by a party spirit they will stoop to almost anything to get their ends and to ensure the success of their party; and so you get these unholy alliances. They are a blot upon the Presbyterian record during that whole period. Thank God, the men whose names are most frequently mentioned in this conference—John Owen and Thomas Goodwin—cannot be charged with that. They had this other view of Church government to which I have already referred. They did not look to the State connection; they but wanted liberty to worship as they understood God to teach in the New Testament; and therefore they never resorted to these shameful practices and subterfuges. May God preserve us from developing a narrow party spirit that is more interested in the success of its point of view than in the glory of God and the purity and the welfare of the Church. If that does not come as a lesson to us from 1660 to 1662, well then I say God help us—our cause is already lost.

The Puritan Conscience in Action

My final word is this, and it is a still more practical one. A great lesson that comes to us from this period is to be alert to the danger of being ensnared and bought by the subtlety and the craftiness and the wiliness of men. All this was practiced upon the Puritans, and especially on the Presbyterian party, from 1660 to 1662. The principle on which the Laudians acted was the principle on which they are acting today. It can be seen in ecumenical circles at the present time. The Roman Catholics, and the present pope in particular, are acting on it. The principle is this: stand inflexible on the essentials, but having done that, be affable, be ready to concede on irrelevancies and matters that really do not matter at all, speak kindly, fraternize with and flatter members of the opposing group. It was a deliberate part of the policy of the Laudian party to bribe some of the Puritans. Richard Baxter was offered the bishopric of Hereford, Calamy was offered the bishopric of Lichfield, Reynolds was offered the bishopric of Norwich, and Thomas Manton was offered the deanery of Rochester. Bates was offered the deanery of Lichfield, Bowles was offered the deanery of York. The only one who accepted was Reynolds, who actually became the Bishop of Norwich.

I do not want to say anything about Reynolds, but I do say this about the others: there is the Puritan conscience in action! It cannot be bribed, it is not "taken in" by the affability and the niceness and the flattery of men. It does not say, "You know, some of these other men are much nicer than our people." It sees through all that, and it sees beyond it. Attempts were made in that way to divide the Puritan party by offering preference to some of their leaders; but it was rigidly and sternly and conscientiously rejected and refused. These men could not compromise on these matters, their consciences could not be bought. They preferred to go out into the wilderness, and to the suffering that followed to so many and in such a terrible manner. That, I say, is the Puritan conscience in action. The scrupulosity, the carefulness, and particularly the carefulness not only to have the right view, but to act upon it whatever the consequences might be.

In other words, the ultimate lesson to be learned from this period, is this: "The arm of flesh will fail you, ye dare not trust your own." We must "trust in the Lord, and in the power of His might." We must be "strong in the Lord, and in the power of His might." We must indeed realize that "the weapons of our warfare are not carnal, but mighty through God to the pulling down of strongholds." It does not matter what they are, or who they are; it does not matter how small we may be. If we see what the Truth is, well then, I say, we must hold to that and fight for that, and refuse to compromise about that, whatever it may cost us. We must refuse every enticement, every offer, every form of flattery and honor, we must be wise to detect the devices that will be used against us—the offering of offices, preferences, positions of honor, places in our denomination, or whatever else it may be— we must reject it all as these men rejected it all, in order that we may fight for the faith and the purity of the Church, the honor of God and of His Christ.

We thank God for the memory of these men, who, having seen the position clearly, acted upon it at all costs. May God give us grace to follow in their train!

Notes

Foreword

1. Iain Murray, *D. Martyn Lloyd-Jones,* vol. 2, *The Fight of Faith, 1939-1981* (Edinburgh: Banner of Truth, 1990), p. 352.

Chapter 2, Jonathan Edwards and the Theology of Revival

1. Jonathan Edwards, *Works,* 2 vols. (London, 1840), 2:7. The sermon begins on page 3.

2. Ibid., 2:17. The sermon begins on page 12.

3. Ibid., 1:237-38.

4. Ibid., 1:394.

5. Ibid., 1:391.

6. From Timothy Dwight's Memoirs of Edwards, in Edwards, *Works,* 1:ccxxxii.

7. Samuel Hopkins, *Life and Character of the Late Reverend Jonathan Edwards* (1761).

8. Edwards, *Works,* 2:261.

9. Ibid., 1:369.

10. Ibid., 1:375.

11. Ibid., 2:273.

12. Ibid., 2: 266-69.

13. Ibid., 1:376-77.

14. Ibid., 1:584.

15. Ibid., 1:583.

16. Ibid., 1:380. Edwards refers in the context to Psalms 2 and 110.

17. Ibid., 1:539.

18. Ibid., 1:379.
19. Ibid., 1:380.
20. Ibid., 1:374.
21. Ibid., 1:397.
22. Ibid., 1:426.
23. Ibid., 2:291.
24. Ibid., 2:312.

Chapter 4, The Puritan Doctrine of Apostasy

1. Thomas Goodwin, *Works* (1861), 9:195.
2. John Owen, *The Nature of Apostasy from the Profession of the Gospel and the Punishment of Apostates Declared, in an Exposition of Hebrews 6:4-6,* in John Owen, *Works,* ed. W. H. Goold, 24 vols. (1850-55), 7:13.
3. Ibid., 7:33-34.
4. Ibid., 7:19.
5. Ibid., 7:20-21.
6. Ibid., 7:60.
7. Ibid., 7:84.
8. Ibid., 7:85.
9. Ibid., 7:183.
10. Ibid., 7:185.
11. Ibid.
12. Ibid., 7:213.
13. Ibid., 7:251.

Chapter 5, Knowledge—False and True

1. George Whitefield, *God a Believer's Glory,* a sermon on Isaiah 60:19.
2. Charles Haddon Spurgeon, sermon on 1 John 1:3, September 15, 1861.
3. Isaac Watts, *Evangelical Discourses* (1746).
4. John Flavel, *Treatise of the Soul of Man.*
5. Jonathan Edwards, *Personal Narrative.*
6. Robert Bolton, *Comforting Afflicted Consciences* (1635).

Chapter 6, The Puritan Idea of Communion with God

1. *Westminster Shorter Catechism,* 1.
2. John Owen, *Works,* ed. T. Russell, 28 vols. (1826), 10:95.
3. John Bunyan, *Grace Abounding,* pp. 37-38.
4. John Owen, *Of Communion with God the Father, Son, and Holy Ghost, Each Person Distinctly, in Love, Grace, and Consolation,* in Owen, *Works,* 10:9.
5. Ibid., 10:28.
6. Ibid., 10:11.
7. Ibid., 10:24.

8. Ibid., 10:28-29.

9. Ibid., 10:30.

10. Ibid., 10:63-64.

11. Ibid., 10:72.

12. Ibid., 10:239.

13. Ibid., 10:253.

14. Ibid., 10:306.

15. Thomas Goodwin, *The Object and Acts of Justifying Faith,* in *The Works of Thomas Goodwin,* in James Nichol, *Nichol's Series of Standard Divines* (1864-65), 8:376ff.

16. Ibid., 7:193.

17. Ibid., 7:197ff.

18. Ibid., 8:379.

19. Robert Bruce, *The Mystery of the Lord's Supper: Sermons on the Sacrament . . . Preached in A.D. 1589,* ed. and trans. Thomas F. Torrance (London: James Clarke, 1958), p. 64.

20. Richard Baxter, *The Divine Life,* in Richard Baxter, *Works* (1838), 3:816.

21. Ibid., 3:815.

22. Richard Alleine, *Heaven on Earth* (1838), p. 334.

Chapter 8, Missions in the Reformed Tradition

1. John Calvin, *Institutes,* 1.6-7.

2. Ibid., 3:6-10.

3. Ibid., 1.3.1.

4. Ibid., 1.5.4, 11.

5. Ibid., 1.4.1-4.

6. Ibid., 1.5.13-15.

7. Ibid., 2.2.13-14.

8. John Calvin, *Commentary on the Psalms,* on Ps. 110; John Calvin, *Commentary on the Gospel of Matthew,* on Matt. 24:14.

9. John Calvin, *Commentary on 2 Corinthians,* on 2 Cor. 2:12.

10. Calvin, *Institutes,* 3.20.42.

11. John Calvin, *Sermons,* on Isa. 7:5.

12. Calvin, *Institutes,* 3.24.8; cf. 3.22.10; Calvin, *Sermons,* on 1 Tim. 2:15.

13. Calvin, *Sermons,* on Deut. 33:18.

14. Calvin, *Institutes,* 4.3.4.

15. Ibid., 3.24.14. Quoting Augustine.

16. Johannes van den Berg, *Constrained by Jesus' Love* (Kampen: Kok, 1956), pp. 72-73.

17. *Canons of Dort,* 2:5.

18. Olav G. Myklebust, *The Study of Missions in Theological Education,* 2 vols. (Oslo: Land og Kirke, 1955-57), 1:40.

19. J. H. Bavinck, *Introduction to the Science of Missions,* trans. David Hugh Freeman (Philadelphia: Presbyterian and Reformed, 1960), p. xiv.

20. *Westminster Directory* (1644).

21. Kenneth S. Latourette, *History of the Expansion of Christianity,* 3:217-18.

22. Ibid., 3:45.

23. Van den Berg, *Constrained by Jesus' Love,* pp. 87-88.

24. Charles Henry Robinson, *History of Christian Missions* (Edinburgh: T. & T. Clark, 1915), pp. 92-93.

25. George Smith, *William Carey,* p. 12.

26. *Form of Agreement* (1805), introduction.

27. A. H. Oussoren, *William Carey,* p. 140.

28. *Heads of Agreement,* 5.

29. Ibid., 8.

30. Smith, *Carey,* p. 149.

31. Richard Lovett, *The History of the London Missionary Society, 1795-1895* (1899), pp. 48-49.

32. Eugene Stock, *History of Church Missionary Society,* 4 vols. (London: 1899-1916), 1:97-98.

33. See John L. Nevius, *Planting and Development of Missionary Churches* (1958).

34. *The Muslim World* (1952).

35. Ned B. Stonehouse, *J. Gresham Machen: A Biographical Memoir* (Grand Rapids: Eerdmans, 1955), p. 475.

36. Latourette, *History of the Expansion,* 3:29.

37. Van den Berg, *Constrained by Jesus' Love.*

38. John McNeile, *History and Character of Calvinism,* p. 384.

39. Payne, p. 235.

40. P. T. Forsyth, *Missions in State and Church* (London: Hodder & Stoughton, 1908).

Chapter 9, Preaching—Puritan and Reformed

1. Richard Sibbes, *Sermons,* 2:98.

2. Ibid., 2:372.

Chapter 10, The Puritan Concept of Divine Intercession

1. Oliver Heywood, *The Whole Works,* vol. 3 (1825), pp. 132, 149.

2. John Bunyan, *Works,* ed. George Offor, 3 vols. (1853), 1:152.

3. Heywood, *Works,* 3:144-45.

4. Thomas Goodwin, *Works,* in James Nichol, *Nichol's Series of Standard Divines* (1864-65), 4:57-60.

5. John Owen, *Works,* ed. W. H. Goold (1850-55), 22:541.

6. John Owen, *Forty Six Sermons upon the Whole Eighth Chapter of Romans* (1674), pp. 556-57.

7. Bunyan, *Works*, 1:212.

8. Ibid., 1:203.

9. Anthony Burgess, *CXLV Expository Sermons upon the Whole 17th Chapter of John* (1656), pp. 227-28.

10. Owen, *Works*, 22:538, 540.

11. Bunyan, *Works*, 1:206.

12. George Offor, "Advertisement," in Bunyan, *Works*, 1:151.

13. Nathaniel Hardy, *The First General Epistle of John* (1865), pp. 124-25.

14. Bunyan, *Works*, 1:169.

15. Ibid., 1:161.

16. Hugh Binning, *Works* (1735), pp. 474-75.

17. Bunyan, *Works*, 1:193, 196-97.

18. William Gouge, *Works*, vol. 2 (1627), p. 230.

19. Henry Lukin, *The Interest of the Spirit in Prayer* (1674), pp. 14-15.

20. Owen, *Works*, 4:287-88.

21. Ibid., 4:295.

Chapter 12, The Casuistry of William Perkins

1. Blaise Pascal, *Lettres Provinciales* (1656).

2. W. R. Forrester, *Christian Vocation: Studies in Faith and Work* (London: Lutterworth, 1951), p. 65.

3. Karl Barth, *Church Dogmatics,* trans. G. T. Thompson (Edinburgh: T. & T. Clark, 1936ff.), 3.4.8.

4. William Perkins, *Works* (1631), 2:2; 2:22.

5. Francis Bacon, *Works*, ed. James Spedding, 14 vols. (1857-74), 1:92.

6. William Perkins, *Cases of Conscience,* Epistle Dedicatory.

7. Perkins, *Works*, 2:1.

8. Ibid., 2:2.

9. William Ames, *Conscience with the Power and Cases Thereof* (1643), Preface.

10. T. Hill, *A Quatron of Reasons* (1600), p. 79.

11. Perkins, *Works*, 3:173.

12. Ibid., 1:553.

13. Ibid., 3:28.

14. Richard Hooker, *Ecclesiastical Polity*, 2.8.6.

15. Perkins, *Works*, 2:88-91.

16. Ibid., 2:91.

17. Ibid., 2:9.

18. Ibid., 2:5.

19. Ibid., 2:25-26.

20. Ibid., 2:49.

21. Ibid., 2:114.

22. Ibid., 2:113.

23. Ibid., 2:114-17.

24. Ibid., 2:116.

25. Ibid., 2:131.

26. Ibid., 2:133.

27. Ibid., 2:449.

28. Ibid., 2:451.

29. Ames, *Conscience*, Preface.

Chapter 13, The Puritan Conscience

1. William Ames, *Conscience with the Power and Cases Thereof* (1643), p. 2.

2. David Dickson, *Therapeutica Sacra . . .: The Method of Healing the Diseases of the Conscience Concerning Regeneration* (1664), p. 3.

3. Thomas Goodwin, *Works*, in James Nichol, *Nichol's Series of Standard Divines* (1864-65), 6:272.

4. Dickson, *Therapeutica Sacra*, p. 4.

5. Ibid., p. 3.

6. Richard Sibbes, *Works* (1862), 3:209.

7. Thomas Brooks, *Works* (1867), 5:281.

8. William Gurnall, *The Christian in Complete Armour* (1837), p. 374.

9. Sibbes, *Works*, 3:210-11.

10. John Bunyan, *Works*, ed. George Offor (1859), 3:260ff.

11. William Fenner, *A Treatise of Conscience*, in *Works* (1651), second pagination, p. 24.

12. David Clarkson, *Works* (1864), 2:475.

13. Richard Baxter, *Practical Works* (1838), 1:116.

14. Ibid., pp. 115-16.

15. Ibid., p. 116.

16. Fenner, *A Treatise of Conscience*, pp. 108-9.

17. Sibbes, *Works*, 7:490.

18. Fenner, *A Treatise of Conscience*, pp. 79-80.

19. John Bunyan, *Pilgrim's Progress*, in *Works*, 3:242.

20. Ames, *Conscience*, p. 20.

21. Fenner, *A Treatise of Conscience*, pp. 143-44.

22. John Owen, *The True Nature of a Gospel Church and Its Government*, ed. John Huxtable (London: James Clarke, 1947), p. 66.

Chapter 14, Thomas Boston of Ettrick

1. Robert Blair and William Row, *The Life of Mr. Robert Blair*, ed. Thomas M'Crie (1848).

Chapter 15, John Owen's Doctrine of Christ

1. W. H. Goold, in John Owen, *Works*, ed. W. H. Goold (1850-55), 1:274.

2. John Owen, *Of Communion with God, the Father, the Son and the Holy Ghost* (1657), in John Owen, *Works*, 2:49-50; 2:71-78.

3. John Owen, *The Person of Christ—God and Man* (1679), in Owen, *Works,* 1:4.

4. Ibid., 1:5.

5. John Owen, *The Death of Death in the Death of Christ* (London: Banner of Truth, 1959), p. 51.

6. Owen, *Of Communion with God,* 2:9.

7. Ibid., 2:18.

8. Ibid., 2:66.

9. Ibid., 2:59-60.

10. Ibid., 2:63-64.

11. Ibid., 2:66.

12. Ibid., 2:54.

13. Ibid., 2:64-65.

14. Ibid., 2:66-67.

15. John Owen, *The Person of Christ,* 1:224.

16. Ibid., 1:225.

17. Ibid., 1:228.

18. Ibid., 1:234.

19. Ibid.

20. Ibid.

21. Ibid., 1:46.

22. Ibid., 1:47-48.

23. Ibid., 1:55.

24. Ibid., 1:57.

25. Ibid., 1:63.

26. Ibid., 1:65.

27. Ibid., 1:69.

28. Ibid., 1:79.

29. John Owen, *Of Communion with God,* 2:51.

30. Ibid.

31. Ibid., 2:52.

32. Owen, *The Person of Christ,* chap. 7.

33. John Owen, *Meditations and Discourses on the Glory of Christ* (1684-96), in Owen, *Works,* 1:323.

34. Owen, *The Death of Death,* p. 55.

35. Ibid.

36. Ibid., p. 56.

37. Ibid., p. 58.

38. Ibid., pp. 53-54.

39. Owen, *Of Communion with God,* 2:156.

40. Ibid., 2:158.

41. Ibid., 2:161.

42. Ibid., 2:162.

43. Ibid.
44. Ibid., 2:163.
45. Owen, *The Death of Death*, p. 64.
46. Ibid., p. 68.
47. Ibid., p. 147.
48. Ibid., pp. 147-48.
49. Ibid., p. 157.
50. Ibid.
51. Owen, *Of Communion with God*, 2:168.
52. Owen, *The Death of Death*, p. 64.
53. Ibid., p. 69.
54. Owen, *The Person of Christ*, 1:254.
55. Owen, *The Death of Death*, p. 65.
56. Ibid., p. 72.
57. Ibid., p. 89.
58. Ibid.
59. Ibid., p. 119.
60. Ibid., p. 157.
61. Ibid., p. 91.

Chapter 16, Puritan Perplexities: Lessons from 1640–1662

1. Stuart Barton Babbage, *Puritanism and Richard Bancroft* (London: SPCK, 1962).

2. Robert S. Bosher, *The Making of the Restoration Settlement: The Influence of the Laudians, 1649-1662* (London: Dacre, 1951). A second edition was released in 1958.

3. Oliver Cromwell, letter 31.